Distributive Politics in Developing Countries

Distributive Politics in Developing Countries

Almost Pork

Edited by
Mark Baskin and Michael L. Mezey

LEXINGTON BOOKS
Lanham • Boulder • New York • London

Published by Lexington Books
An imprint of The Rowman & Littlefield Publishing Group, Inc.
4501 Forbes Boulevard, Suite 200, Lanham, Maryland 20706
www.rowman.com

16 Carlisle Street, London W1D 3BT, United Kingdom

British Library Cataloguing in Publication Information Available

Library of Congress Cataloging-in-Publication Data

Distributive politics in developing countries : almost pork / edited by Mark Baskin and Michael L. Mezey.
pages cm.
Includes bibliographical references and index.
ISBN 978-0-7391-8068-6 (cloth : alk. paper) — ISBN 978-0-7391-8069-3 (electronic)
1. Income distribution—Developing countries. 2. Distributive justice—Developing countries. 3. Economic development—Developing countries. 4. Democracy—Economic aspects—Developing countries. I. Baskin, Mark. II. Mezey, Michael L.
HC59.72.I5D57 2014
339.209172'4—dc23

2014026231

™ The paper used in this publication meets the minimum requirements of American National Standard for Information Sciences—Permanence of Paper for Printed Library Materials, ANSI/NISO Z39.48-1992.

Printed in the United States of America

Contents

Preface

It was no accident that we undertook a research project that led to this book on Constituency Development Funds (CDFs) and distributive politics in developing countries. We believe in the unity of theory and practice. The State University of New York Center for International Development (SUNY/CID) at the University of Albany has been implementing development programs and projects for well over a quarter century in areas as diverse as economic development, decentralization, civil society, strengthening rule of law, and legislative development. In this work, we have always strived to remain abreast of current approaches to working effectively with networks of academics, policy makers, development professionals, and ordinary citizens. This work has generated practical assessments, program evaluations, and training and guidance manuals that reflect the latest insights from academic, policy and development research. This intellectual dimension has contributed significantly to the success of our practical work in improving aspects of governance and reform in our partner countries.

Following from this approach to development, we listen carefully to the issues, agendas and real challenges facing our partners abroad in their efforts to improve governance in their countries. So we naturally took notice when CDFs dominated our conversations with members of parliament (MPs) and legislative development experts at a Global Conference on Enhancing the Effectiveness of Parliaments at Wilton Park in late 2008 that had been sponsored by the UK's Department of International Development, The World Bank Institute and the Commonwealth Parliamentary Association (CPA). The discussions on CDFs, an increasingly popular distributive spending scheme that gives MPs a voice in constituency-level development spending, overshadowed discussions on virtually all traditional areas of legislative development at that conference. Upon investigation, we learned that very little space in the academic or development literatures had been devoted to exploring both the possibilities and challenges of CDFs. The emerging and interesting critical literature on CDFs among civil society organizations (CSOs) did not reflect a broader program of research or other activities on this type of distributive spending mechanism in practice. And in our practical engagement with several parliaments in Africa, we could turn to no emerging and constructive body of research on this type of distributive spending to inform our work. This was more the pity given the real popularity of this type of spending and for real differences and conflicts surrounding the operations of CDFs in each country where it is employed—as the reader will find in the following chapters in this book. On one hand, it appeared that these constituency funds were addressing real needs of citizens that had often been ignored in regional and local-level development and administration. On the other hand, the operations of these funds were already generating public controversy. So it was time, as Mark Baskin puts it in the Introduction, to reduce the heat-to-light ratio on this interesting and important development. We felt it important to examine this increasingly popular, yet controversial, type of spending and provide a balanced view on CDFs.

Our project began with two exploratory workshops in Albany—one on CDFs and the other on distributive spending in New York State—and led to a fruitful partnership with the CPA in developing a set of principles for CDF development and tools to guide their use. Our work with CPA is especially helpful for enabling us to collaborate with MPs from all over the world with a range of experiences with CDFs, as well as with staffers and civil society professionals with knowledge about CDFs. This practical collaboration aims to place the operations of CDFs within a broader, good governance framework that is rooted in transparency, good management and accountability. Thus far, we have developed a set of Principles for Constituency Development Funds and have designed a toolbox that would enable all stakeholders in CDFs, including MPs, CDF managers, CSOs and ordinary citizens—to approach them constructively and practically. The first part of this collaboration can be found in the appendices and we aim to complete this tool box with CPA by 2015.

The comparative case studies that comprise this book have provided important background to our collaboration with CPA. They provide political and historical perspective into each CDF in an effort both to better understand this type of distributive spending and to offer some insights into distributive spending in developing countries more generally. We now offer this research to a broader public. It is our hope that *Distributive Politics in Developing Countries: Almost Pork* contributes to the scholarly and practical inquiries into distributive politics that lay at the intersection of comparative politics, parliamentary development, decentralization, and participatory budgeting, to name just a few fields implicated by the topic. Above all, this book exemplifies well our commitment to marrying in-depth research to development practice and inculcating a culture of continuous learning that can inform locally relevant policy and institutional reforms.

Malcolm Russell-Einhorn, Director
SUNY Center for International Development
Rockefeller College of Public Affairs and Policy
University at Albany

Acknowledgments

We are pleased to acknowledge our many debts from friends, colleagues and students along the way for their considerable contribution to this work. Above all, we would like to thank our collaborators in this project: Joel Barkan, Bob Mattes, Nelson Kasfir, Harry Blair, Stephen Hippo Twebaze, Horace Bartilow, Diana Evans, and David Ndii. We thank them for their excellent work and collaborative spirit that made this project easy and fun.

Much of this work took place in gatherings of academics, public servants, development professionals and nonprofit activists. In two workshops in Albany, we are grateful for the contributions of: Bob Nakamura, David Rousseau, Jeff Straussman, Ned Schneier, Joel Barkan, Kevin Deveaux, Rick Stapenhurst, Rasheed Draman, Scott Hubli, Shem Baldeosingh, Diana Evans, Erzsebet Fazekas, Helen Desfosses, Michael Malbin, Jeffrey Stonecash, Sally Friedman, Marika Dunn, Frank Mauro, Jim Ketterer, Robert McEvoy, Charles Dawson, Barbara Bartoletti, John Burke, Peter Baynes, Kevin Crawford, Michael Hoblock, Marc Levigne, Malcolm Russell-Einhorn, Paul Gumpper, Jim Utermark, Lisa Petter, Andrea Wolfe, Kimberly Pease, Heather Senecal, Gaby Carrascal and Susan Crowdy.

We were grateful for the chance to present our work at a workshop on CDFs at Monash University in Melbourne and particularly value the insights of Professor Ken Coghill Kevin Rizzoli and Abel Kinyondo. We are very grateful to the work we have achieved in partnership with the the Commonwealth Parliamentary Association (CPA) and especially thank Secretary General Dr. William Shija, Shem Baldeosingh, Meenakshi Dhar and Arlene Bussette, Saidi Yakubu and Elsie Simpamba for their cooperation and support, and to the CPA affiliates in Jamaica and Tanzania for organizing two excellent and helpful workshops. In Jamaica, Moveta Munroe and her colleagues in the CDF Unit in Jamaica's Office of the Prime Minister provided valuable insights and assistance. In Tanzania, Abel Kiyondo and Dr. Severin Rugumamu both made useful and helpful contributions to our thinking. We are grateful to all the participants from parliaments in Africa, the Caribbean and Asia at the CPA workshops in Kingston Jamaica and Dar es Salaam, Tanzania.

Professor John Rohrbaugh made several helpful suggestions on how to present this work more effectively. Our student fellows at SUNY CID provided considerable assistance in research: Simone Grant, Susan Appe, Ari Renoni, Andrew Vitek, Stephen Pampinella, Blair Williams, Haibo Li, Heather Senecal, and Zorana Lavin all contributed useful research. Our colleagues Gaby Carrascal and Mihaela Muntean helped to ensure that the project ran smoothly at all times.

We owe special thanks to some colleagues at CID. Paul Gumpper's intelligent collaboration and contributions at all stages of this project considerably eased its burden and was essential in its completion; Malcolm Russell-Einhorn's full support and well-considered comments on different aspects of the project improved it considerably; Steve Pampinella's efforts in support of our work went far beyond the the call of typical graduate research assistance; and Blair Williams' well-organized support helped us complete this project in all its many details.

We owe a special debt to the late Joel Barkan, whose contribution to this volume goes far beyond his written contribution. Joel was an early champion of the study of CDFs and distributive politics in developing societies, more generally, and helped to shape our thinking on this interesting set of issues. He blended his training in social science with a nuanced understanding of African societies and politics, and a practical bent to contribute to improving the capacity of governing institutions to respond constructively to citizens. His contributions in several workshops, phone conversations and emails have made this a better book. We miss him for his insights and intelligence.

At Lexington Press, Lenora Lautigar, Justin Race, Alissa Parra, Brian Hill, and Emily Natsios provided tremendous support and encouragement to complete this project and get it out.

Michael Mezey would like to acknowledge DePaul University's continuing support for his scholarly agenda and for his contributions to this volume and Mark Baskin would like to acknowledge the support of SUNY/CID to this work on CDFs and as a place to hatch an effort to blend practical work in development with a deeper consideration of our work. Sometimes it makes sense just to stand there and think.

Chapter 1

Introduction

Are Constituency Development Funds a Policy Tool?

Mark Baskin

CDFs: A POLICY TOOL WHOSE TIME HAS COME?

This book explores the increasing use of Constituency Development Funds (CDFs) in emerging democratic governments in Africa, Asia, the Caribbean and Oceania. CDFs dedicate public money to benefit parliamentary constituencies through allocations and/or spending decisions influenced by Members of Parliament (MPs).[1] On the first glance, these funds appear to resemble the *ad hoc* pork barrel policy making, often called earmarks, employed in the US Congress for the past 200 years, and much public commentary on the funds cites this similarity.[2] However, unlike earmarks, CDFs generally become institutionalized in the government's annual budget and are distributed according to different criteria in each country. They enable MPs to influence programs in their constituencies that finance education, and build bridges, roads, community centers, clinics and schools. In this sense, a CDF is a politicized form of spending that can help fill in the important gaps in government services in constituencies that have not been addressed in the government's larger, comprehensive policy programs.

It seems that CDFs are an "idea whose time has come (Figure 1.1)." Legislation has been proposed in a number of countries, such as Indonesia, Trinidad and Tobago, Solomon Islands, South Sudan, and Myanmar. But there are more than a few skeptics among donor agencies, multilateral institutions and good governance nonprofit organizations, and the funds are, indeed, controversial. Supporters argue that they represent a policy tool that strengthens relationships among constituents, representatives, and decentralized administrators, thereby reducing the domination of centralized bureaucrats and technocrats and enabling citizens to gain some measure of control over local policy initiatives. Critics reply that CDFs are designed

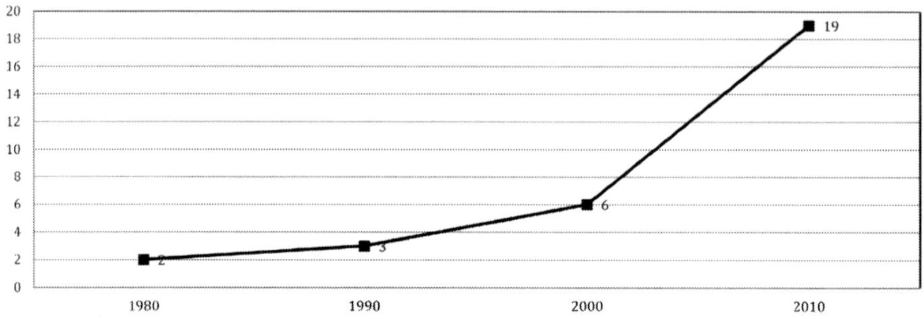

Figure 1.1 Growth of CDFs Over Time

mainly to enhance prospects for MPs' reelection. They are said to strengthen premodern social hierarchies and open up opportunities for corruption and stalled development.[3] This volume aims to reduce the heat-to-light ratio on CDFs by assessing the significance, merit and shortcomings of this emerging policy tool, as well as the dynamics that underlie the emergence of this form of distributive politics in developing countries.[4] It adds to the burgeoning literatures on democratic transition and on distributive politics by exploring the operations of one type of distributive mechanism across several countries.[5]

As is the case with earmarks, CDFs implicate important normative and theoretical dimensions of representation and effective public policy making. In what type of electoral and representative systems are CDFs most likely to emerge? What is the appropriate role of the representative when it comes to generating government funds for his constituency? Does the representative engage in such behavior for the benefit of his constituents, to bolster his own political career, or both? Are citizens with needs the most likely beneficiaries of such funds, or do they go disproportionately to monied and powerful interests? Do CDFs divert scarce resources from high-priority items of national import to local and less important projects? Do the projects completed with CDF financing contribute to enhancing the quality of life in the constituencies or do they contribute to "fiscal illusions" and waste?

This first comprehensive treatment of CDFs in the academic and development literatures emerges from a project at the State University of New York Center for International Development (SUNY CID). This project has explored CDFs in 19 countries and has developed indicators on their emergence, operations and oversight. SUNY/CID hosted two workshops at the University at Albany. The first was an exploratory roundtable on CDFs with academics, policy makers, and legislative development professionals from the United Nations Development Program (UNDP), the World Bank, the National Democratic Institute, the Canadian Parliamentary Centre and the Commonwealth Parliamentary Organization (CPA). The second was an in-depth exploration of earmarks and member items in New York State with officials from New York state government and local government, lobbyists and good government advocates, and academics from SUNY CID. We also presented papers at a number of professional, political science conferences.[6] On a more practical side, we presented a paper at a workshop on "the role of parliamentarians in facilitating grassroots projects" at the 56th CPA conference in Nairobi, Kenya in September 2010. Together with CPA, we organized a workshop with over 20 MPs and staff in Kingston, Jamaica that led the CPA to publish "Principles and Guidelines for Constituency Development Funds" in 2011. The following year, we met again in Dar es Salaam, Tanzania to design a tool box for CDFs and to adopt the first tool on public participation. We are continuing this collaboration that develops tools to inform good practice in CDFs.[7]

The authors explore the emergence, institutionalization and accountability of these funds, and analyze key issues in their operations. They provide detailed case studies of the emergence and operations of CDFs in Kenya, Uganda, Jamaica and India, as well as an analysis of earmarks in the US Congress and offer some provisional conclusions of what the emergence and operations of these funds say about the democratization of politics in developing countries and current approaches to international support for democratic governance in developing countries.

CDFs can be seen from different angles. Political scientists might view them as part of an MP's "home style" and the "electoral connection" for the legislature.[8] At workshops organized by SUNY/CID and the CPA, MPs spoke at length about the importance of maintaining contact with their constituencies and said that CDFs are the first routine tool through which they can demonstrate improvement in government services to their constituents. In this sense, CDFs can be viewed as an innovation in legislative development among governments that are undergoing democratization: legislators are involved in the political project of distributive spending that is associated with "pork barreling" and/or that can lead to greater local public participation and legitimacy in policy making.[9]

Economists and students of public administration view them as a policy tool that enables one type of fiscal decentralization and can explore the problems of coordination of different streams of funding for essential services to constituents and the extent to which this tool enables an efficient use of resources.[10] If CDFs represent a government program that is subject to the externalities and inefficiencies of other government programs, it can be explored, along with other policy tools, as a problem in implementation and coordination.[11]

A third perspective is provided by the international good governance community that views CDFs against an upwardly sloping standard of the march towards globalized, liberal governance that prevails among donor agencies in international development and in the social science we practice and teach. And against this standard of policy reform and good governance, observers in this community have viewed CDFs as manifestations of undemocratic politics, clientelism, cronyism, corruption, inefficiency in developing and providing services to communities.[12]

This collection provides a broad introduction to the emergence and operations of these funds in a set of comprehensive case studies that capture their rich and diverse character. The case studies serve as a basis for further work about CDFs, and can provide background to ongoing efforts to pass legislation and regulations on CDFs and to frame them as one policy tool for service delivery and local-level development. In what follows, we provide a broad comparative overview of CDFs against the background of the conceptual and policy issues that make them controversial, and conclude with an introduction to the individual chapters in the volume.

CDFs can be seen as a response to common problems facing MPs. In workshops on CDFs, MPs from Jamaica, India and Pakistan reported that "we have no choice but to respond to our constituents when they visit from the provinces . . . [they] depend on us and we depend on them in the election."[13] They cited a wide range of projects and constituency support services, such as building classrooms in schools, providing scholarships for students, financing funerals of constituents, road construction, street lighting in villages and urban areas, building additions to hospitals, and emergency relief and response to natural disaster, with "money for small things" described in David Ndii's chapter in this volume. MPs further pointed out that CDFs help to fill holes created by the absence of a consistently rule-bound administrative environment: "In our part of the world, people build houses . . . first, then we have to provide them with gas, electricity and roads. That is the biggest problem of the constituencies and people come to the MPs with these problems."[14] MPs from Uganda, Zambia, Ghana, Kenya and Swaziland maintained that they collaborated with stakeholders from local through national levels of government. They said that MPs have unique responsibilities in their constituencies that extended beyond the act of representing the views of constituents in formulating policy and overseeing the executive. One MP proposed that "constituency service should be embedded in the constitution" and affirmed that CDFs "will not go away anytime soon" because they address real needs and fill serious gaps.[15] In short, MPs claim that these funds provide essential services that will not be otherwise supplied.

A properly constituted CDF is not the only type of distributive policy making that has become popular over the past few decades in emerging democracies, as Joel Barkan and Robert Mattes suggest, in Chapter 2, with respect to constituency funds in Nigeria and district level funds in Ghana. The African Legislatures Project has produced research that demonstrates the importance of constituency-based politics in Africa in both the supply and demand for constituency service.[16] As Dianna Evans further shows in Chapter 7, the age-old system of US earmarks and member items provide members with resources to invest in their constituencies. Barry Weingast characterizes distributive legislation as *divisible*; i.e., projects that are local and varied in size, scope, and dollar amount independently of one another; an omnibus of many divisible projects in a policy area; designed mainly for expenditure or allocation of funds; and making eligible a supermajority of districts for funds.[17] Research on distributive policy in the US over the past century has focused on how all districts receive something that is instrumental in the reelection efforts of each individual legislator and distributive programs are assumed to confer visible concentrated benefits, whose costs are distributed invisibly across the entire taxpaying public.[18]

No two CDFs are structurally identical. They vary cross-nationally in point of origin, precise purpose, percentage of allocated budget, amount provided to each constituency, type of mechanisms of selection and implementation, and type of oversight and accountability. In the allocation of funds, some governments ensure that impoverished areas receive more funding than developed areas, or in employing them to address natural calamities. There are great differences in the capacity to mix CDF funds with donor funds, the capacity to carry unused funds from one year to the next, methods of disbursing funds for projects, and methods for oversight and monitoring, to name a few cross-national differences in the employment of this policy tool.

The table in Appendix 1 demonstrates these variations. First, where do CDFs come from? Philippines' Priority Development Assistance Fund was passed as part of a general appropriations act. Kenya's CDF was passed in parliament in 2003, and amended in 2007 and in 2013.[19] Solomon Islands Rural Constituency Development Fund was created in 1989 with no legislation. Regulations governing legislation passed in early 2013 at the initiative of the executive has been undergoing a process of consultation and possible revision since the middle of that year. Jamaica's CDF was initiated by the Office of the Prime Minister. In Malaysia there is a fund only for MPs of the coalition in power. Proposals to establish formal CDFs in Indonesia, Ghana and Trinidad and Tobago have not been approved, but there are district-level funds in Ghana, for example. Barkan and Mattes very precisely explore the CDFs in Africa in their elegant treatment on CDF origins.

CDFs appear almost exclusively in Westminster systems where MPs have clear, geographically defined constituencies in first-past-the-post plurality/majority electoral systems. The creation of funds in such governments give to members of parliament direct influence over a set of resources that is dedicated to investment and services in their constituencies, and MPs usually believe that the funds can assist them in their reelection efforts. And while they can be contentious in the same way that earmarks have recently been controversial in the US, CDFs are not considered in individual pieces of legislation, but are institutionalized in the annual budget process and almost always cuts across party lines.[20]

The funds are designed to fill holes in development and service delivery. Bhutan's constituency development grant (CDG) can be used for poverty alleviation, rural road construction, and advancement of women and children, but not for recurrent expenditure, purchase of vehicles or acquisition of land and buildings.[21] In Kenya, the CDF shall "ensure that a specific portion of the national annual budget is devoted to the constituencies for purposes of development and in particular in the fight against poverty at the constituency level."[22] It mandates spending on healthcare, education, security, electricity, sanitation and water treatment. In India, the Member of Parliament Local Area Development fund (MPLAD) "provides a mechanism for the Members of Parliament to recommend works of developmental nature for creation of durable community assets and for provision of basic facilities including community infrastructure, based on locally felt needs."[23] It permits projects in water, healthcare, infrastructure, sanitation and emergency assistance, but none in education. In Jamaica, the CDF "seeks to improve the effectiveness of Members of Parliament as a designated funding mechanism for constituency projects . . ." and "[t]he main thrust of the Fund is to promote human and infrastructure development at the community and constituency levels through the establishment of sustainable development projects."[24] Legislation in Solomon Islands indicates that the "funds may be allocated for development purposes to individuals, group income generating projects or community projects."[25]

MPs confirm that, in practice, these funds provide an essential catalyst to address problems in service delivery in their constituencies.[26] Constituents routinely approach MPs and their offices concerning the delivery of services—far beyond the traditional type of support for weddings and funerals—in education, health, roads, transportation and similar services. MPs claim that CDFs help to fill gaps in delivery of services—e.g., providing toilets in schools, giving scholarships to poor students, fixing roads—that have not been provided by ministries and for which local government lacks sufficient resources. So by design, a CDF is less a major development program than a catalyst to facilitate the delivery of essential services. The MPs who have participated in SUNY/CID and CPA workshops believe that they play a crucial role in filling the gaps between the ministries and local/regional government.

Each government takes a unique approach to managing these funds and to developing relationships between communities, MPs, parliamentary committees and executive agencies. Central governments work more closely with local government in some CDFs than in others. The Ministry of Local Government sometimes plays a substantial role in managing the funds, while the Prime Minister's Office or the Ministry of Rural Development can also play a substantial role. Formulas for allocations of funds to constituencies differ in each country, as well. At workshops conducted by SUNY/CID with the CPA, MPs have argued that it was important to adopt an approach to managing CDFs that fit within the national political and administrative cultures.[27]

Further, each CDF's formula of distribution addresses a unique set of conditions and problems. Kenya's CDF distributes 75% of funding among all constituencies and the remaining 25% of funding to those constituencies, which fall below a poverty line. In Tanzania, 25% is equally distributed to each constituency, 45% is distributed according to population, 20% to poorer constituencies and 10% according to size. In short, the template for fund allocation involves finding a distributional formula that reflects the particular social, political and economic circumstances of each country that will provide some flexibility for service delivery outside of the existing institutional channels, and can add some flexibility in the capacity of government to respond to needs for service or infrastructure in constituencies.

The funds command widely varying amounts of resources from the government budget as seen in Figure 1.2. In Kenya, CDFs have taken 2.5% of the budget, while in India it has taken 0.14% of the budget and in Jamaica 0.23% of the budget, and in Bhutan 0.314% of the national budget, although in many cases, these are moving targets and the percentage changes between conception and policy. Not only do the funds take up different percentages of the government budget, but they allocate different amounts to MPs. For example, the research of the International Budget Project shows that Uganda's CDF gave to each constituency $5,187, while in Malaysia, constituencies received $577,951. So in some places, the funds have come to constitute significant sources of funding, while in others it has remained quite modest in its potential impact on service delivery or development.

Nor are the funds consistently managed cross-nationally. Some governments' funds are directly disbursed to MPs. In Papua New Guinea, for example, the Electoral Development Fund releases funds to MPs who identify projects and finance them. Or in Uganda the Clerk to Parliament disbursed funds to each MPs personal account and the MPs then funded projects as they saw fit. In other places, CDFs resemble a typical government program, but one in which the MP and constituents themselves can play a role in identifying projects to be supported by the funds. In Jamaica MPs consult with locally-based committees and submit plans to the Office of the Prime

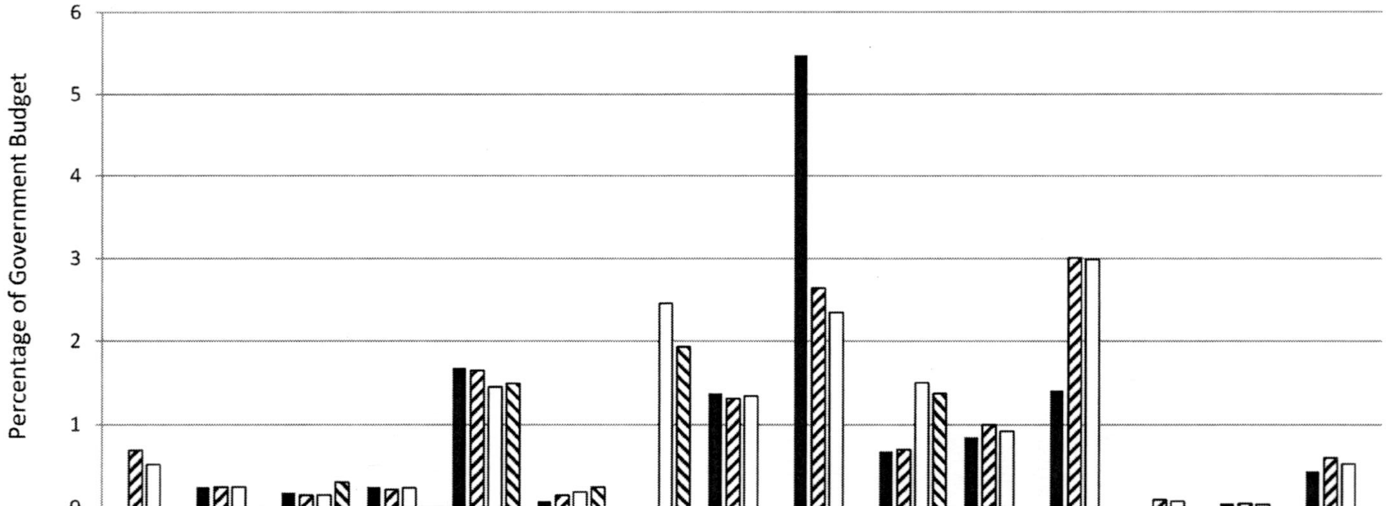

	Bhutan	Ghana	India	Jamaica	Kenya	Malawi	Nigeria	Pakistan	Papua New Guinea	Philip-pines	Solomon Islands	South Sudan	Tanzania	Uganda	Zambia
■ FY 2009	0	0.25	0.18	0.25	1.68	0.08	0	1.37	5.48	0.68	0.85	1.41	0	0.05	0.44
◪ FY 2010	0.69	0.25	0.15	0.22	1.65	0.15	0	1.31	2.64	0.7	1	3.01	0.1	0.05	0.6
□ FY 2011	0.52	0.25	0.15	0.24	1.45	0.19	2.45	1.34	2.34	1.5	0.92	2.99	0.08	0.04	0.53
⧅ FY 2012	0	0	0.31	0	1.49	0.25	1.93	0	0	1.37	0	0	0	0	0

Figure 1.2 Changes in CDF Funding. *Source*: Appendix 1, Characteristics of Selected Decentralized Funds

Table 1.1 Amounts Allocated per MP in USD

	Average Amount Allocated per MP (USD)
Philippines	$4,270,001
Bhutan	$43,000
Solomon Islands	$140,000
Kenya	$794,464
Malaysia	$577,951
Jamaica	$456,361
India	$420,790
Sudan	$317,543
Pakistan	$240,000
Malawi	$21,352
Tanzania	$13,761
Uganda	$5,187

Source: Tsangana, Alison Hickey. "Constituency Development Funds Scoping Paper," *International Budget Project*, 18 January 2010 http://internationalbudget.org/wp-content/upload/Constituency-Develpoment-Funds-Scoping-Paper.pdf., pp. 4–5. The paper does not indicate for which year the allocation took place.

Minister (OPM), which provides an analysis of the proposal and then sends it to the CDF committee in parliament for final approval before the OPM's Finance Officer releases the funds to the appropriate agency. In Kenya, Jamaica, Malawi and India, the funds are indirectly disbursed via implementing agencies, partner ministries or local government.

It is the same with oversight and administration of the funds: a wide range of government agencies, ministries, audit institutions and independent organizations oversee the employment of the funds. Far from instances in which CDFs are swept under the rug in some form of iron triangle, they generally provide much fodder for public discourse.[28] Some governments, such as Kenya and India, provide a great deal of public information on the funds in websites and publications. The Controller and Auditor General conduct regular audits to CDFs in Kenya; the Public Accounts Committees pay close attention to the funds in Zambia, for example, and several governments have Freedom of Information Laws.[29] Robust civil society networks in Africa have closely monitored the use of funds, and the mass media pay close attention to the use and misuse of CDFs among these governments, in Solomon Islands and Jamaica, as well.[30] This is not to suggest that oversight is perfectly accomplished in any of these examples, but to say that oversight of the funds provides a good opportunity for much public information about the funds to come to light and for the funds to become a significant object for the legitimate public controversy and advocacy that is standard in democratic societies.

What becomes clear from this bottom-up survey of CDFs' institutional development in emerging democracies is the unsurprising finding that each one reflects distinct political and administrative circumstances. Critics employ loaded terms such as "politicization," "pork barrel," and "patron-client networks' with a broad brush. And as in so many other policies, institutions, and delivery mechanisms, there is no shortage of inefficiency, ineffectiveness and malfeasance in this policy process and no shortage of public controversy; therein lay a set of challenges.

THE COMMON CHALLENGES AND CONTROVERSIES FACING CDFs

How effective are CDFs in practice? Good governance organizations have typically argued that CDFs provide little real value to the constituencies while their operations violate good governance and classical democratic practice. This vision is predicated on the assumption that parliamentarians are primarily responsible for lawmaking, representation and oversight. In this classical vision, the most constructive contribution of MPs to service delivery is thorough parliamentary oversight of the agencies that are constitutionally responsible for these functions of government. The involvement of MPs in the implementation of policy, it is held, blurs important and constitutionally defined distinctions among different actors in government and opens up avenues for ineffective and corrupt governance.[31] For example, two Kenyan critics of the CDF find that MPs' "expenditure of public funds is commingling of roles of the different organs of state in a manner that is unacceptable . . . it would be against the constitutional principle of the separation of powers for Members of Parliament to take part in actual spending, then submit their annual estimates to themselves in Parliament through the Public Accounts Committee."[32] Of course, such problems may be typical in all branches of government. A vast literature on US policy making and international development suggest that all new government programs typically face implementation challenges.[33] Against this background, CDFs face three broader sets of challenges in their operations: representation and separation of powers, efficiency, and accountability.

Do CDFs violate the separation of powers in violation of classical approaches to parliamentary representation? Good governance professionals argue that, in a system with a well-defined separation of powers, "[p]arliaments provide the vital link between the public and the system of government, serve as the principal forum for airing issues of public concern and continue to perform functions that cannot be replicated by any other institution."[34] In this view, CDFs undermine MPs' national policy making role, and the time taken to manage funds is subtracted from their real responsibilities of considering legislation and oversight of executive's implementation of this legislation. John Patteson Oti, a member of Solomon Island's opposition at the time, argued that the two functions were not mutually exclusive. In parliamentary debate he "anticipated that MPs can be relieved from the burden of being reduced to acting like project managers" and that "[r]emoving MPs from direct responsibility of the Constituency Development Funding will also enable Members of Parliament to concentrate and focus on the very roles and functions for which they were elected in the first place, and that is to be legislators and policy makers."[35] In the same spirit, at workshops organized by SUNY and CPA, MPs neither gainsaid traditional parliamentary responsibilities of representation and oversight nor rejected their efforts to strengthen service delivery in their constituencies.

It also seems that the classical approach to parliamentary representation misses just how contemporary representation has grown into a more complex set of relationships, wherein MPs relate to multiple geographic, status-based and issue-based constituencies. Representation now takes place in programs of outreach with a two-way flow of communication between members and voters. It is increasingly transparent and involves a wide array of actors, including parliamentary monitoring organizations that attempt to hold parliaments accountable for their work. Representation concerns multiple internal and external constituencies, such as ordinary citizens, business, regional, ethnic and gender interests, among others. These days, it involves constituency service as much as it does reflecting the views of constituents in national debates over policy.[36]

The "new representation" also concerns the manner in which the MPs serve their constituents in these funds. There remain controversies over the fairness of distribution of CDF funding for there is no universally accepted formula for distribution of funds among districts and within districts—both over the amount of spending and over the types of needs that are addressed by the different projects. How are the priorities determined within constituencies? Does funding go disproportionately to campaign supporters, members of a specific party or ethnic community? Will all annual distribution be spent or will MPs in safe seats not feel the need to use the spending? If it were possible for CDFs to coordinate with other government agencies, they can help to enhance local-level service. And a range of participatory mechanisms—from constituency consultative meetings, and constituency-based budget proposals—can enhance the responsiveness of CDFs to local needs.[37]

Second, CDFs face the challenge of efficiency in project implementation. The International Budget Project has argued that, "CDFs have a negative impact on accountability and service delivery" in comparison with "other options for strengthening legislatures and improving local project delivery."[38]

As with all government programs, the misallocation, misuse or underutilization of CDF disbursements can come from *fiscal illusions*, or expenditure with unanticipated hidden costs that must be picked up by local, regional or central government agencies as part of a budget outlay.[39] In this respect, CDFs can be treated as "free money" that does not come directly from a constituency's revenue or tax base.[40] When the central government ministries or agencies incur the long-term cost of these projects, they contain unanticipated, hidden costs. Poor coordination among different levels of government can lead to the duplication of projects with development efforts of national and local government or development efforts funded by the donor community.

Another frequent assertion is of the low capacity for *administration* in local government that may be ill equipped to administer project funds due to the technical complexity of management practice. At our workshops, MPs have reported continuing challenges to ensure that local committees have the capacity to work effectively and to provide sufficient resources to make a difference in important matters of small infrastructure, provision of health and other types of services. There is the possibility that some constituencies receive too many projects, that projects are abandoned in midstream following the turnover of an MP, that political interests can be the determining factor of a project far more than an objective consideration of needs, that poor coordination with ministries to take over CDF-built facilities means that CDF projects can remain idle after construction and that the quality of construction in projects is poor. These challenges provide opportunities for improving the design and implementation of CDFs in practice.

A final set of challenges concerns the transparency and accountability of these funds that can result from the absence of effective oversight. This can lead to unaccounted-for financing because balance sheets are improperly reported. This goes together with the potential for corruption, when MPs use funds mainly to buy political favors or votes; when decentralized levels of government, administration and CSOs fail to maintain and submit to central CDF administration detailed records of money used; and/or project designers or implementers are selected on the basis of clientelism or nepotism. The International Budget Partnership's documentary examining MUHURI's social audit in Mombasa, Kenya demonstrated the problems in the operations of institutions that are charged with accountability and/or transparency in Kenya's CDFs.[41] Enhanced transparency and oversight through report cards and social audits are increasingly being employed both by government institutions and by those in civil society.[42] The National Taxpayers Association in Kenya continues to provide comprehensive audits of constituencies with report cards throughout the country supported by the UK Department of International Development.[43] At our workshops, MPs accepted the utility of reaching out to good governance organizations in order to ensure that the funds operate according to the good governance principles of probity, transparency and accountability. They supported efforts of national and regional anti-corruption agencies and civil society to engage in oversight of CDFs with, reporting, social audits, report cards and the like as part of making CDFs politically and socially acceptable.

EXPLORING THE INSTITUTIONALIZATION AND ACCOUNTABILITY OF CDFs

We saw above that a summary critique would argue that CDFs are not held accountable for their performance; they are relatively noninstitutionalized forms of slush funds that are employed as "pork" and to buy votes; and that MPs employ the funds in inefficient and even corrupt ways. There are too few cases for a conclusive cross-national assessment of these claims, although a number of studies have explored different dimensions of national experiences.[44]

We made an initial exploration of CDF performance across 19 governments in developing countries with CDFs and/or other distributive spending schemes. We coded the formal rules that govern these schemes to ascertain the extent to which they are accountable and institutionalized, and the extent of involvement of the individual MP. We defined these terms in the following manner. *Accountability* refers to the extent to which the funds are subjected to reporting, oversight and audits. *Institutionalization* refers to the extent to which the funds become routinized in the number of steps to award and implement projects, and *MP Involvement* refers to the degree of participation by individual members of parliament in the management of funds.[45] CDFs with higher degrees of institutionalization are likely to be a more routine type of policy tool than those with lower degrees of institutionalization. Similarly, CDFs with higher degrees of accountability are likely to be subject to the type of reporting requirements and transparency norms characteristic of better governance tools than those with lower degrees of accountability. Finally, the less that an MP is directly involved in appointing the CDF local committees, selecting projects, awarding contracts and disbursing, the more that CDFs will resemble a policy tool.

We coded each practice or activity uniquely in one of the three variables, so that an activity that is considered part of "institutionalization" was not also coded as part of "accountability" for example. To be clear, this coding is not of actual behavior or operation of the CDFs but of administrative regulations, legislation and publicly available accounts of the rules, so that it reflects a formal commitment and not reported activity. Figure 1.3 demonstrates the variation of 17 governments for which we could collect data on all three variables. Following this, we expected to find the following patterns in relationships among accountability, institutionalization and MP involvement:

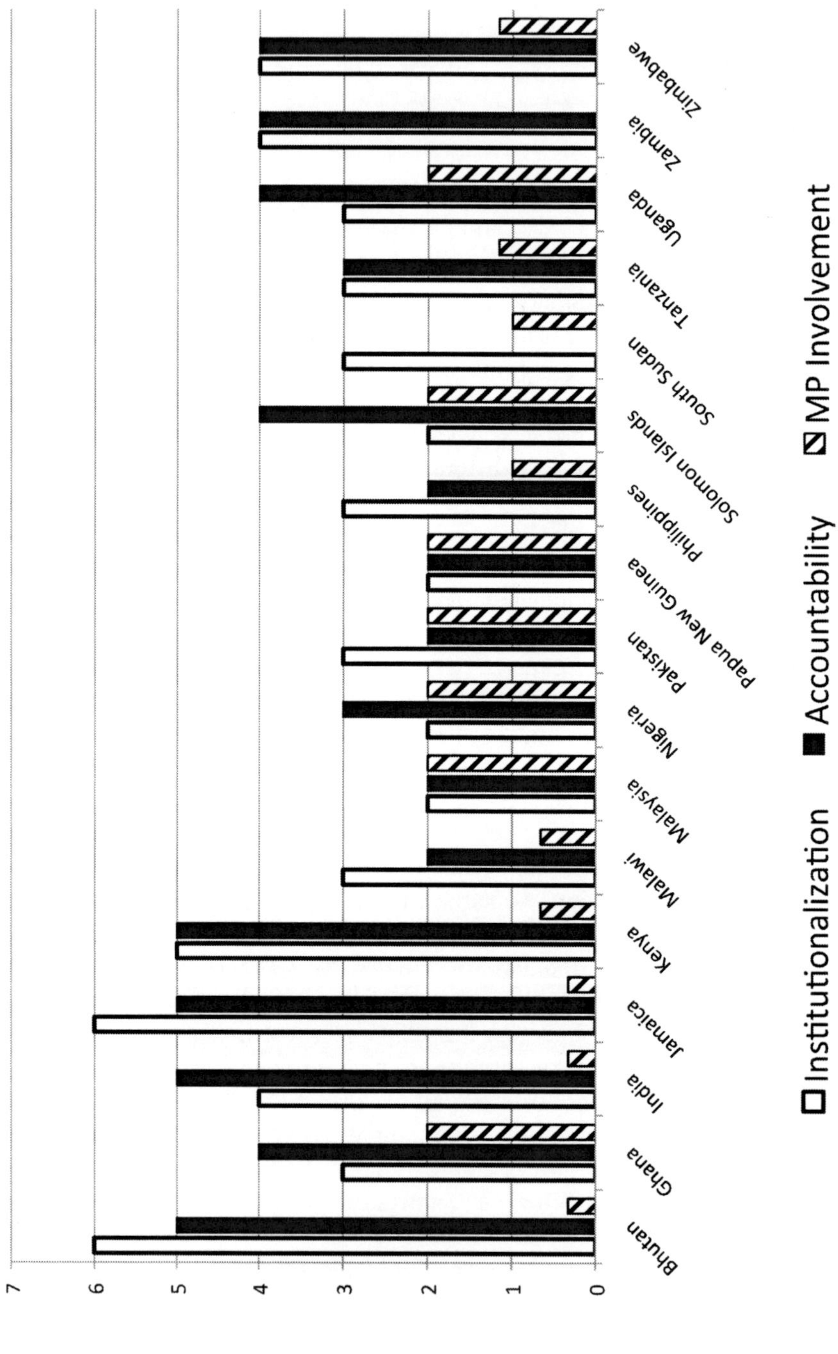

Figure 1.3 Measures of CDF Institutionalization, Accountability, and MP Involvement

1. CDFs that are more institutionalized also have more "accountability" built in to them; and
2. CDFs with more accountability and institutionalization also would have less direct involvement of the MP in its operations.

In Table 1.2 and Figure 1.4, we show that two-thirds of CDFs with low formal MP involvement have medium amounts of accountability and one third of these CDFs have high levels of accountability. This is shown graphically in Figure 1.4.

Similarly, Table 1.3 shows that in the one third of CDFs with low degrees of institutionalization, we also find low degrees of accountability. Two thirds of the CDFs with medium levels of institutionalization have low degrees of accountability; 72% of CDFs with medium degrees of accountability have high degrees of institutionalization; and all CDFs with high degrees of accountability also have high degrees of institutionalization. This is shown graphically in Figure 1.5.

Table 1.2 Correlation Between MP Involvement and MP Accountability

	Low Involvement	*Medium Involvement*	*High Involvement*
Low Accountability	—	>66%	60%
Medium Accountability	>66%	>33%	40%
High Accountability	>33%	—	—

N = 13 Kendall's tau-b = −0.4209 ASE = 0.210 Gamma = −0.5556 ASE = 0.252.

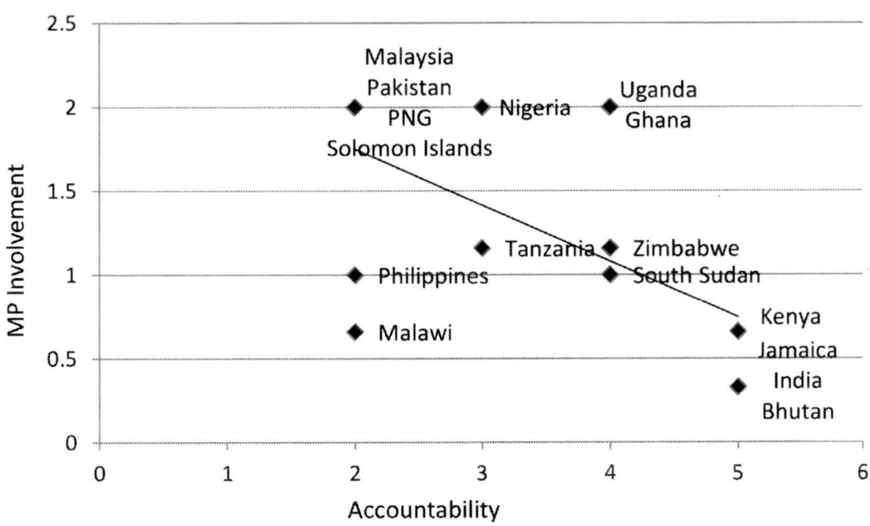

Figure 1.4 MP Involvement and Accountability

In sum, our survey of CDFs show that funds, which are more institutionalized, also have built in to them greater formal accountability mechanisms and that these funds are also likely to have less formal involvement of MPs. To be sure, this finding may speak mainly to the capacity of the government to draft legislation and/or administrative regulations that are in accordance with prevailing norms of good governance, but it might also suggest that such a government also has the capacity to implement such a policy, as well. So the problem with corruption and inefficiency may stem less from the CDF itself than from a broader set of institutional practices, the incentives that are built in to these institutions, and the norms and values that guide this process of design. It is the same in our meetings with MPs and in most of the chapters in this volume: CDFs are a messy "fact of life" in the institutional landscape in developing democracies: they provide resources for multiple service, development and political purposes in parliamentary constituencies and provide MPs with opportunities to curry favor at home.

Table 1.3 Correlation Between CDF Institutionalization and MP Accountability

	Low Institutionalization	*Medium Institutionalization*	*High Institutionalization*
Low Accountability	>33%	>66%	–
Medium Accountability	–	>28%	>72%
High Accountability	–	–	100%

N = 14 Gamma = 0.7255 ASE = 0.182 Kendall's tau-b = 0.5446 ASE = 0.153.

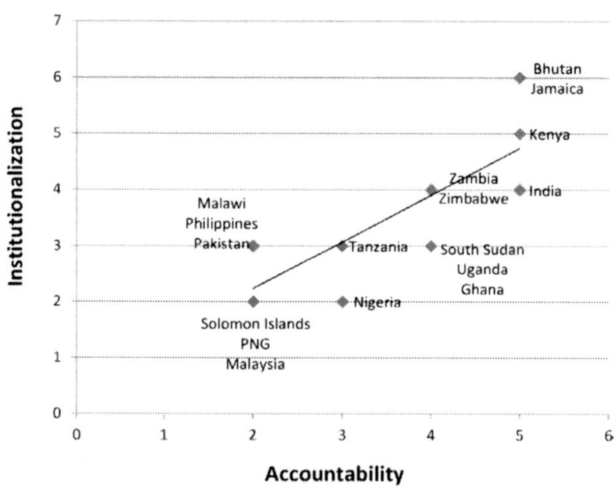

Figure 1.5 Institutionalization and Accountability

MAKING CDFs SAFE FOR DEMOCRACY

It is surprising that there have been very few systematic studies of this emerging institution in developing democracies. The academic studies cited in this chapter have explored the vote-buying character of this type of pork barrel policy, have described individual CDFs, and/or made a series of recommendations concerning CDFs. Donors have displayed little interest in CDFs, possibly because they appear to be politicized schemes that fit outside a technocratic, top-down development "formula" of good governance in developing countries.[46] And support for or interest in CDFs could seem like crossing a red line between good and bad governance. Good governance NGOs have employed donor financing to produce very informative and critical work on CDFs with the broader goal to develop finances for local level development and service delivery that are more in line with liberal good governance as this is putatively practiced in developed countries. It soon became clear that this research and donor-funded activity has not satisfied the demand for useful and constructive information on these distributive funds, a conclusion we drew in meetings, conversations and correspondence with MPs and CDF managers who were interested in spurring the same kind of local development and service delivery favored by the international good governance community.

We sought to conduct a thorough, comparative and context-rich exploration of CDFs that could shed light on this emerging institution and help to frame a set of norms and practices that find the balance between bottom-up solutions to development problems and good governance norms. This exploration has taken two tracks. First, SUNY/CID has collaborated with the Commonwealth Parliamentary Association (CPA) to articulate a set of norms for CDFs that would bring them in line with international standards of good governance. This collaboration brings together members and staff concerned with CDFs from parliaments across the commonwealth. The *Principles and Guidelines for Constituency Development Funds* develop a framework that emphasizes responsiveness to citizens' needs; transparency in the awarding and implementation of projects with CDF funds; effective and efficient administration of CDF funds; ensuring accountability and oversight into the operations of CDFs in order to avoid corruption and abuse; and monitoring and evaluation of fund operations as a key element in learning what works best in the administration of these funds.[47] This has led to the development of a toolbox intended for MPs and professional staff that includes guidance on Sourcing and Financing; Rules and Procedures; Public Participation; Procurement, Tendering and Contracting; Implementation and Operations; and Impact Assessment, Monitoring and Evaluating CDFs.[48] As we go to print, this collaboration continues from the first tool on participation.[49]

We did not wish that this exploration be a typical effort to identify "best practices" and templates that could easily be transferred to any government seeking a theoretically sound formula for development: in our experience no single template of a "best" practice can be employed in multiple societies. So we worked with social scientists with long experience in particular countries with CDFs, and employed a modified version of the field network study methodology.[50] It aims to capture the range of experience with CDFs with cases from different regions of the world, from large and small countries, from older and newer CDFs, from big and small CDFs, from CDFs that appeared to be institutionalized and those that were more fleeting in character. We asked each author to provide the political-economic background and context underlying the creation of a politicized, distributive scheme of development or service delivery; a history of the emergence of the CDF; a description of its legal context; its financing and budgeting; its manner of operations in selecting and implementing projects; the challenges faced by the CDFs; how effective oversight of the CDF has been; and lessons learned and selected commentary on the CDF. We found great variation among the stories that have been told. The initial drafts for these papers provided the background to SUNY/CID's collaboration with the CPA in helping to formulate the principles and guidelines for CDFs and the toolbox of CDF practices. Taken together, these chapters provide an extensive introduction to constituency development funds as a policy tool.

Joel Barkan and Robert Mattes employed data from the Afrobarometer and the African Legislators Project (ALP) to explore political and societal contexts that give rise to constituency development funds against three competing explanations. A "pork-barrel" argument maintains that CDFs represent a response to the pressure MPs feel to deliver both private and public goods to their constituents in order to increase their chances for reelection. A second, institutionalist, explanation suggests that by freeing up MPs to address the needs of constituents, CDFs assist them to become better legislators within the parliament. Third, a counterintuitive "mismatch" argument holds that MPs believe that their constituents seek constituency service when they actually seek stronger representation of their needs at the center. While their evidence supports the "mismatch" hypothesis, Barkan and Mattes also suggest that CDFs may also contribute "what citizens do want—better social service delivery, infrastructure, etc. back in their constituency. . . ."

David Ndii suggests that CDFs may be one of Kenya's most successful development policy innovations. MPs have long provided development patronage and welfare to their constituencies as a "response to the executive's inadequate provision of services and a reflection of the socio-cultural role and responsibilities of leaders and elites to their communities." This broader political and policy context opened a door to a fund that could provide "small things" demanded by constituents at the grassroots, which were provided neither by central state agencies nor by donors. He demonstrates the CDFs' popularity in helping to assist school and health facilities and other infrastructure projects, and suggests that its rate of project execution is superior to that of executive agencies. His review of a series of public controversies on CDFs provides background to an account of the evolution of Kenya's CDF from its origins in 2003 through changes in 2007 and through a potentially significant transformation under Kenya's 2010 constitution that explicitly has decentralized administration and created a bicameral parliament.

Nelson Kasfir and Stephen Twebaze trace the rise and fall of Uganda's CDF in a war-torn, impoverished society in which a no-party political system placed the burdens of MP campaigns entirely on the candidates themselves. It emerged from the MPs' demands for relief from constituent financial pressures and helped MPs to reduce costs of constituency service and to maintain voting support. They show how Uganda's CDF provided miniscule funds for MPs to invest in their constituencies and how it has subsequently been eliminated. They explain the emergence of Uganda's CDF as a function of Uganda's prohibition on political parties, governance through clientage, executive dominance over the legislature, corruption, and increasing tolerance for the misuse of official funds. Ugandan CDFs emerged from MPs demand for relief from constituent financial pressure but never became an institutionalized form of financing of services or development in constituencies.

In her account of US national policy making, Diana Evans explores the politics of earmarks against the background of the other CDFs treated in this volume. Her discussion of these funds, which are "carved out of the operating and capital budgets of federal agencies by Congress," draws on a long and distinguished tradition of scholarship in the United States. The desire of congressmen and senators to ensure that funding in science, homeland security, military construction, defense, transportation and commerce—to name a few areas—is directed to their districts has permeated the tradition of lawmaking in the United States since the founding of the republic. She unpacks the complex process by which earmarks are created and distributed to members on both sides of the aisle in a win-win relationship between executive agencies and the politicians that oversee their budgets. She reports that earmarks take a miniscule fraction of total federal spending and of discretionary spending, and concludes with accounts of reforms and moratoriums of US earmarking that have led to "lettermarking" and "phonemarking," which enables members to side-step the legislative process entirely and directly request agencies to direct spending in their districts.

Horace Bartilow places his analysis of Jamaica's CDF against a political and economic context that has given rise to poverty-stricken garrison communities controlled by "Dons" or strongman community leaders with the financial and political capacity to challenge the authority of public institutions. The Office of the Prime Minister initiated the establishment of a CDF as one way of directly providing services to constituencies against organized crime. In this sense, the development of CDFs represent an attempt to break with a particular type of clientelistic past and to strengthen an MPs relationships with her constituency so that she can be responsive to community needs.

Harry Blair explores the emergence and operations of India's Member of Parliament Local Area Development Scheme (MPLADS) out of the desires of politicians to maintain linkages with voters and from the example of state and municipal-level funds to enable members to devote to municipal works at their own discretion. It has become an extraordinarily complex program: taken together, national and state level representatives can invest more than half as much as the entire governmental apparatus has at its discretionary disposal for investment within the boundaries of the average MP constituency. He succinctly summarizes the mixed results from empirical studies on the existence of a political business cycle in which MP spending in constituencies may lead to reelection, and turns to a discussion of the controversies in operations that include political patronage and corruption, as well as series of irregularities and excesses in implementation that have been identified in formal evaluations and that have led to technocratic calls to end the program that is so popular with legislators. He concludes that enhanced transparency safeguards, and monitoring procedures and external watchdogs in the media will assist the system to become more accountable in nurturing a critical connection between elected representatives and their constituents.

Finally, Michael Mezey's conclusion lowers the heat-to-light ratio in discussions of CDFs and distributive policy making by placing these studies against broader considerations of representation, legislative development, and democratic policy making. The issue may well be not whether CDFs lead to "confusion and inefficiencies" or whether CDFs are "consistent, corruption free instruments for democratic participation in development decisions" but whether these projects "better reflect the needs of the constituency than projects that are identified by central authorities" and/or whether they contribute to a greater sense in constituencies that their voice matters. We believe that the stories of the emergence and operations of CDFs matter for what they say about the evolution of democratic and democratizing political systems today.

GLOSSARY OF KEY TERMS

ALP – African Legislators Project
CPA – Commonwealth Parliamentary Organization
CDF – Constituency Development Funds

CDG – Constituency Development Grant
MPs – Members of Parliament
MPLAD – Member of Parliament Local Area Development Fund
OPM – Office of the Prime Minister
SUNY CID – State University of New York Center for International Development
UNDP – United Nations Development Program

NOTES

1. We will refer to these funds as CDFs or constituency development funds as a generic term although such funds have a different names, such as Electoral Development funds (Papua New Guinea), Constituency Development Catalyst Funds (Tanzania), Member of Parliament Local Area Development Fund (India), and the like. See Appendix 1 for more details on the various funds.

2. See, for e.g., Ketan 2007.

3. Zyl "Constituency Development Funds: African Parliaments' Faustian Bargain."

4. See, for example, Lowi 1972; Zimmerman (1973) developed a comparative typology with distributive policy as one of several types of policy making.

5. Kramon and Posner 2013; Golden and Min, 2013.

6. We presented papers on CDFs at Western Political Science Association in March 2010, at the Research Committee for Legislative Specialists at the Southern Political Science Association in 2011 and 2012, and at the Ninth Workshop of Parliamentary Scholars and parliamentarians in July 2010. We gave the keynote speeches at a Monash University workshop on CDFs that built on our research in March, 2012; and presented on CDFs at the Parliamentary Network of the World Bank in Brussels in December 2010.

7. See this work on: http://www.cid.suny.edu/our_work/related/cdf.cfm and in appendixes 4–6.

8. Fenno, 1978; Mayhew, 2004; and Kitschelt and Kselman, 2013.

9. Keefer and Khemani 2009; Keefer and Vlaicu 2008.

10. Kimenyi 2005; Bagaka 2008; Salamon, ed., 2002.

11. See, for example, Nakamura 1987; Pressman and Wildavsky 1984; Pritchett 2012.

12. See, for example, Tsangana 2010, and "Constituency Develoment Fund in Tanzania: the Right Solution?"

13. Commonwealth Parliamentary Association and SUNY/CID 2011, 5.

14. *Ibid.*, p. 6.

15. *Ibid.* This point has been repeated regularly: "It was only in 1989 . . . that the government decided to use Members of Parliament because they would be close to their people and therefore can identify the needs of their people and because of this they must have funds not only to deliver services to their people but also to help them." Hon. Fred Fono, Deputy Prime Minister and Minister for Rural Development and Indigenous Affairs, Hansard, August 29, 2008.

16. See http://www.africanlegislaturesproject.org/ for more information on ALP. 2010 working paper: http://www.cssr.uct.ac.za/sites/cssr.uct.ac.za/files/pubs/WP277.pdf

17. Weingast 1994, 320–321.

18. Bickers and Stein, 1994, 329–330.

19. It was renamed the "Countrywide Development Fund" in 2000.

20. Malaysia is an exception, where members of the opposition do not gain access to constituency funds.

21. Ministry of Finance Tashichhodzong Thimphu 2009.

22. Constituency Development Fund Act 2003, 3.

23. Member of Parliament Local Area Development Scheme (MPLADS), *Annual Report, 2010–2011*, 3.

24. "Constituency Development Fund," http://opm.gov.jm/agencies/constituency-development-fund.

25 Constituency Development Funds Bill 2013, Section 5 (1): http://www.parliament.gov.sb/files/legislation/9th%20Parliament/Bills/2013/Constituency%20Development%20Fund%20Bill%202013.pdf

26. See Commonwealth Parliamentary Association and SUNY/CID, "Workshop on Constituency Development Funds in Dar Es Salaam, 9–11 October 2012."

27. Commonwealth Parliamentary Association and SUNY/CID "Roundtable and Workshop on Constituency Development Funds," Dar Es Salaam, Tanzania, 9–11 October, 2012.

28. For a discussion of iron triangles, see, Thurber 1996: 76–104. In the United States, the term refers to mutually supportive relationships between executive agencies, special interest lobbying organizations and legislative committees with jurisdiction over a specific functional area, which dominate policymaking in that area, and which present a united front to all "outsiders" who seek influence in that area.

29. For information on the Kenyan CDF see its web portal: http://www.cdf.go.ke/ Note to the Kenyan web site; the India reports and to "Councillors and Councils paying themselves heft allowances from Constituency Development funds," Lusakatimes.com, March 17, 2014: http://www.lusakatimes.com/2014/03/17/councillors-council-employees-paying-heft-allowances-constituency-development-funds/

30. "Politicians Rake Up Almost $200 Million in Discretionary Funds Last Year," The Island Sun, February 28, 2013; Caritas Zambia 2011; Zambian Governance Foundation, 2013.

31. Murray 2011.

32. Ongoya and Lumallas 2005.

33. See footnotes 10 and 11 above for some of this literature.

34. Powers 2012, 28. Also see Mezey 2011.

35. Solomon Islands Hansard, August 29, 2008. For a longer discussion of this point, see Gumpper, Baskin and Li, 2011.

36. See Powers 2012, 28; Mezey 2011; Barkan 2009; and Lindberg 2010, 117–142.

37. See the CPA's Public Participation Tool for CDFs in Appendix 6.

38. Zyl, "What is Wrong with the Constituency Development Funds," 2010, 1.

39. This would be the case when a clinic constructed with CDF funding made no provisions for ongoing procurement of equipment and medicine or salaries for personnel.

40. For example, see Kimenyi 2005: "There are indications that CDF is helping provide services to communities that for many years did not benefit substantially from government services. In particular, the poor have in the past experienced serious problems accessing basic services that are now made available through CDF. Nevertheless, there are increasing concerns about the utilization of CDF which suggest that the funds are not being utilized optimally."

41. See a program on social audit of a Kenyan CDF project at: http://www.youtube.com/watch?v=z2zKXqkrf2E

42. See, for example, Gikonyo 2008.

43. See, for example, National Taxpayer Association, where all the reports are available.

44. Keefer and Khemani 2009; also see Banerjee, Kumar, Pade and Su 2011; and Banerjee; Kraman and Posner.

45. Our coding methods and sources are found in Appendix 3.

46. The term is from Pritchett 2012; Also see Andrews, Pritchett and Woolcock 2012.

47. See Appendix 4.

48. See Appendix 5.

49. See Appendix 6.

50. Lurie 2000; Nathan 1982, 73–99; and Nathan 2000.

REFERENCES

African Legislatures Project. "Welcome to the African Legislature Project." http://www.africanlegislaturesproject.org/.

Andrews, Matt, Lant Pritchett and Michael Woolcock. "Escaping Capability Traps through Problem Driven Iterative Adaptation (PDIA)." United Nations University World Institute for Development Economics Research, Working Paper No. 2012/64 (July, 2012).

Bagaka, Obuya. "Fiscal Decentralization in Kenya: The Constituency Development Fund and the Growth of Government." *Association for Budgeting and Financial Management*, October 23–25, 2008: http://coppfs1.asu.edu/spa/abfm2008/new/Bagaka.pdf.

Banerjee, Abhijit V. Selvan Kumar, Ronii Pade and Felix Su. "Do Informed Voters Make Better Choices? Experimental Evidence from Urban India." Accessed March 31, 2014. http://www.hks.harvard.edu/fs/rpande/papers/DoInformedVoters_Nov11.pdf.

Barkan, Joel, ed. "African Legislatures and the 'Third Wave' of Democratization." *Legislative Power in Emerging African Democracies*. Boulder, CO: Lynne Reinner, 2009.

Barkan, Joel D., Robert Mattes, Shaheen Mozaffar and Kimberly Smiddy. "The Africa Legislatures Project: First Findings." *Center for Social Science Research*. http://www.cssr.uct.ac.za/sites/cssr.uct.ac.za/files/pubs/WP277.pdf.

Bickers, Kenneth N and Robert M. Stein. "Response to Barry Weingast's Reflections." *Political Research Quarterly*, vol. 47, no. 2 (1994): 329–330.

Caritas Zambia. "A Study Report on the Development of the Constituency Development Fund (CDF)." September 2011: http://www.caritaszambia.org.zm/images/stories/CDF_Research_Report.pdf.

Commonwealth Parliamentary Association and SUNY/CID. "Roundtable and Workshop on Constituency Development Funds: Dar Es Salaam, Tanzania, 9–11 October, 2012." *SUNY/CID*. http://www.cid.suny.edu/publications1/SUNY-CPA_CDFs_Jamaica2_June2011.pdf

———. "Workshop on Constituency Development Funds: In Dar Es Salaam, 9–11 October 2012." *SUNY/CID*. http://www.cid.suny.edu/publications1/Tanzania%20CPA%20CDF%20Mtg%20Report.pdf

"Constituency Development Fund in Tanzania: the Right Solution?" *Policy Forum*, February 11, 2009: http://www.policyforum-tz.org/files/ConstituencyDevelopmentFund.pdf.

"Constituency Development Funds." *Office of the Prime Minster*. Accessed August 10, 2013 http://opm.gov.jm/agencies/constituency-development-fund/.

Constituency Development Funds Bill 2013. Section 5 (1): http://www.parliament.gov.sb/files/legislation/9th%20Parliament/Bills/2013/Constituency%20Development%20Fund%20Bill%202013.pdf

Fenno Jr., Richard F. *Homestyle: House Members in Their Districts*. Boston: Little, Brown and Co. 1978. 31–53.

Gikonyo, Wanjiru. "The CDF Social Audit Guide, a Handbook for Communities." *Open Society Initiative of East Africa*, February 2008. http://www.soros.org/initiatives/osiea/articles_publications/publications/cdf_20080201/resource_20080808.pdf.

Golden, Miriam and Brian Min. "Distributive Politics Around the World." *Annual Review of Political Science,* vol. 16, (2013), pp. 73–99.

Gumpper, Paul, Mark Baskin and Haibo Li. "Constituency Development Funds and the Separation of Powers." paper prepared for the Southern Political Science Association, 82nd Annual Conference, New Orleans, Louisiana, January 8, 2011.

Keefer, Philip and Razvan Vlaicu. "Democracy, Credibility and Clientelism." *Journal of Law, Economics & Organization,* vol. 24, no. 2 (2008): 371–406.

Keefer, Philip and Stuti Khemani. "When Do Legislators Pass on Pork? The Role of Political Parties in Determining Legislator Effort." *American Political Science Review*, vol. 103, no. 1 (February 2009): 99–112.

Ketan, Joseph. "The Use and Abuse of Electoral Development Funds and their Impact on Electoral Politics and Governance in Papua, New Guinea." *Center for Democratic Institutions Policy Papers on Political Governance*, no. 2 (2007). http://www.cdi.anu.edu.au/.png/2007-08/D_P/2007_08_PPS4_PNG_Ketan/2007_08_PPS4_KETAN.pdf

Kimenyi, Mwangi. "Efficiency and Efficacy of Kenya's Constituency Development Fund: Theory and Evidence." University of Connecticut Department of Economics Working Paper 2005-42 (April 2005): http://ideas.repec.org/p/uct/uconnp/2005-42.html.

Kitschelt, Herbert and Daniel M. Kselman. "Economic Development, Democratic Experience and Political Parties' Linkage Strategies." *Comparative Political Studies,* vol. 46, no. 11 (2013): 1453–1484.

Kramon, Eric and Daniel Posner. "Who Benefits from Distributive Politics? How the Outcome One Studies Affects the Answer One Gets." *Perspectives on Politics*, vol. 11, no. 2 (2013): 461–473.

Lindberg, Staffan I. "What Accountability Pressures Do MPs in Africa Face and How Do They Respond? Evidence from Ghana." *Journal of Modern African Studies*, vol. 48, no. 1 (2010): 117–142.

Lowi, Theodore. "Four Systems of Policy, Politics and Choice." *Public Administration Review*, vol. 32, no. 4 (1972): 298–310.

Lurie, Irene. "Field Network Studies." Rockefeller College of Public Affairs and Policy, State University of New York at Albany, February 2000.

Mayhew, David R. *Congress: The Electoral Connection.* New Haven, CT: Yale University Press, 2004.

Member of Parliament Local Area Development Scheme (MPLADS). *Annual Report, 2010–2011* Government of India Ministry of Statistics and Programme Implementation.

Ministry of Finance, Tashichhodzong Thimphu. "Constituent Development Grant Rules 2009." *Royal Government of Bhutan*, (2009). http://www.mof.gov.bt/publication/files/pub7vr2029rk.pdf.

Mezey, Michael. "Representation and Constituency Relations Comparative Assessment of Parliaments (CAP) Note." *SUNY Center for International Development*, December 2011, http://www.cid.suny.edu/capnotes1/Mezey_Cap-Note_011912.pdf

Muhuri. "It's Our Money. Where's it Gone?" YouTube Video, 18:08, posted by "centerforbudget," September 21, 2009, http://www.youtube.com/watch?v=z2zKXqkrf2E

Murray, Christina. "Constituency Development funds: Are they Constitutional?" *International Budget Project*, Budget Brief, 12, 2012. http://internationalbudget.org/budget-briefs/brief12/

Nakamura, Robert. "The Textbook Policy Process and Implementation Research." *Policy Studies Review*, vol. 7, no. 1, (1987): 142–154.

Nathan, Richard. "The Methodology for Field Network Evaluation Studies." In Walter Williams, ed., *Studying Implementation.* Chatham, NJ: Chatham House, 1982: 73–99.

Nathan, Richard P. *Social Science in Government, the Role of Policy Researchers.* Albany: Rockefeller Institute Press, 2000.

"NTA Reports." National Tax Payer Association. http://www.nta.or.ke/nta-reports.

Ongoya, Z. E and Eunice Lumallas. "A Critical Appraisal of the Constituency Development Fund Act." November 2005. http://www.kenyalaw.org/Downloads_Other/CDF%20Fund%20-%20Ongoya.pdf.

Pressman, Jeffrey and Aaron Wildavsky. *Implementation,* 3rd ed. Berkeley: University of California Press, 1984.

Pritchett, Lant. "Folk and the Formula: Pathways to Capable States." *UNU World Institute for Economic Research (WIDER), Annual Lecture* 16, (2012): http://www.wider.unu.edu/events/annual-lecture/Past-annual-lectures/en_GB/27-09-2012/.

Powers, Greg. "The Global Parliamentary Report, The Changing Nature of Parliamentary Representation." *IPU and UNDP*, April 2012, 28. http://www.ipu.org/gpr/.

Salamon, Lester M, ed. *The Tools of Government, A Guide to the New Governance*. Oxford University Press, 2002.

Thurber, James A. "Political Power and Policy Subsystems in American Politics." In B. Guy Peters and Bert A. Rockman (eds.), *Agenda for Excellence: Administering the State,* (Chatham, NJ: Chatham House Publishers, 1996).

Tsangana, Alison Hickey. "Constituency Development Funds Scoping Paper." *International Budget Project*, 18 January 2010 http://internationalbudget.org/wp-content/uploads/Constituency-Development-Funds-Scoping-Paper.pdf.

Ward, Bernie. "How can Zambian Citizens Engage with Government in its Efforts to Deliver Quality Services." *Zambian Governance Foundation*, November 2013: http://www.zgf.org.zm/downloads/WorldCaf%C3%A9_Workshop%20Report_November%202013.pdf

Weingast, B. R. "Reflections on Distributive Politics and Universalism." *Political Research Quarterly,* vol. 47, no. 2. (1994): 320–321.

Zimmerman, William. "Issue Area and Foreign Policy Process: A Research Note in Search of a General Theory." *American Political Science Review,* vol. 67, no. 4 (1973), 1204–1212.

Zyl, Albert van. "Constituency Development Funds: African Parliaments' Faustian Bargain." *International Budet Forum.* http://internationalbudget.org/blog/2010/08/12/constituency-development-funds-african-parliaments-faustian-bargain/

———. "What is Wrong with the Constituency Development Funds?" *International Budget Partnership.* Budget Brief, III, no. 10, 2010. http://www.internationalbudget.org/resources/briefs/brief10.pdf.

Chapter 2

Why CDFs in Africa?

Representation vs. Constituency Service

Joel D. Barkan and Robert Mattes

INTRODUCTION

The purpose of this chapter is to explore the political and societal contexts that give rise to constituency development funds generally, and across sub-Saharan Africa in particular. Since 2002, constituency development funds (CDFs) have been established in nine African countries,[1] and another two countries have created "approximations" of CDFs in that they address the perceived need by members of the legislature for budgeted funds to spend on the development of the districts they represent.[2] Thus, just under one-quarter of the 48 countries in sub-Saharan Africa have adopted some type of CDF.

In this discussion we consider three alternative explanations for the apparent popularity of CDFs. The first potential explanation revolves around the conventional wisdom or "pork-barrel" argument. In Africa, this argument would proceed from the basic fact that CDF's and their approximations exist only in countries that elect their legislators from single member districts. It would conclude from this that CDFs or their approximations have been created by African MPs as a response to constant and intense constituent pressure "to deliver" both private (such as jobs or cash handouts for school fees, health dispensary bills) and public goods (such as development projects to build schools, roads, and health clinics) and thus increase their prospects for reelection. Even in one-party dominant party systems, MPs still have good reasons to worry about reelection. On average, between half to two thirds of incumbent MPs lose their seats in African elections, often through party primaries as much as in the general election. Stated simply, these MPs view CDFs as a critical element of their job security.

The "pork-barrel" explanation would also appear to make intuitive sense given two conditions that are widely prevalent across Africa. First, most African countries are both ethnically plural and agrarian societies. The result is that most people tend to define their political interests in terms of their geographical place of residence and the dominant identities of those areas. Second, political parties in Africa are weak with the result that election campaigns for both the executive and the legislature tend to be driven by candidate-centered clientelist organizations, often fuelled by the distribution of private goods to political supporters, rather than by programmatic political parties with clear alternative programs for public policy. Indeed, the prevalence of clientelism is a product of the composition and economy of African society. When combined with the election of members of parliament (MPs) from single-member districts, these conditions put pressure on MPs to provide for the geographic constituency they have been elected to represent.

The "pork-barrel" explanation is also consistent with early research on what legislators do when back in their districts. In his landmark study *Homestyle* published in 1978, Richard Fenno found that members of the US House of Representatives spend considerable time identifying "pork barrel" type projects desired by their constituents because they were preoccupied with the prospects of reelection.[3] Barkan found the same type of behavior in an early study of Kenyan MPs under the "competitive one-party regime" in which MPs faced competitive elections within the single ruling party similar to American party primaries. Indeed, the variance in the vote share obtained by incumbents was largely explained by citizen evaluations of how successful their MPs were at delivering development projects back to the constituency.[4]

A second explanation for the emergence of CDFs is a "counter-intuitive" argument about MP *mis*perceptions, or what we call the "mismatch" argument. Here, MPs rightly perceive the need to maintain close contact with their constituents, but *wrongly* believe that their constituents look to them mainly for "pork." Instead, African constituents' primary expectations of their MP is that they regularly visit the district to learn what is on their minds, and to then quite literally "re-present" or transmit these views back to the central government via the legislature. In other words, while citizens desire *stronger representation of their needs at the center*, MPs respond by delivering services and favors at the periphery (i.e. the district) thinking mistakenly that the CDFs are the answer to what the public wants. One indication of the validity of this mismatch argument is the finding that reelection rates in the countries that have established CDFs do *not* appear to have risen compared to the period before there were CDFs.

The third potential explanation focuses on the role of a category of MPs we call "institutionalists" or "institutional reformers"; that is to say, "members who are intent on transforming their institution from a weak rubber stamp of the executive into a modern autonomous legislature."[5] The logic is as follows. As Richard Fenno pointed out over thirty years ago, legislators' personal goals cannot simply be reduced to reelection. At least some legislators desire a greater degree of personal influence in the political process. Under Africa's one-party regimes, African MPs often satisfied this need by making themselves crucial links in "big man" networks, frequently becoming "little big men" in their own constituencies. Since the return of multiparty politics, however, some things have begun to change.[6] As Barkan and his colleagues have noted, at least some African MPs have started to pursue political influence not through their role back in the constituency, but through the legislature as an institution. Though they are a minority of all MPs, these "institutionalists" have in some cases been able to join together with a larger group of "opportunists" to bring about crucial reforms that have strengthened the capacity and power of their institution.[7]

However, "institutionalists" face a key problem. While they want to devote much of their time to writing legislation and conducting oversight, this comes at the cost of less time for travelling back home to visit and listen to constituents and conduct constituency service. Thus, "institutionalists" incur the greatest risk of losing the support of their constituents when they stand for reelection. For this reason, institutional reformers are sensitive to the need to provide all MPs with adequate salaries, travel allowances, and other forms of support to enable them to devote more time and energy to legislating and oversight while simultaneously tending to constituents' needs. Viewed from this perspective, a major goal behind the establishment of CDFs is quite clear. CDFs not only help MPs deal with their constituents and raise their prospects for reelection, they also free MPs to become better legislators *within* the legislature and by so doing contribute to the emergence of the institution.

Some critics, usually civil society activists concerned with "good governance" have argued that CDFs often lead to corruption. Although these downside risks are real, the establishment of CDFs is part of a larger process of institution-building by those committed to advancing that project. As such, CDFs are also part of the larger process of democratization. This is because legislatures—as institutions of countervailing power—are essential institutions for the realization of democracy because they scrutinize and check the power of the executive branch and hold the executive to account.

Legislatures are particularly important for democratization across Africa because of the continent's history, since independence, of neo-patrimonial or "big man" regimes. With a few exceptions,[8] all of sub-Saharan Africa's 48 countries have resumed multiparty elections since 1989, though as of the end of 2012, only eleven were classified by Freedom House as "liberal democracies,"[9] and another six as "electoral democracies."[10,11] Pointing to Steven Fish's cross-national evidence of the impact of increases in parliamentary power and democratization, we would argue that many of Africa's liberal and electoral democracies are the countries with the strongest and most powerful legislatures vis-à-vis the executive branch. Their legislatures are no longer rubber stamps, but periodically challenge and limit executive power.[12]

The remainder of this chapter is divided into two sections. In the first, we test the three arguments we have just laid out for the popularity of CDFs and why some African countries have them while others do not. In the second, we examine the consequences of CDFs. Thus, our focus is on what compels parliamentarians to look to CDFs as a mechanism of distributive spending. We will not, however, explore their size, nor how they function. In both sections, our approach will be cross national and comparative using evidence from 17 countries included in both the African Legislatures Project and Afrobarometer.

Before we turn to the relevant data, three caveats about CDFs should be kept in mind. First, their establishment in Africa is a recent development of the first decade of the twenty-first century. They have not been around very long, and they are still relatively few in number. As previously noted, and as indicated in Table 2.1, only twelve sub-Saharan African countries either have CDFs, their approximations, or are considering their adoption. Second, because they are both new and few, little is known about how they operate or vary in the way they are constructed or in the benefits they bring to constituents and MPs. Indeed, a major purpose of this volume, and one addressed in the chapters that follow, is to provide initial insight into the operations of CDFs. Third, notwithstanding the fact that CDFs are new and few, their popularity in the countries where they have been established appears to be high amongst both members of the public and MPs. MPs like them because they are a highly visible mechanism to provide resources to constituents. Citizens like them, because they view the CDF for their constituency as a helpful entitlement that cannot be taken away or reallocated to the members of some

Table 2.1 Adoption of CDFs in Africa*

No	*Ambiguous*	*Has CDF*
Benin	Botswana	Kenya (2003)
Burkina Paso	Ghana	Malawi (2007)
Cabo Verde	Nigeria	Tanzania (2008)
Lesotho		Uganda (2005)
Mali		Zambia (2006)
Mozambique		Zimbabwe (2010)
Namibia		
Senegal		
South Africa		

*Limited to countries included in both Afrobarometer, Round 4 and African Legislatures Project (N = 17) but includes all countries with CDFs or approximations.

"other" region or ethnic community. The number of African countries establishing CDFs is therefore likely to rise, as it is increasing elsewhere around the world. Put simply, CDFs are an idea whose time has come.

EXPLAINING THE PRESENCE OF CDFs IN AFRICA

Country Context Variables

We begin our exploration of the context of CDFs in Africa by examining the impact of three country-level variables: (1) the type of electoral system a country uses to elect the members of its national legislature; (2) whether the country was once a British colony; and (3) whether the country is located in Eastern or Southern Africa.

As indicated above, by the end of 2012, nine African countries had established CDFs: Kenya, Malawi, Tanzania, Uganda,[13] Sierra Leone, South Sudan, Swaziland, Zambia and Zimbabwe. Two countries, Ghana and Nigeria, had established approximations of CDFs while the members of the national legislature in a third, Botswana, had expressed interest in creating such funds. When viewed against the backdrop of all forty-five countries that currently have legislatures elected through multiparty elections, it is apparent that CDFs are more likely to be established in some types of countries than others, and that country context is an important determinant of where CDFs exist, regardless of whether there is a demand for them by citizens and/or MPs. As shown in Table 2.2, and as mentioned at the beginning of this chapter, African countries that elect the members of its national legislature from single-member districts (SMDs) are far more likely to have CDFs than those which do not. In fact, no legislatures elected from multimember districts by proportional representation (PR) have, or anticipate creating a CDF.

Table 2.2 Comparing National Predictors of CDFs (45 SSA Countries)

	Country Elects all MPs from Single Member Districts		*Country is a Former British Colony*		*Country Located in East or Southern Africa*	
	Yes	*No*	*Yes*	*No*	*Yes*	*No*
Country Has CDF	50%	0%	64%	0%	35%	8%
Ambiguous	19%	0%	21%	0%	5%	8%
Country Does Not Have CDF	25%	100%	14%	100%	60%	84%
N =	16	29	14	31	20	25

N = 45: Countries in Sub-Saharan Africa with functioning legislatures chosen through multiparty elections as of 2011. For those countries with CDFs, democracy ratings are for the year preceding passing of CDF enabling legislation.

Thus, legislators elected to respond to the needs of constituencies defined solely by their common geographic area of residence are far more likely to respond to such expectations than legislators elected to respond to constituencies defined by their support for a particular political party.[14]

The seventeen countries included in the African Legislatures Project can therefore be grouped into three categories as depicted in Table 2.1—those that do not have CDFs, those we label as "ambiguous," and those that have established the funds.

SMDs are largely though not exclusively a legacy of British colonialism. Some former French colonies elect MPs from single-member districts, but others employ a second round runoff, a majority run-off, parallel systems featuring multimember districts, or list proportional representation. That said, we note that no Francophone or Lusophone country has created a CDF. At the same time, not all Anglophone countries have created CDFs (e.g. Lesotho). And not all Anglophone countries retained the plurality SMD system (e.g. South Africa). Thus, another important factor appears to be region: countries located in East and Southern Africa are far more likely to have a CDF than elsewhere in the continent

That almost all former British colonies located in Eastern and Southern Africa, who use a common system of running elections, have CDFs suggests the presence of a significant contagion effect. It diffuses through legislators from neighboring countries with a shared colonial heritage and official language who are likely to be aware of each other's efforts to strengthen the legislature and especially efforts to improve the terms of service for MPs. MPs from these countries, especially activists within the legislature, periodically interact with each other at regional forums and meetings of the Commonwealth Parliamentary Association or the Southern African Development Community Parliamentary Forum, where they compare notes on their respective experiences. For example, when members of the Uganda National Assembly raised their salaries in the late 1990s, members of the Kenya National Assembly took note and followed suit in 2001. Similarly, in 2001, the Uganda National Assembly asserted itself again by passing the Budget Act which gave itself increased powers in the budget making powers. The Kenya National Assembly followed with their own and more ambitious budget act in 2007. Conversely, when members of the Kenya National Assembly established CDFs in 2003, the members of neighboring parliaments soon sought CDFs for themselves. Though impossible to measure quantitatively, the likely impact of such cross-national learning appears profound.

However, while these macro level linkages are tantalizing, without micro level evidence, we can only guess the underlying mechanisms driving them. Fortunately, we do have such data. We thus turn to evidence derived from two cross-national research projects conducted in 17 African countries. The first is the African Legislatures Project which carried out surveys of 838 legislators randomly chosen from the legislatures of 17 countries.[15] The standard ALP study conducted face-to-face surveys of random and representative samples of 50 members in each country.[16] The surveys of MPs were conducted between 2008 and 2012. The second is Round 4 of the Afrobarometer public opinion survey, which carried out surveys in 20 countries in 2008–2009. A standard Afrobarometer survey consists of face-to-face surveys of random, nationally representative samples of 1,200 respondents (larger samples are used in Nigeria and South Africa). The rest of this chapter focuses on the 17 countries covered by both surveys.

Citizen Demands

One of the reasons that we see such sharp differences between Anglophone and other Sub-Saharan countries may lie in the political culture that has developed based initially on the traditions inherited from the United Kingdom, but subsequently maintained by SMD plurality electoral systems. In this context, it is likely that the citizens of Anglophone societies have learned to expect their MPs to focus their activities on the local district, listening to people and securing private and public goods for constituents. In contrast to this "localist" orientation, Francophone and Lusophone societies may have inherited a tradition consistent with the centralized political systems of their respective colonial powers where legislators are expected to focus their attention on "*les affaires de la nation*" and citizens develop significantly different orientations toward the role of the MP.

To test the argument that the presence of CDFs is a response to the national political culture, we turn to the responses to two questions from Afrobarometer Round 4. The first question gives respondents a forced choice between two statements that when electing a member of parliament they "prefer to vote for a candidate who can deliver goods and services to people in this community" or "prefer to vote for a candidate who can make policies that benefit everyone in our country." In Table 2.3, we display the relationship between preferences for a locally oriented MP by the country's status with regard to CDFs. *Both* of the countries (i.e. Malawi and Tanzania) with the highest levels of "localist" orientations—over 60%—have CDFs, whereas *none* of the countries with low levels (under 30%) have them. There is a clear and strong relationship between the presence of CDFs and political culture, expressed either in categories (Tau b = 0.736***) or as an absolute percentage of localist orientations (Pearson's r = 0.730***). Moreover, with one exception, all of those with low levels are either Francophone or Lusophone in their colonial heritage.

The second Afrobarometer question asked respondents "Which of the following do you think is the most important responsibility of your Member of

Table 2.3 CDF Status by Citizen Demand for Locally-Focused MPs

	<30%	*30–60%*	*>60%*
Country Has CDF		Zambia (52%) Kenya (44%) Uganda (36%) Zimbabwe (34%)	Malawi (74%) Tanzania (64%)
Ambiguous		Botswana (59%) Ghana (46%) Nigeria (39%)	
Country Does Not Have CDF	Lesotho (29%) Mozambique (22%) Mali (21%) Senegal (16%) Benin (16%) Burkina Faso (13%)	South Africa (38%) Namibia (33%)	

Kendall's Tau b = 0.736**** / Pearson's r = 0.730***, N = 17.
"Which of the following statements is closest to your view? Choose Statement 1 or Statement 2. Statement 1: In electing a Member of Parliament, I prefer to vote for a candidate who can deliver goods and services to people in this community. Statement 2: In electing a Member of Parliament, I prefer to vote for a candidate who can make policies that benefit everyone in our country." Cells display the percentage of respondents in that country who choose Statement 1.
Source: Afrobarometer, Round 4.

Parliament": (1) "listen to constituents and represent their needs," (2) "deliver jobs or development projects back to the constituency," (3) "make laws for the good of the country," or (4) "monitor the president and his government"? The results are displayed in Table 2.4. *All three* countries where 60% or more of the respondents say that MPs should "listen to constituents" have CDFs whereas *none* of the countries with very low expectations of representation (those under 30%) have them or contemplate getting them. Again, there is a strong relationship, whether demand for representation is expressed as ordinal categories (Tau b = 0.664***) or as an absolute percentage (Pearson's r = 0.795***).

MP *Mis*perceptions

We have thus far interpreted the results to these questions as a preference for a "localist" oriented MP. Yet one might be tempted to interpret the responses to the first question ("deliver goods and services to people in this constituency") as a preference for clientelist delivery of private goods. Much depends on whether one focuses on the contrast between "goods and services" only for people of this area versus "policies that benefit everyone" or on the contrast between "community" versus "country." In order to probe this matter further, we look at the percentage who, in the second question, say that the most important role of an MP is to "deliver jobs or development projects back to the constituency" and examine its relationship with a country's CDF

Table 2.4 CDF Status by Citizen Demand for MPs to Listen to their Constituents

	<30%	*30–60%*	*>60%*
Country Has CDF		Kenya (58%) Malawi (53%) Zimbabwe (53%)	Uganda (66%) Zambia (63%) Tanzania (61%)
Ambiguous		Botswana (60%) Ghana (45%) Nigeria (41%)	
Country Does Not Have CDF	Mozambique (26%) Burkina (21%) Benin (20%) South Africa (18%)	Senegal (57%) Mali (41%) Lesotho (35%) Namibia (31%)	

Kendall's Tau b = 0.664*** / Pearson's r = 0.795***, N = 17.
"Members of Parliament have different responsibilities. Which of the following do you think is the most important responsibility of your Member of Parliament: 1. *Listen to constituents and represent their needs.* 2. Deliver jobs or development projects back to the constituency. 3. Make laws for the good of the country. 4. Monitor the president and his government." Cells display the percentage of respondents who choose Option 1.
Source: Afrobarometer, Round 4.

status (Table 2.5). In this case, there is *no* statistically significant association between citizens' beliefs that MPs ought to produce economic goods and whether the country had established a CDF (Tau b = –0.353, Pearson's r = –/247). This suggests that MPs may have established CDFs in response

Table 2.5 CDF Status by Citizen Demand for Jobs and Development in their Constituencies

	<30%	*30–60%*	*>60%*
Country Has CDF	Kenya (29%) Zambia (26%) Uganda (20%) Tanzania (18%)	Malawi (39%) Zimbabwe (35%)	
Ambiguous	Nigeria (25%)	Ghana (41%) Botswana (32%)	
Country Does Not Have CDF	Mali (24%) Senegal (16%)	Lesotho (42%) Mozambique (42%) Namibia (36%) South Africa (34%) Benin (34%) Burkina Faso (31%)	

Kendall's Tau b = –0.353 / Pearson's r = –0.247, N = 17.
"Members of Parliament have different responsibilities. Which of the following do you think is the most important responsibility of your Member of Parliament: 1. Listen to constituents and represent their needs. 2. *Deliver jobs or development projects back to the constituency.* 3. Make laws for the good of the country. 4. Monitor the president and his government." Cells display the percentage of respondents who choose Option 2.
Source: Afrobarometer, Round 4.

to a *mis*perception of what citizens want. To the extent that African MPs establish CDFs as a response to demands for geographically targeted goods and services, they probably are mistaken.

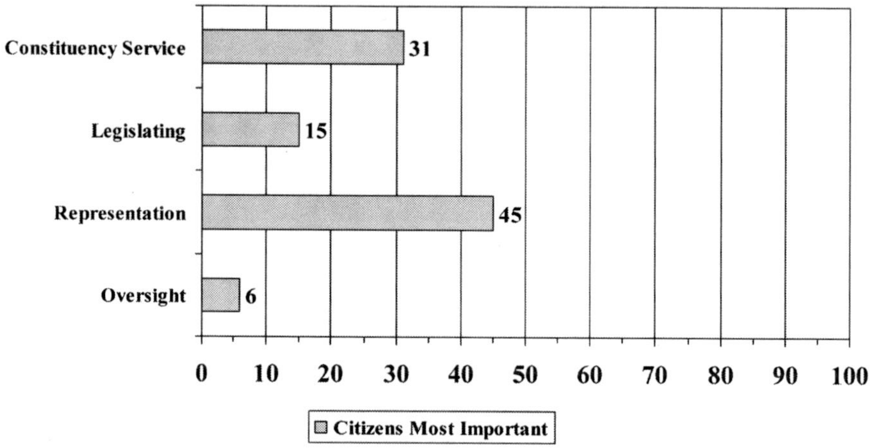

Figure 2.1 Citizen Role Expectations. Members of Parliament have different responsibilities. Which of the following do you think is the most important responsibility of your Member of Parliament? Listen to constituents and represent their needs? Deliver jobs and development to your constituency? Make laws for the good of the country? Monitor the President and his Government? *Source*: Afrobarometer Round 4, n = 20,339.

Additional evidence of the misperception explanation for CDFs is provided when we examine citizens' role expectations of their MPs and then compare them with MPs' own role orientations. Figure 2.1 presents *citizens'* responses to the Afrobarometer question "Which of the following do you think is the most important responsibility of your member of parliament?" As can be seen, citizens express a clear "localist" orientation in that only 13% chose "making laws," or legislating, and just 5% selected "monitoring the president and his government," or oversight. By contrast, a combined 78% expressed the view that MPs should focus on their constituents. However, within this group, far more respondents (45%) indicated that MPs should listen to their views and represent their needs than those who thought MPs should concentrate on constituency service (31%).

The distinction between the two dimensions of "localist" orientations is even more pronounced when citizens' expectations are compared with MPs' own role orientations. In its surveys, ALP asked MPs, "In your opinion, which of these following jobs is the *most* important part of being an MP?" as well as "For you personally, which role brings you the most satisfaction?" Figure 2.2 indicates the emphasis MPs place on constituency service relative

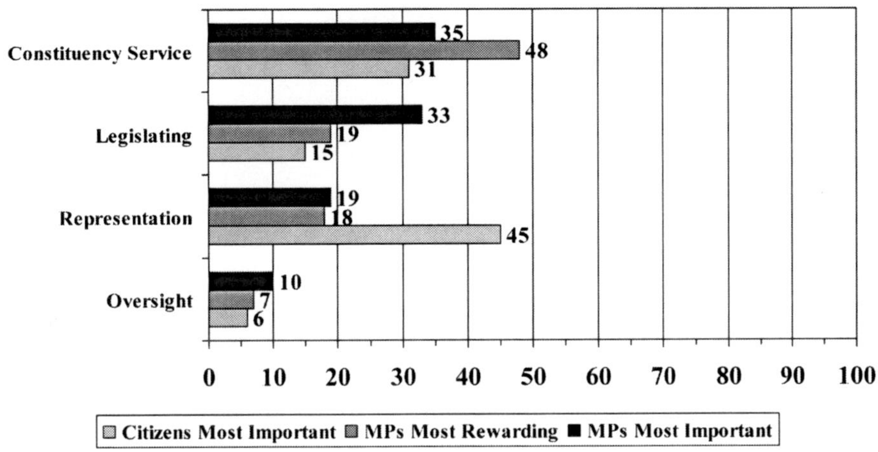

Figure 2.2

to the citizens. When African MPs were asked what is "the most important job of an MP" and what is the "the most rewarding" part of the job, constituency service was not only cited by more MPs than any other function, but it is also the aspect of their job that gives them the greatest job satisfaction.

Across the same 17 countries, there is a 4 percentage point difference between the cross-national percentage of the percentage of MPs (35%) who prioritize constituency service as the most important role they are expected to perform compared to citizens (31%). There is also a 26 point difference between the overall percentage of citizens who selected representation (45%) compared to MPs (19%). The differences are even greater when one compares citizens' expectations to those MPs regard as the most rewarding. Thus, while citizens are more likely than MPs to emphasize representation, they are less likely to focus on constituency service. Although both citizens and MPs emphasize tasks that take place in the constituency and outside the parliament itself, they subscribe to very different interpretations of what this "localist" role entails.

However, the cross-national percentage difference is less illuminating. Once we calculate the citizen-MP gap in emphasis on representation, we find that *the greater the gap between citizens and MPs*, the more likely the country in question will have established a constituency development fund (Table 2.6). In Burkina Faso, citizens are actually *less* likely than MPs to choose representation (−14 point difference). In Uganda and Tanzania, in contrast, the gap between citizens' demands for representation and MP role emphasis is +52 and 51 points.

What we see in Table 2.6 is that CDFs exist in those countries with a very high gap, *or level of misperception* about what citizens want from their MPs (i.e. +30 points or more). Indeed, the relationship is striking (Tau b = 0.830***). MPs in these societies accurately perceive citizen

Table 2.6 CDF Status by Citizens-MPs Gap in Emphasis on Representation

	−30–0	*−1–30*	*+31–60*
Country Has CDF			Uganda (+52) Tanzania (+51) Kenya (+46) Zimbabwe (+37) Malawi (+32) Zambia (+32)
Ambiguous		Ghana (+27) Botswana (+25)	Nigeria (+32)
Country Does Not Have CDF	Burkina Faso (−14)	Mali (+29) Senegal (+25) Lesotho (+25) Mozambique (+8) South Africa (+8) Namibia (+6) Benin (+3)	

Kendall's Tau b = 0.830*** / Pearson's r = 0.792***, N = 17.
The number for each country, is the *percentage point difference* between the percentage of Afrobarometer respondents minus the percentage of MPs from each country who answered that listening to constituents and representing their needs is the most important job for MPs to perform.
Sources: African Legislature Project MP Survey and Afrobarometer, Round 4.

demands for a local orientation, but misperceive this as a demand for goods, services or favors, rather than representation. A crude, but apt analogy might be that of an amorous suitor who showers the object of his affection with jewels and expensive clothes, while the woman secretly confides to her friends that "I just want someone to listen to me."

In sum, although MPs frequently speak about the pressures they are under to provide jobs and development projects back to their districts, and although their establishment of CDFs is a logical response, it appears that when aggregated at the country level—which is the level at which the decision to establish or not establish CDFs is made—the funds are most likely to be found in the countries where MPs misread the desires of their constituents the most.

Parliamentary Reform and Parliamentary Strengthening

As discussed at the beginning of this chapter, a third possible explanation for the spread of CDFs is that they are supported by reform-minded MPs who see it as a way to strengthen the legislature as an institution of countervailing power vis-à-vis the executive branch. Because CDFs are assumed to raise MPs' prospects for reelection generally, it is also assumed that they protect "institutionalists" who are the MPs most vulnerable at the polls. If true, then countries with the highest percentages of MPs who can be classified as institutionalists or "reformers," should also be those with CDFs.

Table 2.7 CDF Status by MP Support for Parliamentary Reform

	<30%	*30–60%*	*>60%*
Country Has CDF		Kenya (56%) Zimbabwe (55%) Uganda (51%)	Malawi (76%) Fanzania (73%)
Ambiguous	Botswana (14%) Ghana (6%)		
Country Does Not Have CDF	Mozambique (28%) South Africa (14%)	Lesotho (43%) Namibia (39%) Burkina Faso (30%) Senegal (34%) Mali (33%)	Benin (62%)

Kendall's Tau b = 0.214 / Pearson's r = 0.539*, N = 15 (Questions not asked in Nigeria or Zambia).
"Regardless of whether your country already has this please tell us whether you support or oppose measures that would allow this Parliament to: 1. Increase the number of sitting days for the Parliament; 2. Set salaries for MPs and Staff; 3. Increase oversight of the executive; 4. Approve senior appointments to the civil service." Cells display the percentage of MPs who support all four reform proposals.
Source: African Legislatures Project MP Survey.

To test this proposition, we turn to a series of questions asked in the ALP MP surveys which attempted to tap support for institutional reform. In particular, we use the responses to four questions asked of MP: (1) Whether parliament should have increased powers to oversee the executive branch; (2) whether parliament should increase the number of days it is in session; (3) whether the salaries of MPs should be increased: and (4) whether parliament should have the power to approve appointments to the senior civil service. MPs answering "yes" to all four questions were categorized as reformers.

With the exception of Benin, the greater the percentage of reformist MPs in a given legislature, the more likely the parliament of that country will have passed legislation establishing CDFs (Pearson's r = 0.539*). Indeed, Benin is a clear outlier where MPs are twice as likely as their colleagues in other Francophone legislatures to support "a full basket of reforms." If Benin was removed from the analysis, the correlation becomes even stronger (Pearson's r = 0.646**). Put differently, this corroborates the argument that MPs see CDFs as part of the same basket of other reforms designed to strengthen their institution even though they address that part of the MPs' job that exists outside the legislature.

THE CONSEQUENCES AND IMPACT OF CDFs

In this section, we move from probing arguments about the spread of CDFs in Africa, to a test of conventional propositions about their impact. In particular, we investigate whether CDFs have changed MP behavior by allowing them to spend less time travelling home and focus more time on activities that build the legislature as an institution. Second, we examine whether or not CDFs have resulted in more positive views of MPs in particular (specific support) or the legislature as an institution (diffuse support).

Constituency Service

In what ways have CDFs shaped the activities MPs undertake back in their constituencies? As we have demonstrated, CDFs tend to occur in those countries where MPs are most likely to perceive intense constituent demands for frequent visits and constituency service, as well as in those legislatures with high levels of support for institution-strengthening reforms. Has the existence of CDFs reduced MPs perceived need to travel home and engage in constituency service? To test this, we examine MP responses to a series of questions in the ALP survey about the frequency of their travel home, and the amount of money they spend on travel and other types of constituency service.

As shown in Table 2.8, the establishment of CDFs makes no difference in the number of trips MPs make back to their constituencies while parliament is in session. In both countries with CDFs and those without, the median MP returns to their constituency two times a month (while parliament is in session). The presence or absence of CDFs also appears to have no impact on the duration of each trip, where the median member stays in the constituency three days per trip (a typical Friday through Sunday stay).[17]

The presence of CDFs makes a sharper difference in the amounts of funds MPs donate to both individuals and local community development projects. In respect to the former, in countries that have established CDFs, the median MP donates roughly one-third more funds to constiuents for personal problems than MPs in countries without a CDF. In terms of donations to local development projects, MPs in CDF countries outspend their counterparts by a four to one margin. These differences are very large, but whether they are due to MPs' access to CDFs, or access to other state-provided allowances that support their work in their constituencies, or to donations that come out of their own pockets—to some combination of all three, cannot be determined from our data. The magnitude of these differences, however, suggests that some of these monies do come from the CDF. Indeed, MPs constantly strive to control or at least influence disbursements from CDFs in countries where they exist. On the other hand, civil society organizations and other watchdog groups argue that CDFs are misused precisely because MPs seek to use the funds to solidify their positions back home.

What about the impact of CDFs on MP's prospects for reelection at the next election? A major motivation of MPs when passing legislation to establish CDFs was the need to address the high probability of electoral defeat.

Table 2.8 MP Behavior in Constituencies by Access to Constituency Funds

		MP Does Not Have Access to Constituency Funds	*MP Has Access to Constituency Funds*	*Test Statistic*	*N*
Mean Monthly Trips Home During Session	Mean	3.0	2.8	Eta = 0.031	736
	Median	(2.0)	(2.0)		
Mean Number of Days per Trip	Mean	6.4	4.4	Eta = 0.126***	712
	Median	(3.0)	(3.0)		
Average Monthly Amount MP Donates to Individuals	Mean	$823	$1207	Eta = 0.099*	599
	Median	($406)	($660)		
Average Monthly Amount MP Donates to Development Projects	Mean	$3492	$948	Eta = 0.046	571
	Median	($146)	($500)		
Electoral Security (MP Expects to Win Reelection by Large Margin)	Percent	33%	58%	Tau b = 0.257***	818
Actual Reelection Rates	Percent	?	?		

Cells display the average response of MPs to each question. For question wording, see Footnote X/Appendix A.
Source: African Legislatures Project MP Survey.

This was particularly true for legislators devoting increased time to their duties inside the legislature. Evidence supporting this interpretation comes from an ALP question that asks MPs about their reelection prospects. A significantly greater percentage of MPs with access to CDFs (58%) expect to win reelection "by a large margin" than those in countries without access to CDFs (33%). Whether the rates of reelection are actually higher in countries with CDFs, we cannot say at this stage of our analysis. Anecdotal data from Kenya and Uganda, however, suggest that CDFs have not raised the prospects for reelection as much as MPs expected.[18] Indeed in Kenya, the reelection rate for incumbents has declined since the CDF was established.

MP Time Allocation

Notwithstanding the finding that MPs appear to view the establishment of CDFs as part of the same basket of reforms that strengthen the legislature, the actual impact of CDFs is not so simple. Table 2.9 examines the relationship between whether or not a country has established a CDF and how members

Table 2.9 MP Time Allocation by Access to Constituency Funds

	MP Does Not Have Access to Constituency Funds	*MP Has Access to Constituency Funds*	*Test Statistic (Eta)*	*N*
Plenary	24%	21%	0.117***	796
Committee	26%	21%	0.181***	761
Party Meetings	16%	11%	0.233***	723
Constituency	24%	31%	0.228***	783

Cells display the average percentage of time MPs report spending on each type of the four listed activities.
Source: African Legislatures Project MP Survey.

of the legislature report allocating their time to various activities. Just as MPs who have access to CDFs are no less likely to travel home, neither are they any less likely to apportion their time to constituency matters or any more likely to devote time to committee or plenary work (in fact, the difference is slightly in the opposite direction). For example, MPs in countries without CDFs devote an average of 24% of their time to participating in plenary sessions of the legislature compared to 21% in countries where MPs have access to CDFs. Similarly, MPs in countries without CDFs devote an average of 26% of their time to serving on committees within the legislature compared to 21% in countries with CDFs.

To be sure, these differences do not only reflect the presence or absence of CDFs, but also the type of electoral system and whether the MP operates in a one-party dominant system or a highly competitive one. Since no country that elects its national legislature via PR has established CDFs, it is not surprising that the percentage of MPs who devote the most time to party meetings and the least amount of time to constituency work, are the countries that have not established CDFs. At the same time, these data caution us against making any simplistic assertions that CDFs, by themselves, have major impacts on MP activities.

Support for MPs

Regardless of their electoral fates, do CDFs allow MPs to deliver a sufficient amount of goods and favors to their constituency to affect citizens evaluations of the legislature and its members in any material way? To test this, we turn to a series of Afrobarometer questions that ask people for their evaluations of the MP in terms of responsiveness, corruption, trust and overall performance. But as demonstrated in Table 2.10, citizens' evaluations of MPs are not substantially higher, and if anything is worse, in countries that have CDFs compared to those that do not. By the tiniest of margins, and well within the margin of error, slightly more citizens in countries with CDFs (30%) report

Table 2.10 CDFs and Citizen Views of MPs

	MPs Have Access to Constituency Funds	*MPs Have Access to Constituency Funds*	*Test Statistic (Tau b)*	*N*
MP In Constituency At Least Weekly	27%	30%	0.040***	20,398
MPs Interested In Public Opinion	22%	19%	−0.020**	20,399
Able to Make MP Listen	44%	50%	0.038**	20,400
All/Most MPs Involved in Corruption	23%	31%	0.060***	20,399
Approve MP Job Performance	50%	46%	−0.086***	20,400

Cells display the average response of respondents to each question. For question wording, see Footnote X/ Appendix A.
Source: Afrobarometer, Round 4.

that their MP visits the constituency at least once a month, compared to citizens in countries without (27%). That said, slightly fewer people (19% compared to 22%) believe their MPs are interested in public opinion and what citizens have to say. On the other hand, the percentage of citizens in countries with CDFs who believe that they are able to make their MP listen to them (30%) is higher than the percentage in countries without CDFs (23%). Citizens in countries with CDFs are also more likely to regard MPs pejoratively than citizens in countries without. The percentage who think "all or most" MPs are involved in corruption is higher in countries with CDFs—perhaps because they have or are perceived as having access to these funds, while the percentage who approve of the job performance of their MP is less (45 compared to 50%). While not definitive, taken together, these findings strongly suggest that CDFs do not provide MPs with a political advantage that some might wish to use if they spend more time engaging the legislative process or exercising oversight within the legislature.

Support for the Legislature

Finally, we turn to the question of whether CDFs materially affect citizens' support for the legislature as an institution, especially its lawmaking and oversight functions. By modest amounts, citizens in countries that have established CDFs are more likely to support legislative autonomy with respect to lawmaking and oversight, two defining functions of the legislature. Citizens in countries with CDFs are also more likely to reject the idea that parliament should be shut down and replaced with presidential dictatorship. Again, however, the differences between the two groups of countries are not overwhelming though

Table 2.11 CDFs and Citizen Support for the Legislature

	MP Does Not Have Access to Constituency Funds	*MP Has Access to Constituency Funds*	*Test Statistic (Tau b)*	*N*
Supports Legislative Autonomy in Lawmaking	60%	69%	0.098***	20,398
Supports Legislative Oversight	57%	63%	0.063***	20,398
Rejects Shutting Down Parliament and Allowing President to Rule	75%	85%	0.128***	20,397
Trusts Legislature a Lot	33%	26%	−0.049***	20,398

Cells display the average response of respondents to each question. For question wording, see Footnote X/Appendix A.
Source: Afrobarometer, Round 4.

they are consistent with the argument that CDFs help strengthen the autonomy of the legislature. At the same time, citizens in CDF countries are *less* likely to trust the legislature as an institution than those in countries without CDFs, perhaps because they are suspicious of MP corruption in the administration of the funds. Once again, however, these finding could be a function of the type of electoral system and whether or not citizens reside in a one-party dominant political system where the legislature is arguably more likely to follow a predictable path in respect to its approach to public policy.

CONCLUSIONS

In this chapter, we first employed relevant data from the African Legislatures Project and the Afrobarometer to test three alternative hypotheses about the spread of CDFs in Africa. In our view, the best evidence supports the MP misperception hypothesis. That is, in the countries with CDFs, MPs have correctly gauged the extent of popular demand for a "localist" MP style, or an African form of "home style." At the same time, this is precisely where MPs get it wrong and interpret these localist orientations as a demand for the delivery of goods and favors to the district, and miss the fact that what citizens want is for their elected representatives to *listen* to their concerns and facilitate a suitable government response. They want to be represented in the decision-making processes of the state so that public policy responds to their needs and their preferences. However, while the establishment of CDFs may be a response to MP misperceptions of public opinion, they may in the long run contribute to what citizens do want—better social service delivery, infrastructure and the like back in their constituency—that is to say, the very public goods they seem to eschew when they emphasize the need for MPs to listen to and represent their concerns. This is a paradox, but one that broadens our understanding of the significance of CDFs and why the spread of these funds to other countries will no doubt increase.

Second, this chapter has explored the contexts within which CDFs operate and has offered some preliminary assessments of the impact of the funds, particularly with respect to contributing to reforms to strengthen African legislatures on the one hand, and sustaining the careers of key parliamentary players on the other. The data presented suggests that the "pork barrel" explanation of why CDFs are established, though logically persuasive, is not supported by the available evidence. CDFs do not appear to enhance the stature of MPs or their prospects for reelection. Though arguably viewed by MPs as part of a larger basket of institution-strengthening reforms, the impact of CDFs may be just the opposite. MPs in countries with CDFs do not spend more time in plenary sessions of the legislature than MPs in countries without the funds. Nor do they devote more time to the work of parliamentary committees, the heart of modern legislatures or less time back in their constituencies. Finally, when back in their districts, MPs in countries with CDFs seem to dish out more cash in the form of both private goods to individuals and public goods in the form of donations to local community development projects. Put differently, CDFs do *not* seem to contribute to the development of the legislature as an institution of countervailing power that is more likely to hold the executive accountable for its actions.

GLOSSARY OF KEY TERMS

CDF – Constituency Development Fund
MP – Member of Parliament
PR – Proportional Representation
SMD – Single Member Districts

NOTES

1. We consider a country to have established a CDF when specific legislation has been passed and signed into law to create such funds, and when the legislation specifies some amount of money or budgetary formula to implement CDFs for all legislative constituencies (i.e. districts). Legislation that establishes CDFs also specifies the procedures to be followed for the allocation of the funds within each constituency,

i.e. whether by the elected representative of the district alone or via a committee of which the representative may or may not be a member.

2. Ghana and Nigeria have approximations of CDFs. In Ghana, 5% of the District Common Fund is automatically re-allocated by law to the parliamentary constituencies existing within each district. In Nigeria, each MP is provided with an annual "constituency allowance" of 2,000,000 Naira ($12,500) to spend as he or she determines. In Ghana, legislation to create a stand-alone CDF was introduced in 2009 and supported by then President John Atta Mills prior to his death and parliamentary elections in 2012, but the legislation has yet to become law. In addition, the possibility of CDF legislation has also been discussed in the Botswana National Assembly, but no legislation has yet been introduced.

3. Fenno, Jr. 1978, 31–53.

4. Barkan 1978, 265–88; and Barkan 1976, 452–55.

5. Barkan 2009, 18.

6. Fenno Jr. 1978.

7. Barkan et al. 2009.

8. Equatorial Guinea, Eritrea and Somalia.

9. Benin, Botswana, Cape Verde, Ghana, Lesotho, Mauritius, Namibia, Sao Tome & Principe, Senegal, Sierra Leone and South Africa.

10. Comoros, Liberia, Malawi, Niger, Tanzania, and Zambia.

11. Puddington 2013, 46–61.

12. Fish 2006.

13. It should be noted that Uganda ended its six year experiment with CDFs in 2011, because MPs regarded the amount of funds allocated to the funds as too small and insufficient for achieving their purpose. See Chapter 4 of this volume for a full account of the CDF in Uganda.

14. In sixteen of these 45 sub-Saharan African countries, all citizens elect a legislator to the lower house of the legislature from a single member district with a plurality rule, though some complement this with members elected by proportional representation from parallel or top-up multimember lists or with appointed members (Botswana, Ethiopia, Gambia, Ghana, Kenya, Lesotho, Liberia, Malawi, Nigeria, Sierra Leone, South Sudan, Swaziland, Tanzania, Uganda, Zambia and Zimbabwe).

15. For a full description of the methodologies employed for the African Legislatures Project and for the Afrobarometer, readers are directed to www.africanlegislaturesproject.org and www.afrobarometer.org.

16. A somewhat larger sample of 60 members was interviewed in Nigeria while smaller samples of 40 MPs were interviewed in Benin and Namibia.

17. In this section, we report medians since the data on travel and spending is skewed by a smaller number of MPs who travel home far more frequently (usually because they live in districts close to the legislative capital) or who spend very large amounts of money.

18. For example, in 2007 in Kenya when the first parliamentary elections were held following the establishment of CDFs in that country in 2003, 72% of the incumbent MPs—a record high—were not reelected to the next parliament.

REFERENCES

Barkan, Joel D. "Bringing Home the Pork." In Joel Smith and Lloyd D. Mulsof (eds.), *Legislatures in Development*. Durham: Duke University Press, 1978. 265–88.

———. "Further Reassessment of the 'Conventional Wisdom': Political Knowledge and Voting Behavior in Rural Kenya." *American Political Science Review*, 70, no. 2, (1976): 452–55.

Barkan, Joel, ed. "African Legislatures and the 'Third Wave' of Democratization." *Legislative Power in Emerging African Democracies*. Boulder, Co.: Lynne Rienner Publishers, 2009.

Fenno Jr., Richard F. *Homestyle: House Members in Their Districts*. Boston: Little, Brown and Co. 1978.

Fish, M. Steven. "Stronger Legislatures, Stronger Democracies." *Journal of Democracy*, 17, no. 1, (2006).

Puddington, Arch. "The Freedom House Survey for 2012." *Journal of Democracy*, 24, no. 2, (2013): 46–61.

Chapter 3

Money for Small Things

Experience and Lessons of Kenya's Constituency Development Fund

David Ndii

INTRODUCTION

"Before last year, women in the expansive Matuga constituency were not a happy lot," so begins a feature in *The Star*, a Kenyan daily. "They had to flock the small cubicle that served as the maternity ward for the Kwale District Hospital. Many a time expectant mothers, most of whom are uneducated, would enter into labor while queuing. Others delivered while on the queue. Some had resorted to visiting backdoor clinics owned by quacks. Others turned to traditional midwives for delivery [who] were unable to deal with complications whenever they arose during or after delivery."[1]

All this has changed, "thanks to the CDF-built maternity wing at the Kwale District Hospital (at cost of Sh. 18,642,963 (US $240,000)) The facility has a labour ward that can accommodate three people at a given time, unlike before when those in labour had to sit outside in the open air and wait for their turn to be attended to. It also has a room with the beds for those who have just delivered, another room with seven beds for those whose time is due but are not yet in labour and an acute room for those with complications and those who need Caesarian-section."

Similar press accounts have become legion in Kenya, and the CDF has consistently received strong public approval across public opinion surveys.[2] On the other hand, a recent International Budget Partnership paper on CDFs attributes the growing popularity of CDFs to the "*perceived* success of the Kenya model."[3] This grudging acknowledgement of success reflects a widespread antipathy towards CDFs in international development discourse. This chapter will address this debate on the value of CDFs.

Critics of CDFs raise two broad concerns. First, they contend that CDFs breach the separation of powers between the legislative and executive arms of government, and encroach on the executive's capacity for service delivery to citizens. This blurring of distinctions, it is argued, adversely affects the performance of both the legislature and the executive. It diverts the focus of MPs from their core functions of representation, legislating and oversight, which do not directly benefit constituents and which distorts the relationship between MPs and their constituents (from "representation" to "bringing home the bacon"). It is further said to undermine both the executive agencies whose responsibilities they encroach on, and local government in particular. This concern suggests that "successful" CDFs, such as Kenya's, may in fact be popular with the public (and MPs, of course), while undermining good governance and the development of democracy.[4]

It is easy to find widespread skepticism among the donor and nonprofit communities regarding the efficacy of CDFs. This is seen in their concern that MPs employ CDFs to pursue political goals (to improve their prospects for reelection) and in the putative absence of requisite development planning and management expertise and capability, such that CDF funds are supposedly more susceptible to corruption and lack of general accountability than other forms of government spending in Kenya, and exacerbated by conflicting executing and oversight roles. As a result, projects and benefits tend to be highly internalized within specific constituencies, making CDF projects more akin to "club goods" than general public goods.[5]

The other side of the coin begins from the political reality in Kenya that development patronage and provision of welfare (such as assistance with medical bills, school fees and funeral expenses) have long been an integral part of the MPs responsibilities. This is both a response to the executive's inadequate provision of services and a reflection of the sociocultural role and responsibilities of leaders and elites to their communities. In this view, the idea that MPs represent their constituents' interests at an "arms length" in national policy that then leads to policies implemented by the executive may have little real meaning to constituents who are in the midst of a medical emergency, for example. Frequently, constituents seek immediate, direct relief rather than a policy intervention on health care. So this view holds that if MPs cannot address these real and immediate needs, representation becomes meaningless, and cynical constituents will sell their votes to the highest bidder. In this "realist" view, CDFs have the potential to strengthen democracy by empowering MPs to deliver more effective constituency service.

This chapter addresses these two views of CDFs with a case study of the Kenya CDF that will also illuminate other controversies in the development and operation of CDFs. The next section provides the political and economic context underlying CDFs. Section 3 describes the history, structure, operations and performance of the Kenyan CDF. Section 4 discusses the challenges and issues that feature in CDF debate, accountability, corruption and the role of MPs. The final section places the Kenyan experience to bear on these development policy and governance concerns/questions raised about CDFs and discusses the evolution of the Kenyan CDF.

BACKGROUND

Political Developments

After three decades of single party rule, Kenya reverted to multiparty politics in 1991, ushering in a turbulent process of democratization that was characterized by intense, highly ethnicized and often violent electoral competition, but also fundamental political change that was associated with expanded political space, media freedom, a vibrant civil society, and an independent and assertive legislature.

There have been four multiparty elections held in 1992, 1997, 2002, 2007, and 2013. The single party era incumbent President Daniel Moi, in power since 1978, and his party KANU (Kenya Africa National Union), in power since independence in 1963, managed to hold onto power in both the 1992 and 1997 elections. In both elections, a fragmented opposition contributed to Moi's victory. The opposition presidential candidates received two thirds of the popular vote in both elections but lost to Moi under the first-past-the-post system. In the parliamentary race, the opposition won 88 out of 210 seats (46%) in 1992 and 103 seats (49%) in 2007.

Moi retired in 2002, in accordance with the two-term term-limit that was introduced alongside the legalization of multiparty politics. In the ensuing election, a united opposition and fragmentation of KANU following Moi's retirement defeated KANU in both the presidential and parliamentary elections. But President Mwai Kibaki's new government led by NARC (National Rainbow Coalition) was a relatively brief marriage of convenience that only lasted from 2002 until 2005. President Kibaki reneged on a preelection power sharing pact that included the creation of the position of prime minister and the appointment of Raila Odinga as the prime minister. This fallout produced the two parties, Mwai Kibaki's PNU (Party of National Unit) and Raila Odinga's ODM (Orange Democratic Movement), that contested the 2007 general election.

The 2007 general election ended in a controversy over the outcome of the presidential race. Amid bitter protest, the incumbent Mwai Kibaki was declared winner and hurriedly sworn in, triggering unprecedented violence that only ended with an internationally mediated power-sharing deal known as the National Accord. The deal involved power sharing between the two candidates by allowing Mwai Kibaki to maintain his office as president while Raila Odinga served as the prime minister. The national accord also restarted the process of overhauling the constitution that had stalled several times in the previous decade. A new constitution was promulgated in August 2010.

The constitution has introduced two fundamental changes in Kenya's political system. First, it marks a more or less complete shift from the Westminster-style parliamentary system of government, to a US-style presidential system, characterized by a complete separation of the executive and legislative branches of government. The second is devolution of political power. The constitution created two tiers of government, a national government, and a subnational tier comprising of 47 counties. The counties are to be governed by a directly elected Governor and legislature (county assembly). The presidential system is also cascaded to the county level. They will have a directly elected governor and deputy governor (elected as running mate) and an assembly with considerable legislative power. Parliament has changed from a unicameral to bicameral legislature with a national assembly and a Senate. Senators will represent counties, and the mandate of the Senate is limited to representing the interests of counties and the distribution of finances among counties.

The long discourse on constitutional reform forged a broad consensus on three grievances to be addressed by the 2010 constitution:

- The concentration of executive power in an all-powerful, unaccountable presidency;
- An electoral system that creates an imbalance of political power between ethnic groups; and
- The geographical (and, in effect, ethnic) development disparities that many attribute in turn to the patronage-driven distribution of public resources.

It is an article of faith among Kenyans that these features of the political system drive tribalism and corruption: the system rewards politicians who are able to control large ethnic blocks of votes, which can only be managed and sustained through corruption and patronage. In response to these grievances, the new constitution seeks to strengthen the legislature and judiciary vis-à-vis the executive, while devolution is intended to diffuse the concentration of executive power in the presidency. Devolution is also envisaged as a means of counteracting the ethnic power imbalance while its fiscal dimension responds to the distributional grievances. The threshold to elect the president (an absolute majority with at least a quarter of the votes in more than half the 47 counties) means that a broad base of support is required for election. In addition, the constitution's presidential system undermines preelection coalitions between ethnic powerbrokers, as the cabinet will be appointed from outside parliament. In the present system, the coalition partners can punish a reneging president by breaking the coalition, as happened to NARC in 2004.

Constitutional change, devolution in particular, has precipitated uncertainty regarding the future of the CDF. It is quite clear that the implementation of the new constitution will necessitate some changes to CDFs because the new constitution assigns local development to the counties, while the CDF is a creature of the national legislature. That the CDF would become problematic in the new dispensation became apparent as soon as the new constitution was enacted. In his first budget policy statement under the new constitution, the Minister for Finance proposed to phase out the CDF, but this was quickly contradicted by his counterpart, the Minister of Planning under whose docket the CDF falls, who announced that the Government would review the CDF Act to make it consistent with the constitution.[6] A task force advising the Government on devolution recommended that the CDF funds should be included in the county governments' share of national revenue, but it did not provide direction on how the fund would be administered and whether MPs would continue to have a role in it.[7]

An updated version of the CDF act was passed in April 2013 in order to bring the program more in line with the new Constitution. The new statute diminishes the role of MPs, and brings the county governments into the picture. But it does not necessarily resolve the tensions. For example, it replaces the District Project Committee with a County Projects Committee in which both the County Governor and Senator are members, but does not designate a chairperson of the committee, adding another theater of an already raging supremacy contest between the two. More ominously, in August 2013, MPs passed amendments to the new law, restoring back some of the power that they had in the old act. This is unlikely to be the last act in the drama.

Development Politics

Kenya began its independence with a devolved structure of government in which seven regions (majimbo) enjoyed significant power. The "majimbo" constitution was a compromise between two visions of the new state, KANU which envisioned a unitary state, and KADU which wanted a federal one. KANU won the independence election with an overwhelming majority and used it to dismantle the devolved system. Within two years, it also co-opted KADU into the Government, making Kenya a de facto one party state (until 1981), when it was legitimized with a constitutional amendment. The devolved power was centralized and the regions were transformed into provinces that were managed by an administration directly controlled by the president. Alongside this, local government was also brought progressively under the control of the central government.

Kenya developed rapidly in the first decade of independence and by the early 1970s, it ranked among the most rapidly developing countries internationally. But even as the country developed rapidly, distributional grievances were fermenting. Against the backdrop of the ideological contest of the Cold War, an intense economic policy debate on whether Kenya should pursue growth or equity culminated in the publication of arguably Kenya's most famous policy document, Sessional Paper No. 10 of 1965 titled "African Socialism and its Application to Planning to Kenya," which declared rapid economic growth as the paramount objective of economic policy. More controversially, it asserted that maximizing growth necessitated neglecting the less developed areas of the country:

> One of the problems is to decide how much priority we should give in investing in the less developed provinces. To make the economy as a whole grow as fast as possible, development money should be invested where it will yield the largest increase in net output. This approach will clearly favour the development of areas having abundant natural resources, good land and rainfall, transport and power facilities, *and people receptive and active in* development [emphasis added].[8]

Dissent on these matters was not to be tolerated—President Kenyatta's preface to the Sessional Paper declared the debate closed. A fallout with the vice president, Jaramogi Oginga Odinga, ensued, and he left the Government to form a left-leaning party, the Kenya Peoples Party (KADU). Following a violent mini election, the party was proscribed and Odinga put under house arrest, which lasted until Kenyatta's death in 1978. A decade later, a populist politician J.M. Kariuki famously proclaimed that Kenya had become a country of 10 millionaires and 10 million beggars. Not long thereafter, he was assassinated, sparking nationwide violent protests.

The erstwhile leader of the federalist leaning KADU, Daniel Moi succeeded Kenyatta as President in 1978. Because his political constituency was the "less developed provinces" that had been marginalized under Kenyatta, it is not at all surprising that his administration reversed the earlier development policy: the economic policy blueprint of his regime, Sessional Paper No. 1 of 1986 declared as its main goal as "raising productivity in all parts of the economy."[9]

In 1983 his government introduced a major decentralization initiative, the District Focus for Rural Development. The goal of District Focus was to change from a top-down, sector-based development strategy to an integrated, participatory, bottom-up development planning budgeting system. The centerpiece of the system is delegation of development planning and coordination to the District Development Committee (DDC), a consultative forum that brings together the civil servants at the district level, elected representatives and community leaders. The DDC is responsible for producing and coordinating implementation of the District Development Plan. A planning unit, headed by an economist (District Development Officer) is the technical arm of the DDC.

By and large, District Focus is considered a failure. This has been attributed to "(i) its lack of basis in an Act of Parliament; (ii) its reliance on an institutional framework that did not facilitate meaningful local decision making and mobilization of resources; (iii) lack of adequate capacity in participatory planning among civil servants; (iv) financial allocations by ministries headquarters which, though insufficient, justified continued control of their field units; (v) dominance of the strategy by civil servants, especially staff of the provincial administration; and lack of people's awareness of and participation in planning and implementation of the strategy."[10]

Despite failing to transform resource allocation, the structures and the rituals—the DDC and District Development Plans—have endured. But perhaps its most enduring legacy is bureaucratic inflation. As the District became a center of patronage and influence, local elites lobbied for creation of more districts. From colonial times to the advent of District Focus in 1983, Kenya had 41 districts. By 1990, there were to 47 districts, which have subsequently been designated as counties under the 2010 constitution. As multiparty politics put more pressure on Moi, as well as on his successor Kibaki, to appease more constituencies, the floodgates opened. The final tally, at the promulgation of the new constitution, was 283 districts.

Even as Moi's public administration expanded, his regime failed to sustain the development tempo of its predecessor. By 1990, most development indicators had barely improved over the levels recorded a decade earlier. These negative trends were exacerbated in the 1990s, compounded by both an aid freeze during the transition to the multiparty system, and by profligate preelection spending that saw inflation reach over 60% in its aftermath. This period also saw ethnically based political violence that severely disrupted agriculture and tourism. The second multiparty election in 1997 also led to a recurrence of both fiscal excesses and political violence, the economy went into a slump that lasted until the change of Government in 2003.

Corruption also exploded. Between 1991 and 1997, the Auditor General documented budget losses amounting to Ksh. 475 billion. This is more than double the cumulative government expenditure on education and health over the same period (Ksh. 210 billion). The period of 1991 to 1993 also produced the Goldenberg scam, which is associated with financing the 1992 general election, and which defrauded the country of Ksh. 27 billion, well over half the education expenditure and more than double the health expenditure over the same period.[11] Public services deteriorated, and Kenya's erstwhile steady development gains either stagnated or worsened. The mortality rate of children under 5 increased from 96 per 1000 in 1993, to 115 per 1000 in 2003.[12] Infrastructure, particularly roads, deteriorated and investment stagnated.

The combination of an overextended, highly centralized, ineffective bureaucracy, poor public services, and runaway corruption was such that by the mid-1990s, the state had all but lost its development credentials.

Harambee and Patronage Politics

"Harambee" is Kenya's national motto—it is inscribed on the national coat of arms. In a literal sense, it means "pulling together." Contextually, it means achieving a common goal through collective effort. Harambee provided a participatory approach to development in which the Government could provide technical expertise and materials and the community would contribute labor. Many development projects were achieved this way. Over time, harambee became captured, first by local elites, and increasingly by national ones. By the mid-1980s, President Moi had become the foremost harambee patron by organizing huge national harambees for various pet projects, in which contribution was increasingly coercive. The political capture of harambees reached its apogee following the return to multiparty politics in the 1990s. Harambee fundraisers became vehicles for bribing voters: all manner of community projects, youth and women groups sprouted up in the run up to the election. They would organize harambee fund raisers and contribute to candidates who would officiate the events, only for the groups to disband soon after elections. A study by Transparency International Kenya (TIK) found that harambee activity increased dramatically, both in number of fundraisers as well as proceeds, around the 1992 and 1997 general elections (Figure 3.1).[13]

Harambee properly came to be seen not just as corrupting politics through patronage and even voter bribery, but also as legitimizing corruption: the

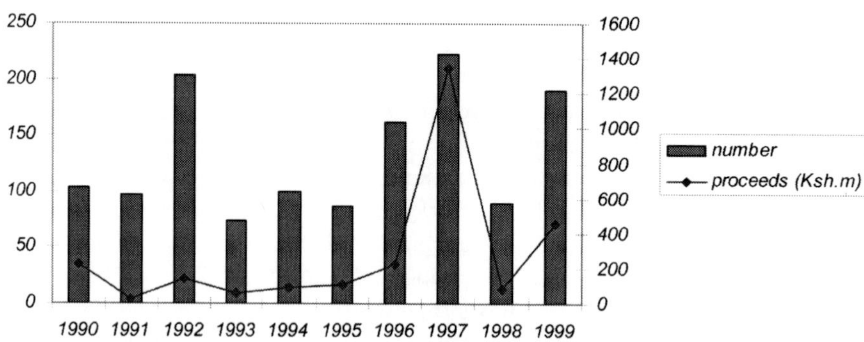

Figure 3.1 Political Harambee Activity 1990–1999. *Source*: David Ndii and Anne Wagiryu, *Harambee: Pooling Together or Pulling Apart*, Transparency International Kenya, Nairobi, 2001, 9, available at www.tikenya.org and http://library.fes.de/pdf-files/bueros/kenia/01394.pdf

biggest harambee patrons were public officials and politically connected individuals. Upon coming to power in 2003, the NARC administration sounded the death knell for political harambees by passing the Public Officer Ethics Act, which bars public officers from officiating in harambees.

Kenya's experience with harambee patronage is an important feature of the political backdrop of the CDF. It is significant that the CDF was proposed by the political opposition, which did not have access to the harambee patronage that was monopolized by the incumbent KANU's access to state resources. Indeed, the TIK study found that nine of the top ten harambee patrons were KANU's top leadership, with President Moi, his vice president, and the secretary general of the party making up the top three. As a result, MPs became dependent on and highly vulnerable to harambee powerbrokers regardless of their party affiliation, although these trends were more pronounced in KANU than in the opposition.

Against this background, the creation of the CDF provided a solution for MPs from the Government and the opposition to resolve financial burdens and free themselves from political clientelism. Further, by limiting incumbent MP's harambee activity, the Ethics Act provided additional impetus to creating some sort of constituency development fund because their opponents, who were not public officers, would still be free to employ harambees to popularize themselves. We will now see how Kenya's CDF is actually just one of several parallel structures that were created to circumvent a central government bureaucracy that had proven unable to deliver services effectively throughout the country.

Devolved Funds

The Harambee was merely the first experiment, and the CDF, the seventh of eight "devolved" funds—as they are now referred to in Kenya—that were established after 1993. In 1993, the World Bank promoted the Road Maintenance Fund on the justification that there was no point of donors financing roads if the Government did not provide money to maintain them. Also in 1993, the Government devolved the administration of a secondary school assistance program that had been managed centrally by the Ministry of Education, to constituency-level committees made up of civil servants, citizens, and elected politicians (councilors and MPs). These were followed by a Rural Electrification Fund (REF) in 1998, and the HIV/AIDs Fund and the Local Authority Transfer Fund (LATF) in 1999.

These precursors laid the foundation for the CDF in two ways. First, they introduced elements of budget entitlement, transparency and predictability to the resources available for local services and development. Second, they introduced the involvement of non-state actors—citizens and interest

Table 3.1 Devolved Funds in Kenya

Fund	*Financing*	*Decentralized to*
Bursary Fund (1993)	Budget	Constituency Committees,
Road Maintenance Fund (1993)	Fuel Levy	Constituency CDF Committee (Community Leaders, appointed by MP)
Rural Electrification Fund (1998)	Electricity Levy + Budget	
LATF (1999)	5% of Income Tax	Local Authorities
HIV/AIDS (1999)	Budget/Donors	HIV/AIDs committee (Govt + Community Leaders, appointed by Govt.
Free Primary Education (FPE) funds (2003)	Budget/Donors	Schools (School Committees/PTAs, appointed by Govt)
CDF (2004)	2.5% of Tax	CDF Committee
Health Sector Services Fund (HSSF) (2010)	Budget	District Health Management Committee (Govt. + comm. leaders, appointed by Govt)

groups—in the management of resources. With the exception of the LATF, which mandated funding to already functioning local authorities, all other funds have entailed the establishment of new constituency-level structures outside of the central government and that included or involved elected politicians (councilors and the local MP).

So notwithstanding some unique qualities, CDFs did not emerge out of the blue, but as part of a broader, two-part process of change: first, they emerged out of the failure of the centralized state—including by donors looking for ways of making aid more effective in the face of bureaucratic inefficiency and corruption—to provide services and good governance in all districts throughout Kenya. Secondly, they resulted from ground-level pressures for democratization, to transfer resources to the grassroots, and to giving local communities greater voice in the management of resources.

HISTORY, STRUCTURE AND OPERATIONS OF THE CDF

Origin

The CDF originated from a motion introduced by an opposition MP, Muriuki Karue, MP for Ol Kalou in central Kenya, north of Nairobi in 1999. The motion sought to have the Government earmark 5% of tax revenue for "grass root" development initiatives. In his own words:

> Whatever a member wanted done for their constituents would be done "when funds became available." The funds never became available for any of the grassroot concerns. It became my concern. In the same country where the

> government was building skyscrapers, villagers could not get a simple culvert to cross a stream that swelled every season. We had world class hospitals but children were dying of minor ailments because there was no clinic anywhere for miles. We boasted of many beautiful universities, yet children in many rural areas were not going to school simply because there was no school to go to. Reason? There was no money. They would be done when money became available. And so I set out on a mission to try and make money available for the so called small things; a primary school, a dispensary, a water borehole, a produce market, a small bridge, education bursary.[14]

The motion passed in October 2000, with an amendment introduced by the Minister of Finance reducing the figure from 5% to 2.5%. After two years of trying unsuccessfully to have the motion implemented, the Hon. Karue introduced a private members bill proposing the establishment the CDF. Parliament's term ended before the bill could be passed. Following the change of Government in 2003, he revived the bill in the next parliament and it was passed, but not before he was compelled to hand over the bill to the Government.

Structure

As noted above, Kenya's CDF is established by statute, the Constituency Development Fund Act of 2003. The law was substantially revised in 2007—the statute itself provides for regular review, in recognition of the fact that the CDF was an experiment whose structure and operation would need to be fine-tuned with experience. The legislation was further updated in 2013 to bring it in accordance with the Constitution that was adopted in 2010. In an attempt to combat corruption and cronyism, the new legislation curtails the influence of MPs in relation to committee appointments and project choices.

The statute earmarks 2.5% of the national tax revenue to be allocated for development projects that are to be identified by citizens in constituencies. The money is allocated to constituencies according to a formula where 75% is divided equally and the other 25% is weighted by each constituency's share of the population below the national poverty line.[15]

It also provides guidelines on how the money is spent. Constituencies are allowed a maximum of 3% of their annual allocation on administrative overhead, another 3% limit on purchase and operation of vehicles and equipment, a maximum of 2% each on monitoring and evaluation, environmental and sporting activities (maximum of 2% on each). They can spend up to 15% on bursaries (school fees grants) to needy students. Each constituency is allowed to maintain up to 5% of the annual allocation for emergencies such as weather related damage, fires etc. With the exception of bursaries, funds may only be spent on acquisition of public assets. Constituencies are required to start a minimum of five and a maximum of 25 projects every year.[16]

The CDF has an elaborate organizational structure comprised of eight organs. This is shown in Figure 3.2, with a summary of the composition and functions of each organ. At the top of the structure there is a parliamentary select committee, known as the Constituency Fund Committee (CFC) and alongside it the Minister of Planning who have shared responsibility for overall governance and policy. The CDF Board is the national fund manager, and is a state corporation (executive agency) in the Ministry of Planning. It controls the money, approves constituency budgets, disburses funds and reports on the performance of the Fund. The Board employs a fund manager in every constituency.

The District Projects Committee (DPC) is envisaged as an oversight and coordination forum that serves as the interface between the CDF and the

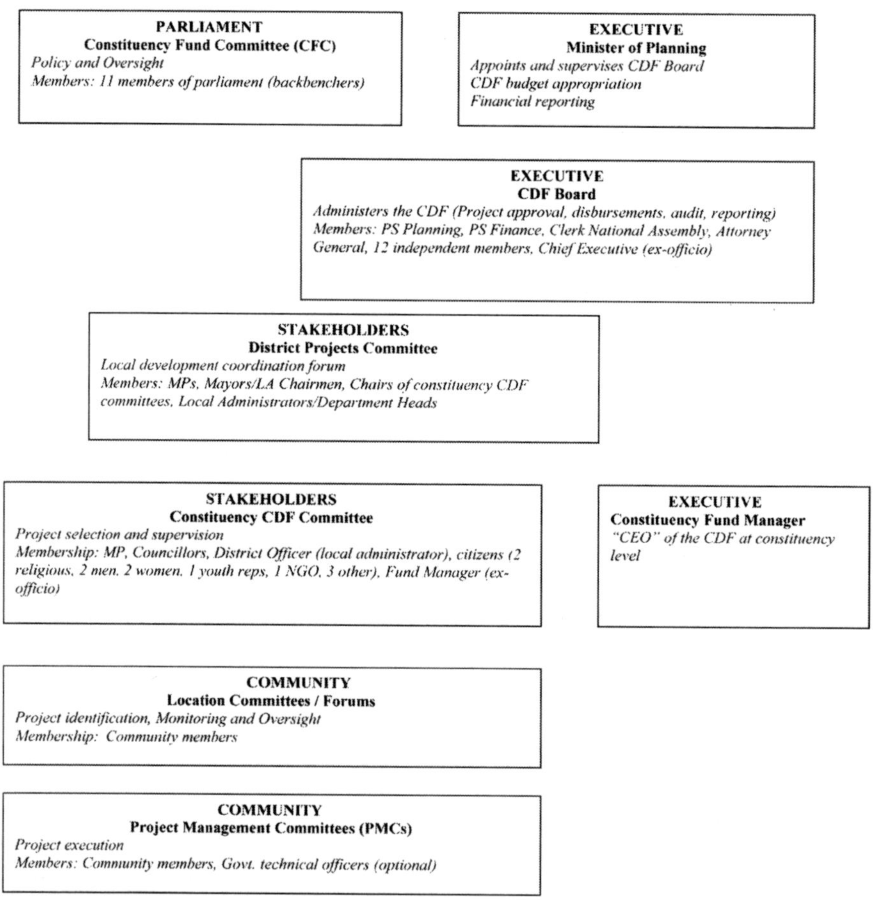

Figure 3.2 CDF Structure in Kenya

central government's development planning and administration. It should be constituted by all MPs in their district, the District Commissioner, as Chairpersons of the CDF in the district, the District Development Officer and District Accountant. However, the subdivision of districts over the last two decades made the DPC superfluous: the number of districts increased from 47 two decades ago, to over 270 today in the period just before the adoption of the 2010 Constitution. Whereas there were previously an average of 5 constituencies per district, by the time the new constitution was adopted, virtually every constituency was a district, and in some cases, there was more than one district within a constituency.

The Constituency Development Committees, referred to as CDF committees (CDFs), are the key operational organ of the CDF. The committee is responsible for selecting and implementing CDF projects. Previously, the CDF constituency committee was constituted by the constituency MP, who was also entitled to be the chairperson of the committee, but also could nominate another member to be the chairperson. Earlier legislation provided for a maximum of 15 committee members, including one government official (District Officer), local government, religious leaders, women, youth, men, and NGOs active in the area. Under the 2013 legislation, the MP, Officer the Board and subcounty administrator join select an eight-member CDFC from a pool of candidates nominated from each of the wards in the constituency "taking into account the geographical diversity within the constituency, communal, religious, social and cultural interests in the constituency and the requirements of gender, youth and representation of persons with disabilities."[17]

At the end of the line are locational committees or fora and project management committees.[18] The locational committees/forums are ad hoc community bodies that meet only to propose projects for their locality. Once a project is funded, a project management committee is constituted. Project management committees are constituted by representatives of the relevant government departments who serve community members in the locality and as technical advisors.

Operations

The CDF budget cycle begins with a wish list of projects proposed by citizens at the location. The MP is responsible for facilitating the identification of these projects. Because the Statute does not prescribe the process, MPs have employed a range of different approaches to the selection of projects. The most common are public meetings and committees that may be nominated by the MP or nominated by designated interest groups, or proposed by citizens in public meetings. Increasingly, MPs have embraced elaborate strategic planning processes. Typically, MPs mobilize the intelligentsia from the constituency—professionals and academics—to facilitate the production of constituency strategic plans. In addition, development NGOs and think tanks support such activities.

The constituency committee reviews the location lists and agrees on a constituency priority list, which is forwarded to the District Projects Committee for review. The MP then forwards the final constituency list to the CDF Board. The CDF Board reviews and approves the constituency proposals for funding, upon ascertaining that the expenditure proposals comply with the law. The legal requirements include limits set on administration expenses at 3% of the annual allocation, buying and operation of vehicles and machinery also limited to 3%, and a limit of 2% allocation each on sporting activities, environmental projects, and monitoring and evaluation. In addition, a constituency is allowed to submit no less than 5 and not more than 25 projects per year. The Board is required to refer the projects that it rejects to the parliamentary committee for direction. The parliamentary committee is, in turn, required to review the projects referred by the board and to communicate its recommendations back to the Board within fourteen days.

The law stipulates that the Board forward the approved CDF projects to the Minister of Planning by the end of February to be incorporated in the national budget, which is tabled in parliament in June. This has turned out to be impractical because the CDF budget allocation is pegged to the revenue forecast that is itself approved in the budget. This means that the actual number of projects to be financed cannot be confirmed until the budget is tabled and the CDF allocation approved by parliament. Thus, in practice, the CDF budget is approved after the national budget. The CDF Board transmits the approved budget to the constituency committees. The Board also disseminates information about the budget publicly through the newspapers and it is also posted on its website.

Upon approval of the national budget, the Treasury transfers CDF monies to an account held by the Central Bank of Kenya in equal quarterly installments. The CDF Board disburses the money to constituency committees' bank accounts. The committees then initiate the implementation of the approved projects.

Budget History and Structure

The CDF was inaugurated in the 2003–2004 financial year with an allocation of Ksh. 1.26 billion (US $16.5 million) which was distributed equally to all constituencies each getting Ksh. 6 million (US $79,000). Table 3.2 shows that full implementation in accordance with the law the following year increased the allocation to Ksh. 5.4 billion (US $70 million) translating to an average

Table 3.2 CDF Allocations

	FY03/04	FY04/05	FY05/06	FY06/07	FY07/08	FY08/09	FY09/10
CDF Allocations, Ksh m	1,260	5,432	7,029	9,737	9,797	9,797	11,959
CDF Allocations, US $m	16.5	70.2	97.1	140.3	156.3	126.1	157.7
Av./Constituency US $	78,802	334,454	462,479	668,098	744,295	600,339	751,116

of Ksh. 26 million (US $330,000) per constituency. The allocation has grown rapidly, reaching Ksh. 12 billion (US $158 m) in 2009/10, translating to an average of US $750,000 per constituency. This growth reflects a similarly rapid increase in tax revenue. In relative terms, the CDF has fluctuated between 1.4 and 2% of the total budget.

Table 3.3 Sectoral Distribution of CDF Expenditure FY03/04–FY09/10

Education	33.9	Administration	2.9
Bursaries	12.3	Environment	1.2
Agriculture	13	Sports	1.2
Water	11	Recurrent	1.9
Health	6.5	Monitoring & Evaluation	1.9
Roads/Bridges	6.2	Emergency	5.1
Energy	5.1	Others	10
Security	4.0		

Data taken from: CDF Board Reports (available on CDF Board website).

Table 3.3 demonstrates that education is by far the most popular sector for CDF, accounting for close to 40% of the CDF budget excluding bursaries, and 45% inclusive of bursaries. Water, health, roads and bridges are the other important sectors, together accounting for just over 30% of the outlays. This pattern of expenditure is broadly consistent with the distribution of public expenditure in Kenya.

Performance

The CDF has financed thousands of development projects in the country. Among the most popular projects are improvements of schools and health facilities, construction of new facilities, water (dams, boreholes and reticulation) and road improvements. Street lighting and sanitation are also popular in constituencies with urban informal settlements. There is as yet no comprehensive statistics on CDF projects, but there is no doubt that its contribution to public infrastructure in these sectors is substantial. For example, the number of public health facilities increased by 30% between 2004 and 2008 (1400 facilities), as compared to 10% (400 facilities) in the period 2000–2004. The difference is attributed almost entirely to CDF-funded facilities.

CDF has enjoyed a high approval rating by the public from the outset. A 2006 survey conducted by KIPPRA, a government policy think tank, asked respondents to rate all the devolved funds on two criteria: decision making and impact. On both criteria, the public ranked CDF second to the Free Primary Education (FPE) Funds (Figure 3.3). A 2009 study by the Kenya

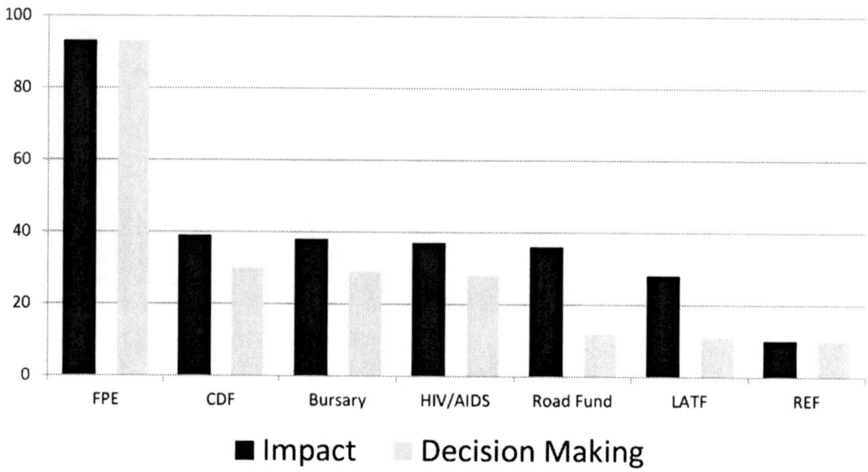

Figure 3.3 Approval Rating of Decentralized Funds. *Source*: KIPPRA. "Baseline Survey Report on Decentralized Funds in Kenya: A Review of Bondo, Bungoma, Nakuru, Machakos, Kirinyaga, Wajir and Mombasa Districts, and Nairobi Province." *Kenya Institute for Public Policy Research and Analysis*. Nairobi, 2006.

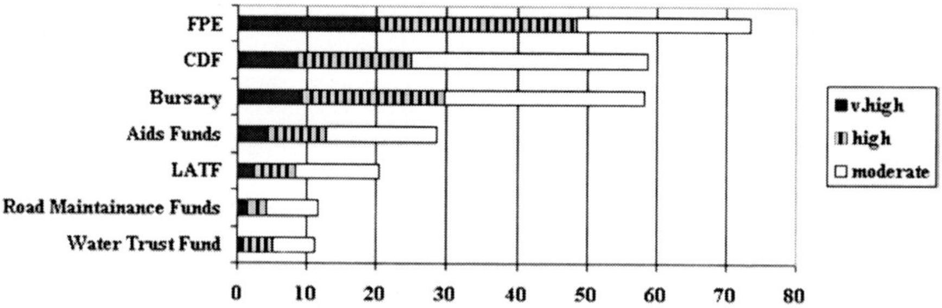

Figure 3.4 Responsiveness of Decentralized Funds. *Source*: "Harmonization of Decentralized Development In Kenya: Towards Alignment, Citizen Engagement and Enhanced Accountability," Kenya Human Rights Commission and Social and Public Accountability Network, www.khrc.or.ke/resources/publications/doc_download/1-harmonization-of-decentralized-development-in-kenya.html.

Human Rights Commission (KHRC) and the Social and Public Accountability Network (SPAN) asked respondents how well the decentralized funds met community needs, and obtained a similar ranking, i.e., CDF ranked second to FPE (Figure 3.4). This study also asked about citizen's participation in various stages of the projects (identification, budgeting/planning, implementation, monitoring). CDF registered the highest average level of citizen participation of all the funds (Figure 3.5).

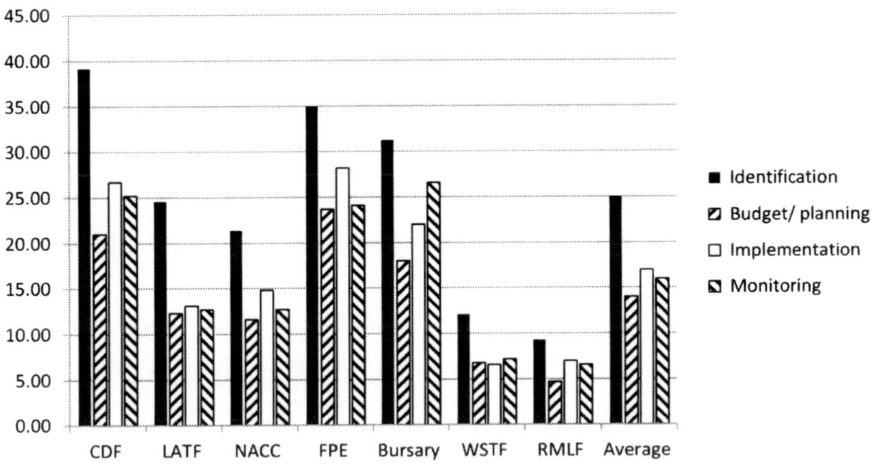

Figure 3.5 Citizen Involvement in Different Project Cycles (%). *Source*: "Harmonization of Decentralized Development In Kenya: Towards Alignment, Citizen Engagement and Enhanced Accountability," Kenya Human Rights Commission and Social and Public Accountability Network, www.khrc.or.ke/resources/publications/doc_download/1-harmonization-of-decentralized-development-in-kenya.html.

A 2006 study by the Institute of Economic Affairs (IEA), an independent think tank, reported between 60 and 90% approval on seven criteria (Figure 3.6). A similar survey conducted for the National Anti-Corruption Steering Committee by the University of Nairobi's Institute of Development Studies in 2008 reported approval ratings very similar to the IEA study (Figure 3.7).

In these surveys, the public rates development dimensions of the CDF, such as project relevance and impact, consistently higher than its governance dimensions, such as participation, transparency, accountability. However, when asked which model they would like adopted for all the decentralized funds, respondents to the KHRC/SPAN, indicated the CDF was by far the most preferred (Figure 3.8).

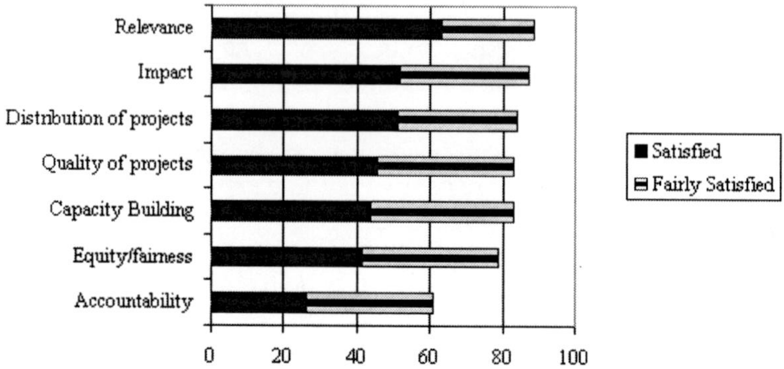

Figure 3.6 Citizen Approval of CDFs (%). *Source*: Kenyans' Verdict: A Citizens Report Card on the Constituencies Development Fund (CDF)", Institute of Economic Affairs. http://www.ieakenya.or.ke/publications/doc_download/236-a-citizens-report-card-on-the-constituencies-development-fund-cdf.

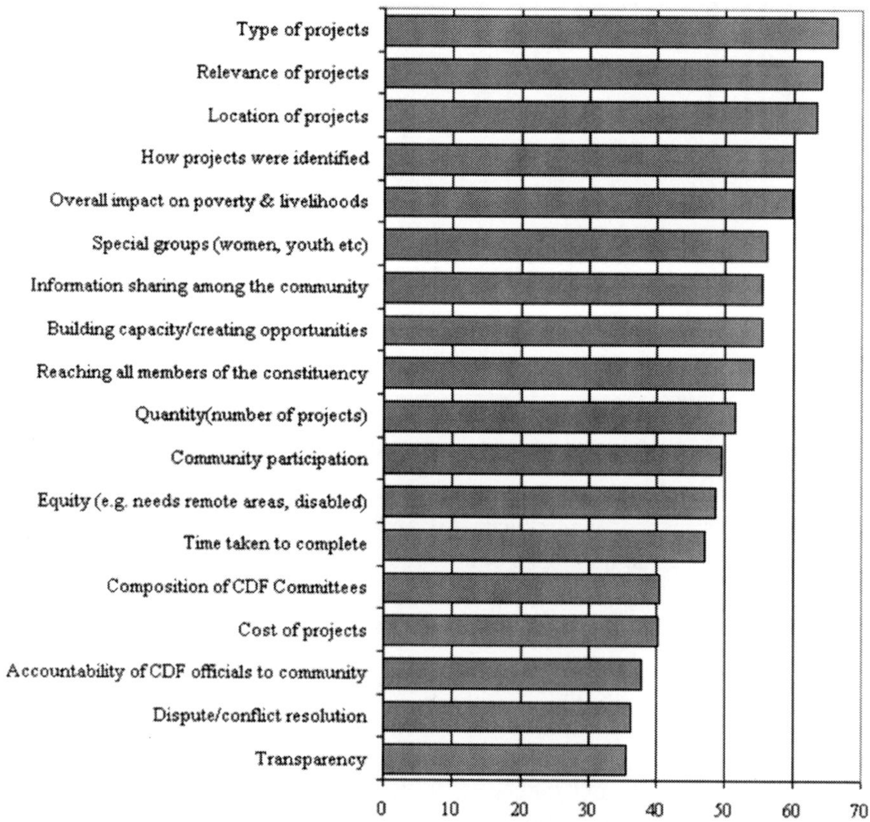

Figure 3.7 Citizen Satisfaction with CDFs—Satisfied and Fairly Satisfied (%). *Source*: National Anti-Corruption Steering Committee. "The Constituency Development Fund: In Examination of Legal, Structural, Management and Corruption Issues in Kenya." 2008.

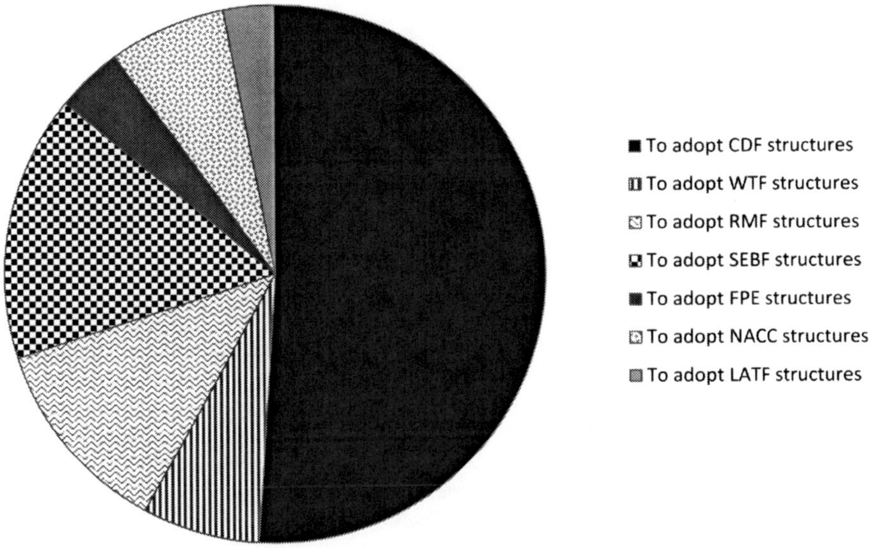

Figure 3.8 Preferred Operational Model for Decentralized Funds. *Source*: "Harmonization of Decentralized Development in Kenya: Towards Alignment, Citizen Engagement and Enhanced Accountability," Kenya Human Rights Commission and Social and Public Accountability Network, www.khrc.or.ke/resources/publications/doc_download/1-harmonization-of-decentralized-development-in-kenya.html.

Table 3.4 Summary of Findings of NTA CDF Project Audits

	Number	*Value**	*% of Projects*	*% of Value*
Well built, complete	955	772.7	36.6	40.1
Well built, (on going)	943	735.7	36.2	38.1
Poor, complete & incomplete	437	293.5	16.8	15.2
Abandoned (failed)	63	34.8	2.4	1.8
"Ghost project" (funded, nonexistent)	209	92.3	8.0	4.8
Total	2607	1,928.9	100.0	100.0

*Value in Kenya shillings.
Source: National Tax Payers Association Reports (authors compilation).

The most comprehensive information on CDF performance comes from independent audits conducted by a consortium of civil society organizations under the banner of the National Taxpayers Association (NTA).[19] At the time of writing this chapter, NTA had published audits of 35 constituencies. Twenty three of them cover only one year FY 2006–7, and the other 12 cover FYs 2006–7 and 2007–8. In total, they cover 2607 projects on which Ksh. 2 billion (US $25 million) had been spent. Of those surveyed, 72% were rated as good value for money, 16% have been rated as poor value for money, 2% were abandoned and 8% as ghost projects i.e. money was allocated but

Table 3.5 Examples of NTA CDF Audits

Project Number	CDF/43
Constituency	Aldai
Project Name	AIC Chepkebuge Secondary
Project Activity	Dormitory Construction
Location/Ward	Chebilat
MPs Name	Hon. Sammy Choge/Hon. Sally Kosgei
Project Status	Ongoing
Total Funds Awarded to Date	2,100,000
Total Funds Spent to Date	600,000
Total Unaccounted Funds	1,500,000
Technical Performance Score	55%
Project Classification	C
Date of Assessment	4/2/09 5.03 p.m.
Comments	Project implementation is ongoing and as at the time of NTA visit, roofing was on course and various materials were on site. The overall workmanship in the project is commendable and the school administration expressed satisfaction with the work undertaken.

Project Number	15
Constituency	Kangema
Project Name	Kihoya health centre
Project Activity	Maternity wing
Location/Ward	Rwathia
MPs Name	Hon. John Michuki
Project Status	Complete
Date of Visit	7/03/09
Total Funds Awarded to Date	8,662,205
Total Funds Spent to Date	5,513,264
Total Unaccounted Funds	3,148,941
Technical Performance Score	63%
Project Classification	A
Comments	The work done on the facility is splendid. There is overall community satisfaction with the project and it indeed reflects value for money.

Project Number	CDF E.01
Constituency	Embakasi
Project Name	Mukuru foot bridge
Project Activity	Rehabilitation
Location/Ward	Mukuru
MPs Name	Hon. Ferdinand Waititu
Project Status	Does not exist
Date of Visit	
Total Funds Awarded to Date	1,000,000
Total Funds Spent to Date	Nil
Total Unaccounted Funds	1,000,000
Technical Performance Score	N/A
Project Classification	Category E

Table 3.5 (Continued)

Comments	There are only two footbridges in the area and none of them was constructed using CDF funds. Although the project status report indicates that 1M is already spent in rehabilitating the bridge, the work is stated to have not started. Whereas it is alleged that the money was transferred to Reuben Primary School, there is no proof of reallocation.

Source: National Taxpayers Association. *CDF Citizen Report Cards.* http://www.nta.or.ke/reports/crc/Eldoret/Aldai_CRC_March_2010.pdf, 20. http://www.nta.or.ke/reports/crc/Nyeri/Kangema_CRC_March_2010.pdf, 8. http://www.nta.or.ke/reports/crc/Nairobi/Embakasi_CRC_March_2010.pdf, 17.

projects could not be physically identified. In financial terms, 80% of the budget was properly used and accounted for. The poor projects account for 12% of the budget while 8% could not be accounted for.

More recent audits conducted by the NTA have continued to indicate a fairly strong return on the CDF-funded projects, with the majority of completed and ongoing projects across the counties receiving high value ratings. On the whole, most constituencies have maintained the 70–80% range of positive returns for CDF funds. Several constituencies have performed even better, with satisfactory returns pushing 90%, and only 1% of the CDF budget unaccounted for.[20]

As observed already, the CDF is one of several funds that have been devised to circumvent the inefficiency and corruption of Kenya's highly centralized executive. Thus it can be argued that the perceived success of the CDF is actually only relative to the failures of executive-led development. There is merit in this argument, as there are two failures of the executive led development that CDF is seen as having remedied.

The first is distribution. As observed above, skewed distribution of development resources has been one of Kenya's most potent political grievances. Although not evidently one of the motivations of setting up, it is one that MPs frequently highlight, as evident from the following contribution to debate in parliament,

> I would like to talk about the gains we have got from the NARC administration. One of the most outstanding and one that I hear about when I visit the rural areas is the constituency development fund. Kenyans are now saying that for the first time in the history of Kenya, they can now taste the national cake.[21]
>
> I was in the last parliament and my constituency only got 30 million shillings in the entire five years for development. This is 0.008 percent. The distribution of wealth must be even . . . Were it not for the CDF, there would be no development in my constituency. I know very well that one constituency, in the year 2007/8—the one we are just about to complete—got 250 million to help with water projects. This is just one constituency! My constituency got only 30 million in five years![22]

> It is important for us to review the CDF. Mvita constituency has only two secondary schools in the last 45 years! You cannot tell me that you will give me an equal CDF to Gichugu which has 56 secondary schools.[23]

The second is implementation of projects. Although it has improved in recent years—the Government's implementation of development projects had been deteriorating for years, to the point where in FY 2004/5, the Government only utilized 45% of the development budget (Figure 3.9). But the low utilization of the budget is only part of the picture. In some ministries, completion rates had fallen to as low as 3% of target. Even with improvement, government performance is still wanting. For example, in 2009, utilization of donor funds was still only 50%.[24] The CDF has established a track record for project execution that is very likely unmatched anywhere else in Kenya's public sector. The CDF achieved a budget execution rate of 70 in its first five years of operation that is, 70% of budget allocation was spent during the year. With the exception of Nairobi, an outlier at 82%, the execution rates for the other 7 provinces range from 68 to 73%.[25]

In the FY 2009/10 budget, the Government introduced an Economic Stimulus Package (ESP) to mitigate the effects of multiple shocks—post election violence, a severe drought and the global financial crisis—on the economy. It chose to channel the ESP through the CDF as opposed to central government ministries or local authorities. The rationale for this was that not only would the CDF system ensure faster utilization, and in effect be more effective as an economic stimulus, it would make for more equitable and accountable utilization of the ESP funds:

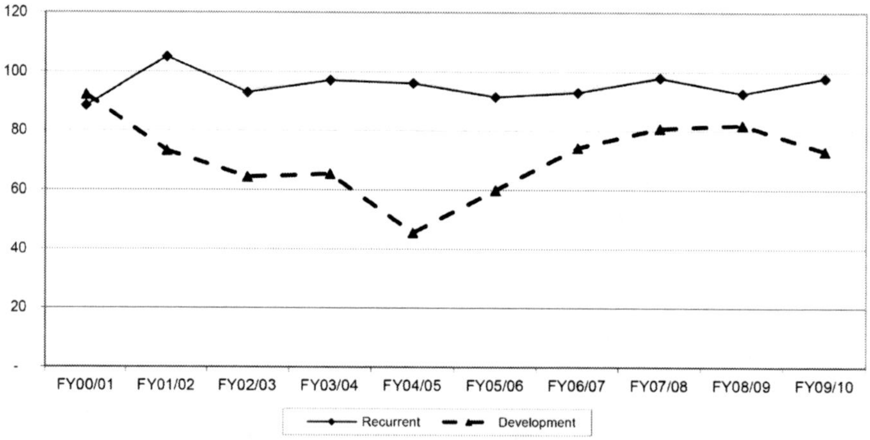

Figure 3.9 Central Government Budget Execution (% of budget utilized). *Source*: Government of Kenya. "Public Expenditure Review 2010." http://www.devolutionplanning.go.ke/index.php?option=com_docman&task=cat_view&gid=64&limitstart=20

> The promotion of equitable regional and social development is a central objective of the Grand Coalition Government. The thrust of this Budget therefore is to ensure that the budgetary resources reach the people at the constituency level. Since, our focus will be to stimulate economic activity at the constituency level, we will channel these resources as conditional grants through the respective ministries, using the existing Constituency Development Fund framework. This will facilitate local accountability, strengthen oversight to ensure all the funds allocated are strictly used for the planned purposes.[26]

One consequence of this is that the CDF has eclipsed the local government system in terms of budget. In FY 2009/10 Ksh. 38 billion was budgeted to go through the CDF system, 30% more than local authorities' expenditure for the previous year (Ksh. 29 billion).

CHALLENGES AND ISSUES

Role of MPs: Conflict of Interest

One of the issues that have dogged the CDF since inception is the question of potential conflict with the legislature's oversight role. This criticism is based on the MP's traditional role as the conveners of the CDF Committee in his or her constituency. Under previous legislation, MPs had been entitled to chair the committees unless he or she chose not to, and the CDF committee was, in turn, responsible for authorizing expenditures from the fund. This gave rise to the contention that if CDF money is not properly utilized or misappropriated, MPs would, in their oversight function, be judges in their own case.[27] The 2013 legislation on CDFs greatly restricts the role of MPs in regards to committee selection, and relegates them to more of an advisory position tasked with assisting community mobilization and project oversight.

Abuse of Power by MPs

MPs are routinely accused of abusing power in CDF. They are accused of rewarding their supporters and cronies with positions on the constituency committees, influencing award of tenders and choice of projects to achieve their political objectives, and outright theft of CDF funds. These accusations are to be found in the media as well as NGO reports, although no systematic evidence in support of the accusation.[28] In two instances, both in 2010, constituents filed civil cases against MPs to court seeking to bar fair allocation, and misappropriation. In one case, the complainants were unable to present evidence of the accusations. In the other, the MP, who was also an assistant minister, the court established that the MP had diverted Ksh.

1 million (US $12,000) to his private bank account, which the court ordered that he reimburse the CDF. The court also ordered a reconstitution of the CDF committee in the constituency.[29]

It is difficult to assess how widespread these incidents are. Part of the challenge is that there does seem to be instances where political adversaries of the sitting MPs are behind smear campaigns—and that seems to have been the case in the suit that was dismissed by the court.

Corruption

Corruption features very prominently in the public debate on CDFs. In a country where corruption is pervasive, it is difficult to discern whether the CDF is just as susceptible to corruption as other public institutions. It does appear however, that incidences of corruption affecting CDF attract more attention in the media than corruption elsewhere in government. While the NTA audits show that the bulk of CDF funds are properly utilized, media reporting of the same audits almost invariably highlights "massive losses" of CDF funds.[30]

The determination to uncover corruption in the CDF is not limited to the media. The first finding reported by the Nairobi Social Audit Report, an audit of three devolved funds, the CDF, LATF and the government's Economic Stimulus Programme published jointly by three NGOs (Institute of Social Accountability, Shelter Forum and Ufadhili Trust), is a summary of "projects with suspected corruption." The title of the table with the summary escalates from suspicion to "Instances of Corruption."[31] However, the table contains a list of incomplete, stalled and poorly done projects. The money spent on the projects is tabulated elsewhere and titled "Summary of Total Amounts Embezzled." The NACCSC/IDS discussed earlier is another example. It asserts "corruption regarding CDFs exists in many forms, at different levels and involves many stakeholders" and further that "bribery was found to be extensive especially in an attempt to secure contracts." Curiously however, the report does not report the data on the question which asked respondents whether they are aware of incidents of corruption in CDF projects (i.e. percentages answering yes or no), but reports only the analysis of a secondary question on the types of corruption witnessed by those who answered yes.

Transparency

The absence of transparency features prominently in the criticism of the CDF, which scores relatively poorly on transparency in all the survey research cited in this chapter. In the IDS National Anti-Corruption Campaign Steering

Committee (NACCSC) survey cited earlier, transparency received the lowest approval rating—two thirds of the respondents reporting their CDF as lacking in transparency, the lowest approval rating of all the attributes listed in the survey. The study reports that, "in a majority of the constituencies, there was no open discussion about the activities and usage of CDF money, in others, mystery surrounds the CDF and its activities at the grassroots level. The implementers are rarely willing to discuss CDF activities freely with the beneficiaries. This has created a feeling that there are underhand activities."[32]

This situation may reflect a weakness of the CDF statute with regard to information disclosure. While the statute obliges the CDF to involve citizens in the identification of projects, the decision making process is not open to scrutiny, neither are the officials required to inform citizens on how decisions are made. Thus citizens cannot learn why some projects were chosen over others, or how contracts are awarded. In addition, the Ministry of Planning is required by law to present an annual status implementation report to parliament, but it had yet to present one by December 2009.[33]

In response to this criticism, the National Management Committee (the precursor to the National Management Board) instructed the CDFCs to erect notice boards in all locations and display on them "accurate and updated information on the CDF projects, their physical location, cost, the contractor, their current status and expected date of completion."[34] An additional step taken by the 2013 CDF legislation is to require election of five CDFC members by constituents. The act requires MPs to convene a public meeting to conduct the election within 45 days of being sworn in. Ideally this will work to bring greater levels of transparency to both the CDFC and the program as a whole.

Absence of the Project Management Committees' Legal Status

The Project Management Committee is one of the most interesting organs in the CDF structure. The original CDF Act (2003) provided for implementation of CDF projects by the "relevant government department in the district." In the 2007 version, this was replaced by "project committee in each case, with the assistance of the relevant department of Government." But the Act does not give structure to the project committees i.e. how they are to be convened and to operate. In fact, this is the only mention of the project committee in the entire statute.

Nonetheless, the PMCs have become the actual executing organs of CDF projects. They procure, maintain and operate project bank accounts—in violation of public procurement law and government financial regulation, which require that only designated public officials can exercise these functions.

In the absence of a clear framework, MPs have appointed members of the PMCs at their discretion—there has been nothing to stop an MP from appointing his or her relatives and cronies. In some cases a PMC is responsible for one project and is disbanded once the project is completed. In other cases, they have become standing committees serving on different projects for the entire tenure of the MP.

Disruptive Impact on Budget and Policy

As observed earlier, the bulk of CDF money has financed education and health projects, which has led to a very significant increase in public facilities. This increase has caused concern about the impact of CDF projects impact on the Government's policy, programs and budget. A review of the Government's Second National Health Sector Strategic Plan (NHSSP II) laments that:

> This rational and restrained building program (of health facilities) is in danger of being disrupted by the uncoordinated construction of dispensaries using Constituency Development Funds, which MOH (Ministry of Health) is then expected to operate. There are anecdotal reports that up to 1,600 such dispensaries have been built, not necessarily to appropriate designs and standards, or in appropriate locations—this may be determined on political grounds as opposed to rationalization of access. Currently, 300 of these CDF-constructed facilities have been reopened and are functioning; in FY 2007/08, an additional 600 dispensaries will be operational.[35]

But even as the report laments the disruptive impact of CDF, it acknowledges that the Government's facilities policy is deficient:

> The current infrastructure norms and standards for the KEPH (Kenya Essential Package for Health) are based on populations and do not take into account of distances travelled by clients. Yet the 2007 Client Satisfaction Survey showed that respondents seeking outpatient services in hospitals live further away (over 13 kilometres) compared with those seeking services in health centres (7 km) or dispensaries (4 km). The overall average distance that patients/clients must travel to reach any type of facility is about 9 km. There is therefore a need to establish additional new facilities particularly in hard to reach areas.[36]

This latter observation resonates with the response of CDF champions, who argue that the CDF outlays are a better reflection of the people's needs than the Ministry of Health's "rational and restrained" building program. They also contend that political pressure to equip and finance the operations of CDF health facilities has translated to an increase in the health budget, which is a stated goal of government policy that the executive had failed to achieve on its own volition.[37]

There is heuristic evidence consistent with this assertion, especially in a very significant improvement in citizen's proximity to health facilities. The percentage of citizens living within 5 km of a public health facility has increased from 70 to 90%—with four of the eight provinces reaching 100% of the population.[38]

Distribution Formula

The CDF allocation formula has been criticized as inequitable, with 75% of funds allocated on a pro-rata basis (i.e. equal amount per constituency) and 25% according to the incidence of poverty. The resulting outcome is seen to favor constituencies with low population density, and to be particularly biased against areas with both high population density and high incidence of poverty. According to an analysis by the Kenya National Bureau of Statistics (KNBS), the disparities measured in terms of transfers per poor person in the sparsely populated areas was 20 times more than the per capita transfers to poor persons living in urban areas.[39]

The KNBS predicated its critique on the principles that apply to income transfers to households. However, CDF is not a transfer to households, but rather a capital transfer for provision of public goods. The more appropriate criteria for evaluating distributive implications of the CDF formula would be indicators of access to the services that the CDF finances, viz. education, health, water. On these criteria, the sparsely populated areas have historically been less well served with public services than the densely populated ones.

CONCLUSIONS

The CDF is arguably one of the most successful and popular development policy innovations in Kenya's recent history. It has certainly realized its founders vision, i.e., making funds available for the local concerns—the so called "small things." Consequently, the performance of CDF must be judged in the context of Kenya's weak state capacity that has, over time, been further eroded by corruption and bureaucratic inefficiency and perhaps more importantly, spatial distributional grievances associated with skewed allocation of budgetary resources. The fact that the CDF, which only commands 2.5% of budget, has become the most visible development effort in Kenya suggests that the historical failure of Kenya's executive-led development may be even more profound than most observers have contemplated. It is also the case that the CDF has also benefited from Kenya's economic recovery since 2003, which has seen a significant improvement in government revenues which translates into substantial resources available to the CDF on account of the fact that the CDF is created as a percentage of revenue.

With regard to the implementation performance, the CDF owes its capacity to implement projects to its highly devolved structure that gives citizens meaningful participation, and potentially strong ownership over projects. With regard to distribution, the CDF owes its success to the fact that its distribution is transparent and not subject to executive discretion. These attributes of the CDF do not necessarily stem from its relationship with the legislature—arguably any other program with these characteristics would be equally successful. Indeed, the FPE funds, which share these characteristics, are more favorably rated by citizens than the CDF.

The MPs' leadership of the CDF is much criticized, and there is no doubt that some MPs abuse the responsibility. But this could also be one of the most important factors driving the overall success of the CDF. The performance of the CDF has become an important criterion by which constituents assess their MPs' performance, which compels the MPs to strive to ensure that CDF delivers tangible benefits. It is doubtful that MPs would be as proactive if they were not directly accountable to their constituents for the CDF.

The CDF has also benefited from a dynamic legal framework. The statute stipulates that it should be reviewed every two years, and is the only Kenyan statute with such a provision.[40] This made it possible to address quickly some of the shortcomings identified in the initial phase of operation. Key among these was to establishment of the CDF Board to address the conflict associated with direct involvement of the legislature in implementation. Another innovation was to transfer the responsibility of project implementation from the central government to the communities by way of establishment of project management committees. This has increased communities' sense of ownership of the CDF.

The question that remains then is whether the development success of CDF is at the expense of democratic governance. In its original structure, the CDF did give the legislature a budget execution function which lent credence to this contention. As observed, this was subsequently addressed by establishing the CDF Board, an executive agency, and transferring to it the execution function. In essence the only formal function that MPs have retained at the national level is as members of the Constituency Fund Committee whose function is no different from other committees of parliament. At the constituency level the MPs retain their roles on the committee, and they do have a substantial amount of influence on the committee. Does this constitute a breach of separation of powers? Arguably yes. But in a parliamentary system, this is not peculiar to the MPs role in CDF committees. Indeed it has been alleged that promises of appointment to positions of assistant ministers are used to compromise MPs oversight performance.

It is far from clear that the CDF will survive in anything close to its current form. In essence, it was a political innovation that sought to address distributional grievances that the constitution has addressed. For constituents, its continued relevance hinges on the responsiveness of county governments' to their local development needs, that is, whether they are able to provide the "money for small things" that has made the CDF an unlikely success story. One the CDF's enduring legacies is its impact on patrimonial politics. The CDF liberated MPs from begging the executive for development projects, which partially explains why it has been unpopular in the bureaucracy, as well as among citizens from wealthy harambee patrons. The CDF has been instrumental in the welcome demise of political harambees.

The tension between the CDF and devolution will continue to play out. Turf battles between MPs and Senators at the national level, and with the county government structures at the constituency level are inevitable. But it is in the interest of all of them to retain it since it provides additional funds to the county from the centre.

GLOSSARY OF KEY TERMS

CDFC – CDF Committee
DDC – District Development Committee
DPC – District Projects Committee
ESP – Economic Stimulus Package
FPE – Free Primary Education
HSSF – Health Sector Services Fund
IDS – Institute for Development Studies
IEA – Institute of Economic Affairs
KADU – Kenya African Democratic Union
KANU – Kenya Africa National Union
KEPH – Kenya Essential Package for Health
KHRC – Kenya Human Rights Commission
KIPPRA – Kenya Institute for Public Policy Research and Analysis
KNBS – Kenya National Board of Statistics
Ksh – Kenya Shillings
LATF – Local Authority Transfer Fund
MP – Member of Parliament
MOH – Ministry of Health
NACC – National Anti-Corruption Campaign
NARC – National Rainbow Coalition
NHSSP – National Health Strategic Sector Plan
NTA – National Taxpayers Association

ODM – Orange Democratic Movement
PMC – Project Management Committee
PNU – Party of National Unity
REF – Rural Electrification Fund
RMF – Road Maintenance Fund
SEBF – Secondary Education Bursary Fund
SPAN – Social and Political Accountability Network
TIK – Transparency International Kenya
WTF – Water Trust Fund

NOTES

1. Otieno, "No more dying while giving birth for Matuga women." *The Star*, 2011.
2. See the studies reported below.
3. Tshangana, 2010.
4. International Budget Partnership "Constituency Development Funds: African Parliaments' Faustian Bargain."
5. Kimenyi, 2005.
6. Kenyatta, "Budget Speech for Fiscal Year 2010/2011"; and Oparanya "Remarks by the Chief Guest (Min of Planning) during Strategic Plan Launch."
7. Task Force on Devolved Government, 2011.
8. Government of Kenya, "African Socialism and its Application to Planning to Kenya," 46.
9. Government of Kenya "Economic Management for Renewed Growth," 1986.
10. Chitere and Ireri, 2004.
11. In the Goldenberg scandal, a politically connected company (one of principals was the head of the national intelligence service, faked gold exports) between 1992 and 1993 (Kenya does not produce gold) to obtain export subsidy from the Government. It is believed that some of proceeds were used to finance Moi's 1992 reelection.
12. World Bank, 2009.
13. Ndii and Wagiryu, 2001.
14. Karue, 2011.
15. The new constitution has established 290 constituencies, up from 210 previously. In the old system, the number of constituencies was reviewed every ten years to take account of population changes. The new constitution provides for review of names and boundaries but the number remains fixed at 290.
16. Constituency Development Fund Act, 2013. Section 23(1).
17. Kenya Gazette Supplement. "The Constituencies Constituency Development Fund Act: 2013." Section 24 (3) (C) *Republic of Kenya Gazette Supplement No. 45 (Acts No. 30).*
18. A "location" is an administrative level of government below the constituency.
19. The audits entail actual site visits to all the projects audited, interviews with stakeholders and review of documents. Physical works are evaluated by independent

professionals (engineers and quantity surveyors). The findings are published in a comprehensive report card for each constituency that includes a listing, including photographs, of every project (see examples in this chapter).

20. National Taxpayers Association. "CDF Citizen Report Cards."

21. Prof. Ruth Oniang'o, opposition (KANU) nominated MP. Hansard June 14 2005

22. Wyclifffe Oparanya, MP for Butere constituency. Hansard March 19 2008

23. Najib Balala, MP for Mvita and Minister for Tourism. Hansard 21 October 2008. Mvita is a constituency within the city of Mombasa, in the coast region of the country. Gichugu is a rural constituency in central Kenya, perceived as having been favored by the Kenyatta administration, while the coast region perceives itself as having been marginalized by the same administration.

24. Kenyatta, "Budget Speech for Fiscal Year 2009/2010."

25. Government of Kenya. "Public Expenditure Review 2010."

26. Kenyatta, "Budget Speech for Fiscal Year 2009/2010."

27. Most of the MPs who were in office when the CDF was started chose to chair the committees, but after the 2007 election, most MPs opted not to chair the committees.

28. For example, a 2009 report by the Institute for Social Accountability asserted that the excessive powers of MPs in CDF implementation resulted in a dearth of technical capacity, poor planning, and other weaknesses that work to undermine the program. CDF Status Report. The Institute for Social Accountability (2009). http://www.tisa.or.ke/about-devolved-funds/constituency-development-fund/

29. See for example, a similar case: "MP Gesami ordered to appear before EACC," *The Star*, March 10, 2012.

30. "Sh. 425 million Misused in Grassroot Projects" (Daily Nation 28 March 2011), "Audit Report Reveals loss of Sh. 500m in CDF Cash (Business Daily 6 April 2011)."

31. Institute for Social Accountability. "Nairobi Social Audit Report," 2010, 17.

32. The Institute of Social Accountability, "The CDF Status Report, December 2009."

33. The Ministry's failure has been raised by The Institute of Social Accountability (TISA) in The CDF Status Report, December 2009. http://www.scribd.com/doc/32513504/CDF-Status-Report

34. Constituencies Development Fund Board, "Constituencies Development Fund: National Management Committee Secretariat. Re: *Erection of CDF Notice Boards.*"

35. Ministry of Health, "National Health Sector Strategic Plan II Mid-term Review Report."

36. Ibid.

37. This assertion was made by the previous parliament's chairman of the Constituency Fund Committee, Hon. Ekwe Ethuro, in meetings attended by the author

38. Ministry of Health, "Mid Term Review Report of the Second National Health Sector Strategic Plan (NHSSP II)."

39. Kenya National Bureau of Statistics, 2008.

40. "The Chairperson of the Constituency Development Fund Committee in consultation with the Member of Parliament for the Constituency, the subcounty

administrator for the Constituency, and the ward administrator for every ward shall, within the first year of a new parliament and at least once every two years thereafter, convene open forum public meetings at in every ward in the constituency to deliberate on development matters in the ward and the constituency."

REFERENCES

Chitere, P.O and O.N. Ireri. "District Focus for Rural Development in Kenya: Its Limitations as a Decentralisation and Participatory Planning Strategy and Prospects for the Future." *Institute of Policy Analysis and Research.* Discussion Paper No., 2004

Government of Kenya. "African Socialism and its Application to Planning to Kenya." Sessional Paper No. 10 of 1965. http://siteresources.worldbank.org/INTAFRICA/Resources/257994-1335471959878/Sessional-Paper-No-10-%281965%29.pdf.

———. "Economic Management for Renewed Growth." Sessional Paper No. 1 of 1986 Government Printer.

———, Constituencies Development Fund Board. *Constituencies Development Fund: National Management Committee Secretariat. Re: Erection of CDF Notice Boards.* October 9, 2007. http://www.cdf.go.ke/downloads/viewdownload/6-cdf-circulars/13-9-th-oct-2007-erection-of-cdf-notice-boards-to-all-constituency-fund-account-managers

———, Ministry of Health. *National Health Sector Strategic Plan II Mid-term Review Report.* November 2007.

———. *Mid-Term Review Report of the Second National Health Sector Strategic Plan (NHSSP II).* 2007.

Karue, Muriuki. "The Tale of CDF" in *Episodes from an MP's Diary.* Nairobi: Lesako Foundation, 2011.

Kenya National Bureau of Statistics. *Constituency Report on Well-Being in Kenya-Based on the Kenya Integrated Household Budget Survey 2005/6.* 2008.

Kenyatta, Uhuru. "Budget Speech for Fiscal Year 2009/2010." (Speech, Nairobi, Kenya, June 11, 2009.) Ministry of Finance. http://www.treasury.go.ke/index.php/resource-center/doc_download/141-2009-2010-budget-speech.

———. "Budget Speech for Fiscal Year 2010/2011." (Speech, Nairobi, Kenya, June 10, 2010.) Ministry of Finance. http://www.treasury.go.ke/index.php/resource-center/doc_download/141-2009-2010-budget-speech.

Kimenyi, Mwangi S. "Efficiency and Efficacy of Kenya's Constituency Development Fund: Theory and Evidence." *Working papers 2005-42,* University of Connecticut, Department of Economics.

National Taxpayers Association. *CDF Citizen Report Cards.* http://www.nta.or.ke/nta-reports.

Ndii, David and Anne Wagiryu. "Harambee: Pooling Together or Pulling Apart." *Transparency International Kenya.* 2001. http://library.fes.de/pdf-files/bueros/kenia/01394.pdf.

Oparanya, Wycliffe. "Remarks by the Chief Guest (Min of Planning) during Strategic Plan Launch" (speech, Nairobi, Kenya, April 20, 2011). http://www.cdf.go.ke/

downloads/summary/4-speeches/39-remarks-by-the-chief-guest-min-of-planning-during-strategic-plan-launch.

Otieno, Brian. "No More Dying while giving Birth for Matuga Women." *The Star*, April 6, 2011.

Task Force on Devolved Government, "Interim Report of the Task Force on Devolved Government: A Report on the Implementation of Devolved Government in Kenya." 2011.

Tshangana, Alison Hickey. "Constituency Development Funds: A Scoping Paper." *International Budget Partnership*, January 18, 2010, accessed at http://internationalbudget.org/wp-content/uploads/Constituency-Development-Funds-Scoping-Paper.pdf on 12-18-12.

World Bank. *Kenya - Poverty and inequality assessment: executive summary and synthesis report.* (Washington, DC, 2009). http://documents.worldbank.org/curated/en/2009/04/10842664/kenya-poverty-inequality-assessment-executive-summary-synthesis-report.

Zyl, Albert van. "Constituency Development Funds: African Parliaments' Faustian Bargain." *International Budget Partnership.* August 12, 2010. http://internationalbudget.org/blog/2010/08/12/constituency-development-funds-african-parliaments-faustian-bargain/.

Chapter 4

In Name Only

Uganda's Constituency Development Fund

Nelson Kasfir and Stephen Hippo Twebaze

Before it was eliminated in August 2011, Uganda's Constituency Development Fund (CDF) was an outlier, sitting at one end of almost every standard used to evaluate CDFs. It poorly served the goals typically ascribed to them. It was tiny, often misdirected to campaign or personal accounts, poorly regulated and rarely accounted. Parliament never legitimated it by passing a statute after it had been introduced into the national budget in 2005. Through 2011 it operated without any increase in its funding for each MP. Only the exceptional MP followed its guidelines and invested what little it provided toward improving the welfare of any constituents.

Its small size made it especially paradoxical. When it was introduced, each MP received U.Shs. 10 million (US $5300).[1] By May 2011 its exchange value had fallen to US $4200—less than 1% of the CDF granted to each MP in next-door Kenya. The Ugandan CDF could not make a perceptible impact on any development goal however development is defined. Nor could it contribute more than marginally to financing an incumbent's campaign for re-election, although it was frequently used that way. It could not meaningfully provide for constituent service. Even so, investing it in constituency projects created accusations of unfairness. To make it useful for any purpose, MPs had to supplement it with other funds. They frequently used it for purposes that violated its guidelines. Its most consequential effect may have been to erode the integrity of MPs. Thus, the puzzles posed by this CDF include the reasons it was created in the first place and contradictions in its intended purposes as well as its actual uses.

Explaining these puzzles involves several interconnecting general factors typical of poor unindustrialized countries, although Uganda's unusual no-party system also played a unique role in the origin of its CDF. Four important explanatory variables are the earlier prohibition on parties, governance through clientage, executive dominance over the legislature and corruption increasing tolerance for the misuse of official funds. These factors frequently intersect in patron-client systems in which top politicians use state resources corruptly to buy the loyalty of followers. Since the executive has the greatest access to resources, MPs often become clients, allowing the executive to exert influence over them. While the process of organizing MPs as clients typically occurs through parties, it can happen without them. MPs, whether or not clients of the President or another high official, typically create their own clients by providing material rewards to constituents in return for their votes.

When Yoweri Museveni became President of Uganda by winning a guerrilla war in January 1986, he called for "fundamental change," which his listeners understood as the end of governance by patronage and corruption.[2] The no-party system emphasized governance based on issues and individual merit. Nevertheless, patron-client relations reappeared under the new National Resistance Movement (NRM) government and steadily became more significant.[3] Corruption scandals multiplied permitting politicians to mobilize political followers.[4] In the first parliament under the 1995 Constitution, MPs did take several initiatives to constrain the executive, making an early effort toward becoming a branch of government separate and equal to the executive.[5] But President Museveni was able to use patronage to blunt this advance and largely restore executive dominance in later Parliaments.

Later sections of this paper explain the origin, shape and operation of the Ugandan CDF as a function of these four factors. In brief, without parties, MPs had much greater responsibilities for personally financing their campaigns, a practice that continued after the shift to party competition in 2005. Voter expectations to be treated as clients by receiving material rewards caused all MPs to spend large sums on constituent service—funerals, medical expenses, school fees, sports equipment and even bridges and roads. Growing executive influence over MPs led them to expect support from the President. Finally, Parliament introduced almost no legal framework to govern the CDF aside from including it in the national budget, leading most MPs' to provide no accounting for spending it.

The reasons for its small size also include the political debate over its adoption, budget constraints and competing conceptions over who should be responsible for development. Given Uganda's elaborate decentralization scheme adopted in 1993, more than a decade before the CDF, the President felt MPs should not be involved in development projects. Rather, the President as well as many MPs wanted a fund for constituency service. The President simply announced the amount in a directive rather than introducing legislation to establish it. Overall, its problem stemmed from calling it a "CDF" when it could not function as one. As Kassiano Wadri, an MP, asserted, ". . . it's the name that brought us problems. After failing to find a name for it, they decided to call it a 'development fund,' yet it was not meant for development."[6]

BACKGROUND

Uganda's CDF resulted in large part from demands for constituent service that emerged from the long period of violence and destruction of its economy. For two decades the country had experienced military coups, lawlessness and a civil war. This instability significantly slowed down its economic growth and caused serious political decay. The economy contracted significantly during the Amin years between 1971 and 1979 and again with the removal of the second Milton Obote regime from 1984 to 1986.

By the time the NRM captured state power, the social infrastructure had become thoroughly dilapidated. The incapacity of the state to provide social services was exacerbated by military challenges to the new NRM regime in different parts of the country, particularly in northern Uganda where civil war lasted 20 years. This pattern of instability initially caused the NRM to focus on rehabilitation. By the time the CDF was introduced, these programs had put the country back on its development path.

The NRM established a no-party democracy as the basis for electing representatives to local and national government during reconstruction of the country. While the rationale changed over time, its core premise was "individual merit" as the basis not only for voters to choose among candidates, but also for MPs to decide personally on which policies to support (Kasfir: 2000). Parties were not banned, but could not hold delegates' conferences, open local branches, raise funds, nominate candidates, or campaign for them at public rallies.[7]

As a new political organization, the NRM was at a disadvantage in competing with the parties that had been established before independence. With some justification, the NRM leadership argued that the country's political instability had been caused by the ethnic and religious mobilization of those parties.[8] However, since the no-party political system undermined the sectarian power base of the old political parties, it helped NRM leaders establish themselves.[9] These restrictions on parties weakened their institutional development and promoted the spirit of MPs acting alone—including claiming credit for development in their constituencies. The no-party regulations also relegated the role of mobilizing campaign finances to candidates.

No-party electoral arrangements also strengthened clientelist relations between candidates and voters. The first no-party elections of MPs in February 1989 were indirect and based on an open ballot.[10] Many candidates paid voters. A candidate for Ndorwa County in Kabale District, nominated four days before the election, campaigned by giving money and U. Shs 6 million [about US $60] worth[11] of alcohol on voting day.[12] The culture of clientelist rewards that started with the 1989 elections repeated in every election afterwards, even though from 1993 elections for national office were conducted on the basis of universal adult suffrage and a secret ballot. The pattern continued through the 2011 elections, despite the success of many government development programs.

With the return to multiparty competition after a national referendum in 2005, restrictions on parties were lifted. However, party politics did not take root. The NRM took advantage of its access to state resources and opposition parties were poorly organized. Of 35 registered parties, only seven were able to field candidates and win seats in the 2006 and 2011 elections. None created a sufficient financial base to sponsor candidates who did not have to resort to personal resources. The high incidence and success of independent candidates in elections also suggest the absence of vigorous multiparty competition. Many Ugandans still preferred the individual merit principle as the basis for choosing representatives. For instance, Miria Matembe a former MP for Mbarara municipality and supporter of an opposition party stood as an independent on the ground that she did not want to divide her constituency on partisan lines.[13] This tendency toward independence helped perpetuate client-based constituent politics that emerged under the no-party system.

Initiatives by the NRM government to reconstruct the economy and eradicate poverty resulted in impressive growth rates and reduction in poverty levels. The amounts that candidates for Parliament had to raise to pay voters grew at an even faster rate. These extra costs greatly stimulated MPs' motivation to find official sources of funds for constituent service.

ORIGIN

The CDF emerged from the demands of MPs for relief from constituent financial pressures stimulated by reckless campaign promises and escalating costs of campaigns. It was promoted explicitly to reduce the costs of constituency service while implicitly intended to help incumbents maintain voting support. Development purposes were distinctly secondary, although MPs wanted relief from their own contributions to local projects.

The growing costs of campaigning were responses to the impact of the no-party system and the underlying culture of patronage relations that led many voters to perceive themselves as clients being wooed by competing MP candidates. The prohibition on party funding resulted in candidates paying for their own campaigns for the 1994 Constituent Assembly (CA) and 1996 and 2001 Parliamentary elections. As one MP put it "the weakness of individual merit is that you are alone" (interview, July 4, 2005). Most voters, particularly rural voters, had an intensely personal view of what constituency service should be. They expected material favors from candidates as a basis for judging whether to vote for them. In their view, an MP should help them solve personal problems such as paying for a hospital visit, school fees, a wedding or a funeral. A candidate who did not reward his followers was not likely to do so after being elected.

Candidates regularly gave small material rewards to voters. As Haji Aziz Kasujja, then a member of the Electoral Commission observed, "MPs bribe voters by using items like soap, salt and money."[14] Even though the CA was created solely to adopt a new constitution while the National Resistance Council (NRC) served as Uganda's legislature, voters ignored this distinction. Instead, as Pecos Kutesa, a CA delegate, remembered, they demanded "candidates for the CA bring water to their cattle, construct schools, health centers, roads among the many needs they had."[15]

Unrealistic promises by MPs during the three national election campaigns prior to the introduction of the CDF in 2005 expanded voters' notions of what representation by their MP could produce for them. The absence of guidance from party leaders, a consequence of the no-party system, may have led many candidates to make more irresponsible promises to constituents. Candidates, particularly those new to politics, promised to build good schools, hospitals, roads and pay better salaries to civil servants.[16] In the 1996 Parliamentary elections, MPs promised to build air-conditioned houses, hospitals, schools and movie theaters in their constituencies.[17] Other promises included increasing the number of places for their constituencies in university admission quotas and reducing school fees.[18] One candidate even offered cooking stoves to all residents in his constituency. Inevitably, constituents attacked them for failing to provide services they had promised.[19]

Large campaign expenses created debts that candidates could not easily repay. Some were arrested for debts incurred in campaigns. Court bailiffs occasionally pursued MPs over these debts. Some were arrested and taken to court for failure to pay them or for issuing bad checks.[20] Others hid in the precincts of Parliament to elude arrest.[21] MPs suffered heavy losses when constituents failed to repay loans they had provided.[22]

Since it would have been a national embarrassment for MPs to be jailed for their debts, the President directed the Ministry of Finance to find a solution. The Ministry negotiated with three major banks to consolidate loans MPs had borrowed from various private moneylenders into one loan portfolio guaranteed by the government. MPs benefited from the reduced interest rates of this new instrument.[23] But the problem of unsustainable debt reappeared in the 2001 Parliamentary campaigns.

After each election, efforts by MPs to maintain voter recognition led them to incur more debt through constituency expenditure. As one MP said "you know, we cannot sit back and make laws only. The only way our people can know us is when we initiate some projects."[24] "MPs would spend on political ventures like weddings, victory parties village by village and paying previous campaign debts. Within one month one would have spent a whole five years' salary."[25]

In a proposal foreshadowing the CDF, Aggrey Awori tabled a motion in Parliament calling for a development fund of Shs. 2.4 million (US $2,200) *per month* for MPs' constituency development projects.[26] To fund this proposal, MPs called for a reduction in the number of government ministers, a rationale unlikely to win favor with the President. They argued that since they spent large sums on development projects, the budget should include funds for that purpose.[27,28]

In early 2002, the President held a non-partisan meeting that Movement MPs below the age of 35 had organized to discuss the President's persistent criticisms of their lack of ideological focus.[29] The meeting digressed to the financial problems of young MPs. One after another told him that they were spending their allowances as well as their salaries on fundraising for development activities and personal needs of constituents. The President promised to find money in the budget to extricate MPs from their debt crisis.

MPs' debts and the cost of constituent service also became an issue in several NRM caucus meetings in late 2004 and early 2005. In those meetings, Movement MPs pressed specifically for a constituency development fund.[30] The President responded by sending a government team to Kenya, headed by his Minister for Parliamentary Affairs, Hope Mwesigye, to examine the Kenyan CDF.[31] Without subjecting the team's report to any form of debate, the President directed the Ministry of Finance to include money in the budget to help MPs contribute to development projects in their constituencies. The President told MPs about this decision in a Movement caucus meeting convened in May 2005 to discuss building support for the constitutional amendment bills.[32]

Museveni's agreement to a CDF at this time may have been related to his political maneuvers to make himself eligible for a third term by removing the constitutional restriction of a two-term limit on Presidential service. His intention to run again faced serious opposition. Since almost all MPs had long clamored for the CDF, creating one was an expedient use of patronage. The President may also have decided to introduce the CDF to "tame the 2001 Parliament to behave differently from the 1996 Parliament as his government approached the critical period of transition to multi-party politics."[33]

The President announced the CDF in his 2005 State of Nation address to Parliament, saying that it would enable MPs to start development projects in their constituencies and insulate them from fund raising pressures. "We need leaders who have no pressure. . . . A leader must be able to see, not to worry. If you are worried, you can't think properly."[34] He accused some MPs of fund raising to hand out money in campaigns: "I remember those who started it. I tried to talk to them, but they would not listen and now it has got out of hand."[35] He complained that they were disorganizing the politics in the NRM. He also proposed to amend the Leadership Code of Conduct to make fundraising from personal resources illegal. "If there is any fund raising, it should be the Constituency Development Fund." However, the President later insisted in an NRM caucus meeting that giving much CDF money to MPs would cause conflicts with local governments as the latter control development budgets under the decentralization policy. He argued that a CDF works better in countries where there is no decentralization.[36] The confusion over the CDF's purpose is telling.

Another reason for the small size of the CDF was the desire of MPs to spend it before elections the following year. The timing of the President's approval meant inserting it in the budget at the last minute. "The decision was reached in negotiations between the Parliamentary Commission and the Ministry of Finance. It is what could be squeezed in the national resource envelope for the CDF without causing an imbalance in budget priorities."[37] In its expenditure process, the Ministry of Finance sets its first figures for budget lines three years in advance. Consequently, the appropriation for the CDF had to be small at least partly because so many other priorities had already been determined. Although the money was tiny by comparison with that of Kenya's CDF, MPs felt it was worthwhile to get the CDF started and work to increase it later.[38]

LEGAL FRAMEWORK

MPs put weak structures in place to regulate their own activities and to account for their expenditures. Although the government had proposed no bill, MPs could have regulated the CDF by passing a private member's bill. They had used that route successfully in two important earlier cases, the Administration of Parliament Act, 1997 and the Budget Act, 2001.[39] Instead, they merely approved the CDF funding contained within the government's budget estimates. The casual manner in which they accepted the President's directive to fund the CDF suggests they were focused more on their own reelections than on development projects in their constituencies.

During its consideration of the Presidential directive as part of the budget estimates for 2005/06, the Legal and Parliamentary Affairs Committee (LPAC) had objected to the Parliamentary Commission's suggestion to delay the CDF until accountability provisions were included. "There is no way this can be postponed on account of lack of an accountability mechanism. This is a presidential pledge."[40] Instead, the committee recommended that the CDF should not be subjected to Parliamentary financial procedures, but rather released to members who would take responsibility to account for it.

During plenary debate, MPs characterized the initial release of CDF funding as "a pilot project pending the regularization and formulation of appropriate guidelines or enactment of enabling legislation."[41] MPs supported the expeditious release of the CDF in accordance with government accounting regulations.[42] Parliamentary election campaigns only a few months away provided a likely motive for their eagerness.

In taking this approach, MPs appeared to subject accountability of the CDF to the Public Finance and Accountability Act, 2003 (PFAA) and to the Treasury's accounting regulations for its enforcement. That meant the CDF would be treated like any other advance to a public official. The PFAA gives accounting officers the authority to control public finance spent within their departments. As the designated accounting officer of Parliament, the Clerk to Parliament became responsible for reviewing CDF expenditures. He found it difficult to get MPs to account for their CDF expenditures (discussed below) and worse had no jurisdiction over MPs who did not return to Parliament.[43]

The CDF *Guidelines* regulated how it could be used.[44] They provided a concept of a CDF that at least resembled conventional expectations. They restricted the CDF to funding activities that directly increased productivity; created employment; boosted food security and promoted poverty alleviation programs especially for women groups and other marginalized groups. They also required MPs to spend their CDF allocation on activities that stimulated sustainable growth and development, triggered rapid transformation and supported non-state social (religious and cultural) institutions. They prohibited CDF expenditure on political, recreation and entertainment activities. MPs were required to form CDF committees of five members. These committees were responsible for identifying and prioritizing development projects to be funded, ensuring equitable distributions of projects to the residents of the constituency and accounting for funds received. At least two members had to be women. The MP was the chairperson of the committee and two of the members had to be appointed secretary and treasurer.

In addition, the *Guidelines* required the accounting officer of Parliament, the Clerk, to disburse the CDF in a lump sum as an advance to each MP within one month of its release. The money was simply posted to each

MP's bank account. MPs had to account for CDF expenditures at the end of each financial year (rather than after six months as the PFAA requires). The *Guidelines* instructed MPs to provide credible documentary evidence, including receipts, minutes of CDF committee meetings that indicated the identity, distribution, location, and cost of each project, as well as acknowledgement letters and distribution lists. The secretary to the Parliamentary Commission had to inform MPs of these regulations before disbursement of CDF funds.

Each MP received the same funding. Thus, no region or political party gained an advantage nor did poor constituencies obtain any subsidy through a special distribution mechanism, as in Kenya's CDF. The exception is a peculiarity resulting from differences in the types of constituencies, a holdover from the no-party period. In addition to conventional "general interest" seats, Parliament contains "special interest," or affirmative action seats for women, youth, workers and the disabled, and for the Uganda Peoples Defence Forces (UPDF).[45] The special interest constituencies differ enormously in the size of their territory and in the number of constituents represented.

Each district must elect a woman as its MP. Three special interest MPs respectively representing workers, youth and persons with disabilities serve each of the four regions. Each of these groups also has a fifth representative who must be a woman. The latter three women MPs have national constituencies. Lastly, there are 10 military MPs, none of whom represent a territorial constituency, so they must be regarded as each representing the state as a whole.

While general interest constituencies are relatively equal in territorial size, constituencies the size of districts, regions and, of course, the state are much larger[46]—making the impact of their CDF funds all the more imperceptible. Thus, Alex Ndezi, MP for the Disabled in Central Region, argued that the CDF should increase by the number of districts an MP represents.[47] Since military MPs have no territorial constituencies, they had to use their ingenuity to decide how to spend their CDF allotments.

BUDGET HISTORY

The failure to enlarge the CDF funds during its first six years provides another indication that the government was unwilling to make the CDF a significant policy tool. Small from the start, the CDF remained unchanged, growing only when the number of MPs increased. That further suggests the CDF was not intended to support development. Meanwhile both the national budget and Parliament's allocation expanded significantly. Considering that MPs authorize the budget and appeared to take intense interest in the CDF, their behavior was puzzling.

Table 4.1 CDF as Percent of National Development Budget by Year (budgets in billions of Shs)

Fiscal Year	*CDF Allocation*	*Total Development Budget*	*CDF % Total Development Budget*
2005/06	2.95	1,741	0.17
2006/07	3.19	1,896	0.17
2007/08	3.19	2,032	0.16
2008/09	3.19	2,673	0.12
2009/10	3.19	3,400	0.09
2010/11	3.19	3,049	0.10

Source: Ministry of Finance and Economic Planning, Approved Budget Estimates for Revenue and Expenditures (2005–2010).

Since each of the 295 elected MP (there were also 10 *ex-officio* MPs) received Shs. 10 million, the Ministry of Finance had to earmark a sum of Shs. 2.95 billion (US $1,550,000). These funds became a line item in Parliament's development budget and increased to Shs. 3.19 billion with the addition of 24 elected MPs at the beginning of the 8th Parliament. Table 4.1 illustrates the growth in the government's development budget and the declining proportion spent on the CDF since it was introduced in 2005.[48]

If Parliament's development budget had declined or remained static despite the rise in the national development budget, pressure to prevent any expansion in the CDF would have been more understandable. But Parliament's development budget almost tripled, growing even faster than the national development budget. As the figures in Table 4.2 illustrate, the CDF percentage share of both Parliament's full and development budgets fell sharply.

Furthermore, the process of squeezing the CDF into Parliament's development budget had disastrous effects for the legislature's other capital projects during the CDF's first years. The Parliamentary Commission had submitted a development budget estimate of Shs. 3.2 billion for 2005/06 before the CDF had been authorized.[49] With the President's directive, the Ministry of Finance included Shs. 2.95 billion for the initial CDF budget but added only Shs. 1.01 billion more for all other projects—amounting to only 31% of the Parliamentary Commission's original requests. The sudden decision to make the CDF a line item in Parliament's development budget encroached on its other capital priorities because the Ministry of Finance sets budget ceilings three years ahead in its medium term expenditure framework (MTEF).[50] In particular, it set back Parliament's plan to build new chambers to accommodate the expansion in MPs elected in 2006. To make

Table 4.2 CDF as Percentage of Parliament's Development and Full Budget by Year (budgets in billions of Shs)

Year	*Recurrent Budget*	*Development Budget*	*Parliament's Full Budget*	*CDF Budget*	*CDF as % of Development Budget*	*CDF as % of Parliament's Full Budget*
2005/06	49.08	4.04	53.12	2.95	73.0	5.6
2006/07	54.74	8.97	63.71	3.19	35.5	5.0
2007/08	68.79	19.04	87.83	3.19	16.8	3.6
2008/09	112.20	16.68	128.88	3.19	19.1	2.5
2009/10	108.87	15.64	124.51	3.19	20.4	2.6
2010/11	117.64	11.47	129.11	3.19	27.8	2.5

Source: Policy Statements presented to Parliament for its debate on the estimates of revenue and expenditure (2005–2010).

matters worse, only Shs. 252 million of the additional Shs. 1.01 billion was released.[51] A backlog of unfunded projects had to be carried into subsequent financial years.

The peripheral role of the CDF as a tool of development is further underscored when its size is compared to funds for government grassroots development programs like the National Agricultural Advisory Services (NAADS). In 2005 the government allocated Shs. 5.5 billion to NAADS compared to the 2.95 billion allocated to CDF. By 2009 funds earmarked for NAADS increased exponentially to Shs. 133 billion while the CDF rose modestly to Shs. 3.19 billion.[52] Budget allocations to local governments are even larger—approved development expenditures rose from about Shs. 176 billion in 2005/06 to approximately Shs. 328 billion in 2009/10.[53]

OPERATIONS

The contradiction between development and patronage was apparent in the design of the CDF and in differences in its use by MPs. The Parliamentary Commission's *Guidelines* stressed development, despite the MPs' demands for using it for constituency service, especially as elections approached. Most MPs, and probably the President, regarded the CDF as a "pocket facility" to support their reelection prospects. Consequently, there was considerable variation between the emphasis on development in the *Guidelines* and the political intentions of many MPs. Even if MPs invested in development, the CDF was so modest that the projects it could initiate had to be small—helpful to only a few beneficiaries. In any case, the *Guidelines* were not closely followed.

MANIPULATING CONSTITUENCY COMMITTEES FOR PROJECT SELECTION

MPs frequently selected, initiated and implemented CDF projects. Often, they did not leave these functions to committees despite the requirement in the *Guidelines*. Some did not even form constituency committees, presumably using the money directly for campaign finance or personal purposes. Whether they were interested in development or patronage, they usually modified committee selection. Where MPs spent their CDF on reelection expenses, committees were mainly composed of political cronies.[54] In one case, an MP from Pader District admitted that he used party chairpersons of every subcounty to compose his committee.[55] In another, an MP from Moyo District chose a group of supporters of his party at subcounty levels to constitute his committee.[56]

On the other hand, MPs with development priorities tended to prefer larger committees than the five members the *Guidelines* stipulated. Frequently they relied on local elected officials. For example, in Isingiro South constituency, the committee consisted of subcounty secretaries for production (interview with a Kikagati subcounty official, December 10, 2010). Likewise, Fred Nkayi Mbagadhi, MP for Kagoma, created a CDF committee composed of 15 local council officials (*Monitor,* February 4, 2008).

Members of committees expected payment for attending meetings, a serious drain on CDF funds. Thus, committee meetings were not held frequently. Two MPs reported that their CDF committees met only once a year due to the costs of holding them (interviews, December 8, 2010). In Nyabushozi constituency, the MP relied on local council chairpersons, who have official funds to attend meetings, rather than form a CDF committee at all (interview, a constituency resident, November 11, 2010). As this MP pointed out, "A CDF committee would be good, but if the funds are little, one can't facilitate it."[57] Another MP complained that the members of CDF committees outside the local government structure were greedy. "They want a share of CDF money. Out of the ten million they want to share two million first and plan for the balance after."[58]

Forming broad committees permitted MPs who wanted the CDF to support development to promote residents' awareness of its availability. CDF projects tended to succeed more in constituencies where the level of awareness was higher. An NGO study in Nyabushozi, where the CDF was invested for development, found that 47% of constituents sampled were aware of it and felt that it had been used transparently.[59] When the MP received this CDF in 2007, she declared the money and suggested development priorities in a meeting with all the subcounty council chairpersons in the constituency.[60] Other MPs, for example Sam Byanagwa, the former

MP for Rukiga County took the same approach each year he received CDF funds. His committee determined how the funds would be invested without his intervention.[61]

Conversely, in Makindye East, an urban constituency in which the MP formed a small CDF committee, only 28% of residents sampled knew about the CDF and they tended to believe that allocation of the funds and identification of beneficiaries were not transparent.[62] Similarly, a local parish official in Kyadondo North constituency heard about CDF for the first time in the NRM primary election campaigns of July 2010 when candidates raised it for debate.[63] His MP had not provided any form of accountability for his CDF. Even after these campaigns, this parish official could not point to anyone in his parish or the subcounty who had benefited from it.[64] Only 7% of constituents in Aruu County were aware of the CDF.[65] Their MP had never formed a CDF committee, had provided no accountability and had misused the fund.[66]

USING PROJECTS TO GAIN SUPPORT

Many MPs used their control over the CDF to select projects in their constituencies that would build their support. Almost all MPs who accounted for their CDF funds supported social activities for youth and women groups at public functions despite the proscription in the CDF *Guidelines*.[67] They also assisted churches, mosques and other faith-based organizations.[68] One MP argued that MPs assist faith-based organizations because they consider them essential building blocks for electoral support.[69] To avoid accusations of favoritism, MPs typically spread what little CDF funds they had over the entire constituency. For example, one MP reported that he used a network of supporters to distribute the fund equally to each of the 210 villages in the constituency.[70]

Nevertheless, MPs faced an impossible situation because demands from their constituents were overwhelming. Grumbling about the inadequacy of the CDF, Henry Banyenzaki (Rubanda West) said "I have hundreds of groups" demanding funds.[71] MPs also discovered that their constituents exaggerated the size of the CDF and how much it could accomplish. "Ten million to an ordinary folk in my constituency is perceived to be able to buy the city of Babylon or tarmac all village roads."[72] Rivals to MPs were able to persuade credulous voters that incumbent MPs received an allocation of 10 million shillings for the CDF every month and then spent it on themselves.[73] "Any slight personal improvement of a business, building, a house in the village or buying a bus by an MP is all perceived to be the CDF at work."[74]

Furthermore, restrictions in the *Guidelines* sometimes worked against MPs. The *Guidelines* did not permit CDF investment in projects the government had already begun to fund, even if it was now neglecting them. Voters paid little heed to such prohibitions. They *needed* the road to be finished. So, they criticized MPs who would not spend their allocations on such obviously pressing needs.[75]

SUPPLEMENTING CDF FUNDS

Because CDF funds were so small, MPs had to invest their own funds or solicit contributions from NGOs or other government sources to create development projects (interview with a Minister of State, December 8, 2010). By the same token, the CDF was only a drop in the bucket for MPs who used it to meet personal constituent demands. An MP who represented an urban constituency in Kampala explained, "I have so far received 40 million [shillings] in four years, but I have spent 180 million to maintain my support in the constituency. That is the way I remain visible."[76] MPs often invested part of their salaries. One MP from northern Uganda claimed that he spent 30% of his consolidated pay from Parliament, 36 million shillings per year (US $16,000), to maintain support.[77]

Successful mobilization of funds from other government sources or from NGOs, depended on an MP's influence and political connections. MPs frequently asked local and central government officials and NGO managers to contribute to their projects. One MP explained "I spend 70 million shillings per year to support CDF projects in my constituency. I solicit this money from a network of NGOs and friends. The CDF only supplements this effort."[78]

APPLYING CDF FUNDS IN SPECIAL INTEREST CONSTITUENCIES

Constituencies for women, workers, youth, disabled and the military are much larger than general interest constituencies. These MPs faced the challenge of expending insignificant funds in extremely large constituencies, and for the ten military MPs, in constituencies without a specified territory. In several cases these MPs responded by choosing projects that would benefit their special interest group—for instance some women MPs devoted their CDF funds to projects exclusively for women and used local women councilors as the committee to select them. Military representatives invested in projects to benefit soldiers or soldiers' wives. Later, the ten members of the UPDF caucus decided to pool their funds and spend them on larger projects for soldiers' welfare.

OVERSIGHT

The absence of rigorous oversight provisions is a good indication that the CDF was intended more for patronage than for development. The absence of a statute meant no detailed mechanisms for accountability and transparency. The *Guidelines* provided broad provisions for accounting but no explicit sanctions. Their main attempt to establish a mechanism for transparency was to require constituency development committees (CDCs). The committees had minimal effect because most MPs did not form them and those who did made little use of them in decision-making and even less in preparing accounts.[79] In the words of a political commentator the absence of strict rules and sanctions made it "a tall order holding MPs who misappropriated the money accountable."[80]

An astonishingly large proportion of MPs failed to account at all for their expenditures. In four consecutive reports covering the first four disbursements of CDF funds, the Auditor General observed that he could not establish whether MPs used their funds in accordance with the *Guidelines* issued by the Parliamentary Commission.[81] The Clerk to Parliament was simply unable to compel MPs, even those who retained their seats, to account to him. The few MPs who submitted their accounts did so irregularly. Only 48 MPs accounted for the first CDF disbursement in 2005.[82] The accounting of only three was acceptable—Parliament's internal auditors rejected the other 45. Only 69 out of 319 MPs accounted for their second CDF disbursement.[83] Again, only a few of them met the required accounting standard.

In a later verification sample of CDF accounting practices, the Auditor General discovered that most of those few MPs who submitted reports persistently violated the *Guidelines* by spending money on political and social activities.[84] Perhaps the most egregious invitation to ignore the rules, one that signaled officials would overlook failure, was the appearance each year of the CDF funds in MPs' personal bank accounts—whether or not they had accounted for the previous year's disbursement.

The Clerk to Parliament tried to do his job. He threatened not to release funds to those MPs who had not accounted for their previous disbursement.[85] In March 2008, he wrote a letter to all MPs threatening to attach their salaries and disqualify them from receiving their next disbursement, if they did not submit satisfactory reports.[86] "Instructions shall be given not to give a new advance to anybody with an unsettled balance. Only those who will have accounted for both advances will be paid."[87] Few responded. Yet, all of them continued to receive CDF disbursements. By January 2010, the Clerk was resigned to their noncompliance. He told the Public Accounts Committee (PAC) that "the problem of lack of accountability would continue for as long as the funds were paid directly to Members of Parliament and if there was no law to regulate accountability of the fund."[88]

With only one exception (to our knowledge), no effort was made to compel or punish MPs who had not accounted. In May 2011, three months before the CDF was abolished, the Inspector General of Government (IGG) brought charges of embezzlement against Yokasi Bihande, an opposition MP.[89] Bihande eventually pled guilty to filing false accounts for the fiscal years 2009 and 2010 and received a suspended sentence and a fine.[90] In August 2012, the IGG requested Parliament to submit CDF accounts for all MPs in the 8th Parliament, so more cases may be forthcoming.[91]

The PAC offered another formal avenue for oversight. The committee threatened noncompliant MPs, but deliberations by the committee on the CDF turned into self-serving arguments proposing increases in its allocation rather than giving unequivocal support to the Clerk's demands for accountability. At first, the chair of the committee, Nandala Mafabi, told the press "the matter is going to be debated in the house and a decision will be taken, but as a committee we want those MPs who never accounted for the money to pay back public funds."[92] The committee made other sweeping recommendations including attachment of MP pensions. They gave MPs whose accountability was queried 60 days to account or refund the money. And they proposed the Parliamentary Commission establish a registry for receipt of CDF accounts and issue certificates to MPs whose accounts were satisfactory. But, the following August, the PAC supported a proposal to increase the CDF allocation from 10 million (US $4,500) to 70 million shillings (US $32,000). While PAC's earlier tough stance appeared in its reports, by the end of 2010 Parliament had not debated its recommendations for stricter standards.

PROPOSED REFORM

Civil society activists recognized that a carefully designed CDF could advance development significantly. At the same time they were deeply suspicious of attempts by MPs to appropriate more public resources for their incomes: ". . . the CDF seems to have been ill constituted, thus falling short of the public interest and susceptible to abuse. . . ."[93] Still, no CSO advocated ending the CDF. AFLI, the CSO most attentive to the CDF, commended the policy as "a useful avenue for contributing towards poverty eradication. It provides direct service delivery to the grass roots . . . [and] ensures equitable development" to overcome potential ruling party bias.[94] A UDN Program Officer agreed: "If the regulations are made stronger, the CDF is a good thing. It has worked elsewhere, in Kenya. Some grassroots development projects will miss out if it is scrapped."[95]

AFLI prepared a model of what a successful Ugandan CDF could look like—its "Proposed Constituency Development Fund Bill (CDF), 2007."[96] The bill increases the funds allocated to each constituency, defines the developmental purposes to which they may be invested, provides a structure of project oversight at the constituency, district and national levels, and establishes a detailed accounting framework. Unlike the actual CDF, the central role of the MP is radically diminished—responsible only for choosing the members and chairing the committee to select projects for the constituency.

The bill raises the amount of the initial CDF expenditure for each constituency to Shs. 50 million [US $29,100]—still only about 4% of the Kenyan CDF.[97] Unlike the basically unregulated choice of activities to fund the present CDF, the bill carefully specifies the kinds of development projects that the CDC can choose as those "that directly increase household income and productivity."[98] These are further defined as "community-based . . . interventions that can trigger rapid rural transformation . . . in agro-processing and marketing of agro-produce." CDF money may not be used for local or central government projects, or to support the interests of political parties or religious or sectarian activities. In addition, the bill removes two categories of special-interest representatives, workers and military, as well as *ex-officio* MPs, from receiving the CDF.[99]

The bill sets up the following structure. The Government would create the CDF under the Parliamentary Commission as a line item in Parliament's development budget. Rather than depositing the annual allocation in an MP's bank account, it would be disbursed through the district government to each MP representing a constituency in the district. However, the Chief Administrative Officer (CAO) for the district, rather than the MP, would pay for the projects and account for their expenditure. As now, the MP would appoint and chair the CDC, but without as free a hand. Instead, the committee's nine members would have to be selected from among certain officers of local councils, a subcounty chief, representatives of women, youth and persons with disabilities as well as a person from a local active NGO. Three members of the CDC would have to come from political parties different from the MP's party.

Rather than simply choosing any projects they wished, as occurs now, each CDC would prepare its list in order of priority and send it to the Clerk to Parliament to be reviewed by a National CDF Committee (NCDFC) chaired by the Minister of Finance and including the permanent secretaries to the Ministries of Local Government and Agriculture, the Clerk and the Chair of PAC. According to the bill, the NCDFC would review the projects, apparently as an oversight committee rather than as planners.[100] Again, unlike the existing CDF, the bill proposes offences with stiff penalties for misappropriation of funds, financial loss or discrimination.[101]

In an implicit invitation to any MP to introduce it, the bill plaintively defines the "bill" as including "both Private members Bill and Government Bill."[102] But AFLI's draft was never considered by Parliament.[103] Nevertheless, if it were adopted, the Ugandan CDF while still smaller than most other countries' CDFs, would become an authentic CDF.

REMOVAL OF THE CDF

The CDF ended as inauspiciously as it began. As part of its budget submission at the beginning of the 9th Parliament, the Parliamentary Commission unexpectedly announced "we have decided to eliminate the CDF basing on the justification that the fund is not performing any productive work, and yet constituents were blackmailing MPs that they eat the funds."[104] Before the decision to remove it, many new MPs in the 9th had begun to organize a coalition to sponsor a private member's bill to better regulate the CDF. Several were irritated by the peremptory cancellation, depriving some of their constituents of continuing programs (*New Vision*, August 4, 2011). Efforts to introduce a new CDF, probably based on appropriating a percentage of the local government budget for the CDF, continue at the time of writing—"an MP must be seen by his constituents to be doing something."[105] Oddly, the decision to scrap the CDF was also "in name only," because the Ministry of Finance continued to supply this line item and Parliament put it into MPs' allowances instead of reverting it to the development budget.[106]

CONCLUSION

The remarkable divergence of the Ugandan CDF from its counterparts tells us more about how Uganda was governed than about how a CDF should function. Uganda's CDF emerged from an impoverished war-torn society in which the victors in a guerrilla war instituted a no-party political system that put the burdens of running for Parliament entirely on the candidates. The costs of raising campaign finance and frequent demands from voters led MPs to a tiny CDF in 2005 just before the first multiparty elections. From the start, whether its purpose was development, constituent assistance, or campaign finance was ambiguous.

As both the national and Parliament's budgets increased over the next five years, the insignificant amount distributed to each MP remained constant. Parliament never passed a statute to regulate it. Only a few MPs invested their CDF allocations in development projects. Since the money was deposited in MPs personal bank accounts, the temptation to misuse it was great.

Despite the imposition of guidelines, many MPs diverted their first allocations to secure their reelections and then mostly failed to account for them. Nevertheless, they were not denied their CDF in following years.

Uganda's experience with its CDF poses a striking illustration of the widely accepted proposition that legislators everywhere shape their policy decisions to achieve their reelections.[107] In a patron-client society, incentives for reelection focus more on material rewards for voters than they do in issue-based societies. Throughout their experience with the CDF in the six years it existed, most MPs considered it a means to reduce their expenses in meeting demands from their constituents. Constituency service also served as the primary justification they put forward in their efforts to increase it. Furthermore, the President and virtually all constituents believed the point of the CDF was to satisfy residents' short-run needs.

This expectation posed the most daunting challenge to allowing the CDF to achieve any mission of development responsive to constituents. The insignificant allocation of the CDF, its lack of oversight and its widespread misuse can all be traced indirectly to this basic attitude. Nor did it fulfill the basic purpose its creators actually intended. It was simply too small to relieve MPs of their burdens of constituency service. Still, a minority of MPs, despite all the defects in the CDF, spent their allocation on useful projects that promised sustained, although limited, improvements in the welfare of a few of their constituents.

The CDF also posed a challenge to Parliament as an institution and to the integrity of MPs. To the extent that the CDF diverted the time and energy of the MPs, it undermined their attention to their core functions of legislation and oversight. But the consequences went deeper. The casual approach taken to the CDF eroded the integrity of MPs and, to some degree, diverted their attention from more important functions of Parliament. Maintaining high standards of honesty among lawmakers is important for making Parliament an independent arm of government and creating respect among citizens for the laws it passes. The failure of MPs to account for the CDF weakened Parliament's oversight role over the executive and the public's trust.

GLOSSARY OF KEY TERMS

AFLI – African Leadership Institute
CA – Constituent Assembly
CAO – Chief Administrative Officer
CDC – Constituency Development Committees
CSO – Civil Society Organization
IGG – Inspector General of Government

LPAC – Legal and Parliamentary Affairs Committee
MTEF – Medium Term Expenditure Framework
NAADS – National Agricultural Advisory Services
NCDFC – National CDF Committee
NRC – National Resistance Council
NRM – National Resistance Movement
PAC – Public Accounts Committee
PFAA – Public Finance and Accountability Act
UPDF – Uganda Peoples Defence Forces

NOTES

1. For exchange rates, we use Oanda.com for 1st October of year cited. http://www.oanda.com/currency/historical-rates/
2. Museveni 1992, 21.
3. Rubongoya 2007.
4. Tangri and Mwenda 2008.
5. Kasfir and Twebaze 2009.
6. *New Vision*, November 28, 2009.
7. Carbone 2008, 137.
8. Makara 2003.
9. Tripp 2010, 40.
10. Kasfir 1990.
11. Oanda rate equivalences between Ugandan shillings and US dollars begin with January 1990, so this conversion is approximate.
12. Interview, Kabale, March 9, 2011.
13. Interview, December 6, 2010.
14. *New Vision*, April 23, 1997.
15. *New Vision*, August 12, 2009.
16. *New Vision*, August 13, 1993.
17. *New Vision*, June 10, 1996.
18. *New Vision*, June 3, 11, 1996.
19. *Monitor*, June 5, 1996.
20. *New Vision*, June 7, 1997.
21. Interview, MP, December 15, 2010.
22. Odonga: 2010, 41.
23. Interview with a prominent media official, January 18, 2005.
24. *New Vision*, July 12, 2007.
25. Odonga 2010, 40.
26. See *Crusader*, May 29, 1997; and *Monitor*, June 11, 1997.
27. See *Sunday Vision*, October 20, 1996; and *Monitor*, June 7, 1997.
28. The government resisted MPs' demand for a monthly development fund for some time, but later gave them a "mobilization fund" of Shs. 2.25 million per month (US$??) to pay for constituency visits twice a month (interview with a former MP,

December 7, 2010). It was increased to Shs. 2.5 million in the Seventh Parliament (2001–2006) and to Shs. 3.5 million in the Eighth Parliament (2006–2011).

29. Interviews, two MPs, December 15, 2010.
30. Interview, senior NRM official, December 7, 2005.
31. Interview, MP, December 15, 2010.
32. *New Vision*, May 12, 2005.
33. Interview, parliamentary official, December 12, 2010
34. *Hansard* June 2005, 14155.
35. *Hansard* June 2005, 14155.
36. Interview, Minister of State, December 8, 2010.
37. Interview, senior parliamentary official, January 10, 2011.
38. Interview, MP, 2 November 2010.
39. Kasfir and Twebaze 2009, 81–83, 90–91.
40. LPAC 2005.
41. *Hansard* 2005, 15756.
42. *Hansard* 2005, 15784.
43. *Report of the Auditor General* 2006, 254.
44. *Guidelines* 2005.
45. Kasfir and Twebaze 2009, 87.
46. Some districts contain only one general interest constituency. In those cases there are two CDF allocations available for exactly the same constituents.
47. *Monitor,* May 1, 2009.
48. If the decline is calculated as a percentage of the growth of the whole budget (recurrent and development) over the same period, it is even steeper.
49. *Policy Statement* 2005, 34.
50. *Policy Statement* 2008, 6.
51. *Policy Statement* 2006, 9.
52. *Budget Speech* 2009.
53. *Approved Budget Estimates* 2005 and 2009.
54. Interview with a Uganda Debt Network program officer, December 19, 2010.
55. Interview, December 15, 2010.
56. Interview, December 8, 2010.
57. AFLI 2007c, 18.
58. Interview, December 15, 2010.
59. AFLI 2007b, 16.
60. AFLI 2007c, 18.
61. Interview, December 6, 2010.
62. AFLI 2007c, 18.
63. *Parliamentary Scorecard*: 2009, 290.
64. Interview, December 8, 2010.
65. AFLI 2007c, 19.
66. *Parliamentary Scorecard*: 2009, 306.
67. Interview, internal auditor of Parliament, December 16, 2010.
68. Interview, MP, December 8, 2010.
69. Interview, December 16, 2010.
70. Interview, December 8, 2010.

71. *Sunday Vision*, November 6, 2005.
72. Odonga Otto: 2010, 46.
73. *New Vision*, May 7, 2007.
74. Odonga Otto: 2010, 46.
75. Interview, former MP, December 12, 2010.
76. Interview, December, 8 2010.
77. Interview, December 15, 2010.
78. Interview, Minister of State, December 8, 2010.
79. *Auditor General's Report* 2009, 354.
80. *New Vision,* March 6, 2008.
81. *Auditor General* 2006–2009.
82. Letter to MPs 2007.
83. *Report of the Auditor General* 2007, 254.
84. *Auditor General*: 2009, 354.
85. *Auditor General* 2007, 254.
86. He cited the Treasury Accounting Institutions Act (2003) which provides that "advances not accounted for within 60 days from date of payment should be deducted from the monthly salary of the debtor" (*Monitor*, 3 August 2011).
87. *Monitor*, March 11, 2008.
88. *Monitor*, January 18, 2010.
89. *New Vision*, May 23, 2011.
90. *New Vision*, April 4, 2012.
91. *Weekly Observer*, August 10–12, 2012.
92. *Monitor,* January 18, 2010.
93. UDN 2007, 2.
94. 2007a, 7.
95. *New Vision*, November 28, 2009.
96. AFLI 2007b.
97. AFLI 2007b, 10.
98. AFLI 2007b, 10.
99. AFLI 2007b, 7.
100. AFLI 2007b, 8,9.
101. AFLI 2007b, 15.
102. AFLI 2007b, 5.
103. Interview, senior Parliamentary official, December 16, 2010 Interview, senior Parliamentary official, December 16, 2010.
104. *Observer*, August 3, 2011.
105. Interview, MP, October 23, 2012.
106. *Observer*, May 16–17, 2012.
107. Mayhew: 2004.

REFERENCES

AFLI 2007a. "A Proposed Constituency Development Fund (CDF) Policy." African Leadership Institute. Kampala. April.

——— 2007b. "A Proposed Constituency Development Fund Bill (CDF), 2007: Submitted to the Government of Uganda for the Regulation of the Constituency Development Fund of the Parliament of Uganda." Africa Leadership Institute. Kampala. April.

——— 2007c. "Development or Politics of Patronage?" Africa Leadership Institute. Kampala. May.

Auditor General 2006–2009. "Annual Reports of the Auditor General for the Financial Year Ended 30th June 2006–2009." Uganda Government. Kampala.

Budget Speech 1997, 2005, 2008, 2010. The Republic of Uganda. Kampala. June.

Carbone, Giovanni 2008. *No-Party Democracy? Ugandan Politics in Comparative Perspective*. Boulder, CO: Rienner.

Constitution of the Republic of Uganda 1995, amended 2006. Kampala: Uganda Printing and Publishing Corporation.

Guidelines 2005. "The Legal, Policy Framework for the Constituency Development Fund in Uganda." Parliament of Uganda. Kampala. October.

Hansard 2005. Parliamentary Debates. June, September.

Kasfir, Nelson 1990. "Uganda Elections of 1989: Power Populism and Democratization." In *Changing Uganda*. Edited by Holger B. Hansen and Michael Twaddle. Kampala: Fountain.

——— 2000. "'Movement' Democracy, Legitimacy and Power in Uganda." In *No-Party Democracy in Uganda: Myths and Realities*. Edited by Justus Mugaju and J. Oloka-Onyango. Kampala: Fountain, 60–78.

——— and Stephen Hippo Twebaze 2009. "The Rise and Ebb of Uganda's No-Party Parliament." In *Legislative Power in Emerging African Democracies*. Edited by Joel D. Barkan. Boulder, CO: Lynne Rienner, 73–108.

Letter to MPs 2007. "Letter to MPs from the Clerk to Parliament." Parliament of Uganda. Kampala. November 30.

LPAC 2005. Report of the Legal and Parliamentary Affairs committee on Policy Statements for the Financial Year 2005/2006. August.

Ministry of Finance and Economic Planning, Approved Budget Estimates for Revenue and Expenditures 2005–2010.

NRM Caucus Minutes 2008. National Resistance Movement Parliamentary Caucus. State House: Entebbe. July 7.

Makara, Sabiti 2003. "Voting for Democracy in Uganda: Issues in Recent Elections, 1996–2001." In *Voting for Democracy in Uganda: Issues in Recent Elections*. Edited by Sabiti Makara, Geoffrey B. Tukahebwa, Foster E. Byarugaba. Kampala: LDC Publishers.

Mayhew, David R. Congress: 2004. *Congress: The Electoral Connection*. Second Edition. New Haven: Yale University Press.

Museveni, Janet 2010. "What is African Leadership Institute up to?" *New Vision*, November 7.

Museveni, Yoweri K 1992. "Ours Is a Fundamental Change." In *What is Africa's Problem: Speeches and Writings on Africa by Yoweri Kaguta Museveni*. Kampala: NRM Publications. Pp. 21–27.

Odonga, Otto 2010. *Theory and Practice of Democracy: A Parliamentarian's Perspective*. Arusha: Roka.

Parliamentary Scorecard 2008–2009. Assessing the Performance of Uganda's Legislators: 2009. Africa Leadership Institute (AFLI). Kampala: Some Graphics Ltd.

PFAA 2003. The Public Finance and Accountability Act, 2003.

Policy Statements 2005–2010. "Policy Statements Presented to Parliament for its Debate on the Estimates of Revenue and Expenditure." Parliament of Uganda.

Rubongoya, Joshua B 2007. *Regime Hegemony in Museveni's Uganda: Pax Musevenica* New York: Macmillan.

Tangri, Roger and Andrew M. Mwenda 2008. "Elite Corruption and Politics in Uganda." *Commonwealth and Comparative Politics*, 46:2. Pp. 177–194.

Tripp, Aili Mari 2010. *Museveni's Uganda: Paradoxes of Power in a Hybrid Regime* Lynne Rienner: Boulder, CO.

UDN 2007. "Briefing Paper on the Constituency Development Fund in Uganda." Uganda Debt Network. Kampala: May.

Chapter 5

Earmarks in the United States

Diana Evans

BACKGROUND

Political Context

Congressional earmarks are the American version of constituency development funds. Of the three branches of the federal government, this case study focuses on the legislative and executive branches, as they are directly involved in earmarking. Congressional earmarks consist of projects that Congress carves out of executive agency budgets, directing the agency to spend a portion of its funds on those projects. The president proposes a detailed annual budget to Congress, a budget that does not normally take into account the particular needs of individual congressional districts; however, Congress has nearly complete authority over the eventual shape of the federal budget, giving it the opportunity to insert its own priorities, including earmarks. Once Congress has passed its own spending bills, the president possesses merely the power to accept or reject the legislation that would enact those plans. Because earmarks are embedded in essential agency funding, presidents rarely threaten to veto a spending bill solely because of the earmarks it contains.

When Members of Congress (MCs) "earmark" funding for their own states and districts, they can claim credit with their constituents for these earmarks.[1] Most MCs cannot believably claim credit for reducing the budget deficit or passing major legislation, but they will be believed when they claim credit for an earmark which exclusively benefits the citizens or their district or state, as no other political actor is likely to be interested enough to provide such targeted benefits.[2]

Although Congress has been characterized by increasing levels of partisan polarization and rancor, the politics of earmarks have until recently been relatively bipartisan. Although Republicans in particular have sometimes condemned earmarks, especially in the 1994 and 2010 elections, during ten years of mostly Republican majorities in Congress (from 1995 to 2005) the number of earmarks grew nearly tenfold. When Democrats won the majority in both the House and Senate in the 2006 election, they reduced spending on earmarks by roughly one-third[3] and instituted reforms that provided transparency and the potential for accountability. The most important such reform was the requirement, instituted at the beginning of the new Congress in 2007, that for all earmarks, the MC who requested it be publicly identified; moreover, MCs were subsequently required to list on their websites every earmark they requested. Prior to those reforms, earmarks were often worded so that it was difficult or impossible for an outsider to identify the sponsor or the recipient. Thus, the 2007 reforms achieved considerable transparency.

However, in the eyes of some earmark critics, these reforms were not sufficient. By the 2010 elections, Republicans were able to capitalize on voters' fears of the economic situation in general and the exploding federal deficit in particular to win back the majority in the House of Representatives and considerably reduce the Democrats' majority in the Senate. Many Republican candidates, particularly those endorsed by ultraconservative tea party activists, latched onto earmarks as a symbol of government waste and corruption and pledged to end earmarking if they won the majority in Congress. Upon winning the House, Republicans did just that, albeit in the form of a moratorium rather than a permanent ban. The Senate was more reluctant; indeed, the Senate Republican leader, Mitch McConnell (Ky.) opposed such a ban; however, under pressure from his caucus, he soon reversed position, and Senate Republicans voted in favor of a moratorium as well. Because Democrats retained the majority, the moratorium was still not the official policy of the Senate. However, Republicans vowed to filibuster any legislation that contained earmarks, a credible threat, given that Democrats did not have the 60 votes to break a filibuster. Making a virtue of necessity, the chairman of the Senate Appropriations Committee announced a moratorium on earmarks for the current congress.[4] In addition, in his 2011 State of the Union address, President Obama vowed to veto any bill containing earmarks.[5] However, given their political usefulness, MCs have devised less visible, more informal ways (discussed below) to gain earmarks from the executive branch for their constituencies.

The Politics of Distributive Policy

Earmarks, more pejoratively known as pork barrel projects, come under the broad heading of distributive policy. Definitions vary, but distributive policy is most often defined as policy that targets discrete benefits to specific populations such as states and congressional districts, spreading the costs across the general population through taxation. Such benefits have so little policy connection to each other that changing or even removing one district's benefit from a bill would have no impact on the benefits given to other districts.[6] Distributive benefits have taken many forms over the years, from lighthouses beginning in the first Congress in 1789 to nineteenth-century pensions for widows and orphans of Civil War veterans to rivers and harbors projects, to transportation bills from 1987 on.[7]

No quantitative data exist on the extent of earmarking prior to the 1990s, although there is evidence that it was done, especially in the Senate.[8] Earmarks have been systematically tracked in recent decades, however. The longest span of time-series data on appropriations earmarks has been collected by the anti-earmark advocacy group, Citizens Against Government Waste (CAGW). Table 5.1 presents their data on the number and value of earmarks in all appropriations legislation since 1991; the third column adjusts their cost data for inflation, showing the true growth in the costs of earmarks. The table shows that, by CAGW's count, the number of projects grew from 546 in 1991 to a peak of nearly 14,000 in 2005, a more than 25-fold increase. Although the numbers declined following the 2006 election, the 2010 total is still nearly 17 times the number of projects granted in 1991. The inflation-adjusted cost of earmarks has grown more slowly, but the cost for 2005 is nevertheless 6 times larger than the 1991 figure. Earmarks in 2010 cost 3.3 times as much as those in 1991, which is a significant reduction from the 2005 peak, but still a significant real increase over 1991.[9]

What accounts for the dramatic increase in earmarks over this time period? The roots of earmark growth surely are found in the reforms instituted by the House of Representatives in the early 1970s, when for the first time, MCs with a direct interest in a particular appropriations subcommittee were no longer blocked from serving on it, giving rise to a growth in spending in general and setting the stage for more earmarking in particular. Once the chairs of the full committee and its subcommittees showed themselves to be willing to distribute earmarks, the demand inevitably became unmanageable.[10] Moreover, Republicans, newly in control of both the House and Senate in 1995, initially followed through on their campaign promise to limit pork barrel spending; however, they soon began to take full advantage of the practice in order to protect their incumbents and their majority. In addition, subcommittee chairs quickly saw that earmarks were useful to buy votes for the bills to which they were attached, providing an impetus for the expansion of earmarking.[11] Finally, lobbyists have played an important role in the growth of earmarks. This practice has introduced another element into the traditional exchange of projects for constituents in return for votes for the representatives.

Table 5.1 Earmarks, 1991–2010*

Year	*Number of Projects*	*Cost in Billions*	*Cost in Billions, Inflation-Adjusted**
1991	546	3.1	5
1992	892	2.6	4
1993	1,712	6.6	10
1994	1,318	7.8	11.5
1995	1,439	10	14.3
1996	958	12.5	17.4
1997	1,596	14.5	19.7
1998	2,143	13.2	17.7
1999	2,839	12	15.7
2000	4,326	17.7	22.4
2001	6,333	18.5	22.8
2002	8,341	20.1	24.4
2003	9,362	22.5	26.7
2004	10,656	22.9	26.4
2005	13,997	27.3	30.5
2006	9,963	29	31.4
2007	2,658	13.2	13.9
2008	11,610	17,2	17.4
2009	10,160	19.6	19.9
2010	9,129	16.5	16.5

**Source:* Citizens Against Government Waste (http://www.cagw.org/reports/pig-book/#trends). Inflation-adjusted figures calculated by author, based on 2010 dollars.

That is, when lobbyists request and receive earmarks for their clients, campaign contributions from the beneficiaries are often forthcoming as well, further enhancing the MCs' electoral prospects. This phenomenon is discussed in more detail below.

Although earmarks are technically controlled by the majority party, especially in the House of Representatives, the distribution process (described in Section 5 below) has traditionally been bipartisan. Given that Congress is now so bitterly partisan and that, moreover, earmarks can be helpful in protecting minority party incumbents from majority party challengers, why has the majority party been so willing to give earmarks to the minority? There are several reasons. First, the majority fears that the minority would use earmarks as a weapon against them at election time (as, indeed, the Republicans did to the Democrats in 2010 after forswearing earmarks for themselves); for that reason, the majority has made the minority part of the practice, in a game of "partisan blame avoidance" to forestall that possibility.[12] Second, particularly in the Senate, partisan control has changed numerous times over the past thirty years; Senate appropriators have thus found it in their interest to follow a sort of golden rule, treating the minority as they hope the minority will treat them when the tables are turned. Third, in passing legislation, it is helpful for majority party to win as many minority party votes as possible; earmarks are awarded to increase the probability that the recipients will support the committee's position on the bill and amendments to it.[13]

The arguments: As noted above, the practice of earmarking is solidly based in Congress's power of the purse as granted in Article I of the Constitution, a point to which earmark defenders often allude. Moreover, congressional proponents of the practice argue that earmarking is an essential component of the constitutional system of checks and balances on the grounds that earmarking gives members of Congress a direct voice as to what individual spending projects will be funded, rather than giving exclusive powers over such spending to the executive branch. Those MCs also defend their right as elected representatives to decide what projects should be funded in their own districts, typically comparing their own assessments of their districts' needs to the assessments of "faceless bureaucrats" who do not know or care about the district or state as the MCs do. Indeed, many members consider obtaining a share of federal spending for their constituencies an essential part of their job. If they are then rewarded by their constituents with reelection, it is a sign that they are performing their obligations appropriately.

Members of Congress also defend earmarks on the grounds of their contribution to the economic development of their districts and states; for MCs, earmarks serve the same purpose as CDFs. Typical of such defenses is a statement by Republican Senator Richard Shelby of Alabama in response to questions from *Science Magazine* about the massive earmarks that he had won: "Shelby says the earmarks he has secured for several of the state's universities have been good for Alabama's economy and its scientists. 'The federal funding [I] have been able to help procure for math, science, and engineering facilities at Alabama universities has directly impacted the State's ability to compete on a national level,' he said in a statement to Science. 'Before [I] began working to bring state-of-the-art math, science, and engineering facilities to universities across Alabama, only a few schools nationwide were able to compete for federal research funding. Now, Alabama has some of the best research facilities in the nation and regularly competes for these dollars.'"[14]

In the current political climate of voter anger over the economy and the rise in deficit spending, Democrats have nonetheless generally favored a continuation of earmarking for their districts, particularly for local governments and not-for-profit entities. Following their ascension to the congressional majority in 2007, Democrats instituted reforms of the earmarking process, described above, intended to create transparency. Subsequently, in March of 2010, the Chairman of the House Appropriations Committee, Rep. David Obey (D-Wisc.), banned earmarks to for-profit entities. This reform reflected Democrats' desire to separate themselves from a series of corruption scandals associated with lobbyists who appeared to be buying earmarks by giving large campaign contributions to the legislators who obtained them.

The Democrats' overall pro-earmark position is consistent with the party's traditional belief in an activist government that taxes at higher levels than the Republicans prefer. Democrats typically argue that government revenues should be used to promote the common good in terms of both economic and social welfare. When Democrats run for office by claiming credit for what they have brought to their districts, they expect to be, and usually are, rewarded by their constituents.[15]

By contrast, earmark opponents, mostly Republicans, consider such spending to be inherently wasteful. At the extreme, they sometimes imply that eliminating earmarks would, in and of itself, substantially reduce the budget deficit. This argument is undermined by the fact that earmarks amount to no more than 1% of federal spending. But Senator Jim DeMint (R-S.C.), a leading opponent of earmarks, made a more subtle point; if earmarks were banned, "You would see spending come down dramatically if you took out all the self-interest that earmarks represent. So I've seen for years . . . that you put a little bit of bacon in for all the Congressmen and Senators, they'll vote for a big bill they would otherwise not vote for. So it is a problem with spending."[16] In addition, earmark opponents implicitly believe (although they rarely argue) that a merit-based competitive process for funding projects, administered by the bureaucracy, produces better spending decisions. Moreover, some critics link earmarks to outright corruption. For example, the Tea Party Patriots emailed the following statement to their supporters following the 2010 election: "Americans are tired of these games and the way that earmarks breed corruption and favor-trading."[17]

Thus, the Republicans, as advocates of lower taxes and reduced spending, have at various times taken clear positions against earmarks, although they have not consistently practiced what they have preached. In their 1994 congressional election campaign manifesto, the Contract With America, House Republicans proposed and later passed a line-item veto in the expectation that the president would veto individual pork barrel projects in appropriations bills. That law was declared unconstitutional in 1998 by the Supreme Court in *Clinton v. City of New York* on the grounds that Congress had unconstitutionally transferred legislative power to the president. Additionally, despite his earlier opposition to earmarks, House Speaker Newt Gingrich soon began to exploit them to protect the Republicans' congressional majority, and earmarking soared to its 2005 peak. Associated with this explosion of earmarks were a number of earmark-selling scandals; the most notorious resulted in a prison sentence for Republican representative Randy "Duke" Cunningham (Calif.) in 2006. These scandals seemed to add to voters' discontent with Republicans and played a role in their loss of both houses of Congress to the Democrats in 2006.

Consistent with his past opposition to earmarks, during the 2008 presidential campaign, Republican presidential candidate John McCain railed against earmarks. Subsequently, House Republicans, in the minority in Congress after 2006, began once again to see the political merits of a moratorium on earmarks. Seeking to use the issue against the Democratic majority and worried that Democrats might outflank them on the issue, House Republicans voted on March 11, 2010 to ban earmark requests for Republicans, only a day after Rep. David Obey (D-Wisc.) banned earmarks to for-profit entities. Although a few Republican House members refused to go along with the party's self-imposed earmark ban, most did so; similarly, the majority of Senate Republicans voted for such a ban, although there was more vocal opposition there and a number of Senate Republicans failed to comply with the ban in 2010.[18]

Once Republicans attained the majority in the House in the 2010 election, they again voted to impose a moratorium on earmarks for the next congress (2011–12); this time, because they controlled the committee chairmanships, they were able to impose the moratorium on Democrats as well. Thus, the House instituted its first formal, if time-limited, ban on earmarks. Under pressure from newly elected Republican senators supported by tea party groups, Senate Republicans followed suit, albeit much more reluctantly. That reluctance was clearly expressed by the Senate Republican leader, Mitch McConnell (Ky.), who initially refused to go along with the move. He eventually reversed himself but continued to express a key argument for earmarks: "I'm not wild about turning over more spending authority to the executive branch, but the only way we will be able to turn the corner and save our future is if elected leaders like me make the kinds of difficult decisions voters are clearly asking us to make."[19]

President Obama, initially reflecting Democrats' more favorable view of earmarks, endorsed House Democrats' reforms of the earmarking process. In a public statement on the earmarks included in a huge omnibus appropriations bill, Obama said

> Done right, earmarks have given legislators the opportunity to direct federal money to worthy projects that benefit people in their districts and that's why I've opposed their outright elimination. And I also find it ironic that some of those who rail most loudly against this bill because of earmarks actually inserted earmarks of their own—and will tout them in their own states and their own districts.[20]

In the same speech, Obama endorsed the House Democrats' ban on earmarks to for-profit entities, noting that such earmarks are "the single most corrupting element of this practice . . ." However, Obama's support for earmarks eventually disappeared. Following the 2010 congressional election, the president in effect signed on to the moratorium, promising in his 2011 State of the Union address to veto legislation containing earmarks.

In recent years, public interest groups from across the political spectrum, including CAGW, Taxpayers for Common Sense, the conservative, anti-tax group Club for Growth and the liberal Public Citizen have opposed earmarks. CAGW offers some of the most biting commentary. For example, their annual compilation of earmarks is known as the *Pig Book.* Their press conferences announcing the release of a new *Pig Book* are often graced with a large, live pig; their awards to the biggest earmarkers are called the "Oinker Awards."

Others have campaigned against earmarks as well. For example, *Science,* a publication of the American Academy for the Advancement of Science, long has criticized academic earmarks as a misuse of federal research funds, which normally are awarded through peer-reviewed grant applications to agencies such as the National Science Foundation, an approach that *Science* prefers. Under the peer-review process, a large share of these funds is awarded to faculty at leading research universities. In response, institutions that do not fare well in this competitive process have appealed directly to their MCs (often through lobbyists) for earmarks to fund their projects.

Legal Framework

Although earmarks are grounded in Congress's constitutional authority to fund the federal government's programs, they are not exactly like CDFs. No formal legislation established the practice of earmarking, and statutory limits on earmarking have been instituted.[21] Unlike CDFs, earmarks are not authorized as separate funds established for the express purpose of distribution to local constituencies. Rather, as the preceding sections indicate, they are funds carved out of the operating and capital budgets of federal agencies by Congress. As such, they are insulated from the processes by which funds are normally allocated by those agencies and diverted from the uses to which they normally would be put.

The legislation that appropriates funds for the federal government is, of course, binding on executive branch agencies. However, most earmarks are contained in the congressional committee reports that are issued when that legislation is reported from committee to the House or Senate. Both House and Senate Appropriations Committee reports have recently been loaded with earmarks, as Table 5.1 indicates, but because the House and Senate versions of a particular appropriations bill normally differ, the two bodies negotiate a final, compromise version, reported by an *ad hoc* conference committee. During the conference, participants negotiate the final list of earmarks to be included in the legislation or more commonly, the conference committee report that accompanies the compromise bill. The bill is then voted on by the House and Senate. If passed by both houses, it goes to the president for his action.

Earmarks contained in these committee reports normally are not mandatory in a legal sense. They are recommendations. However, bureaucrats worry about incurring the wrath of the members of Congress who both produced those reports and provide agencies' funding year after year. The political incentive to honor the wishes of those MCs is strong.[22]

As an illustration, the 2009 House Appropriations subcommittee report on the Agriculture, Rural development, Food and Drug Administration, and Related Agencies Appropriations Act (hereafter Agriculture Subcommittee Report 111–181, 2009) is very explicit in its observance of the new legal requirements for earmarks noted above. The language is as follows:

> **Directed Spending by Congress and by the Executive Branch**
> This bill contains about $1.3 billion in grant funding awarded solely at the discretion of the Administration, and $3.011 million in funding requested by the President for specific projects. In addition to placing a one year moratorium on earmarks in appropriations bills enacted in 2007 so that new rules could be put in place, the Committee has subsequently taken unprecedented action to increase transparency and reduce funding for earmarks. This bill continues to further reduce earmarks in 2010 and is expected ultimately to be 3% below 2009. In this bill since 2006, the total funding earmarked has been reduced by 56%. This year earmarked funding will equal 1% of the cost of the bill. It should also be noted that under the policies adopted by the Committee, the use of member earmarks awarded to for-profit entities as a functional equivalent of no bid contracts is ended. In cases where the Committee funds an earmark designated for a for-profit entity, the Committee includes legislative language requiring the Executive Branch to nonetheless issue a request for proposal that gives other entities an opportunity to apply and requires the agency to evaluate all bids received and make a decision based on merit. This gives the original designee an opportunity to be brought to the attention of the agency, but with the possibility that an alternative entity may be selected.
>
> **DISCLOSURE OF EARMARKS AND CONGRESSIONALLY DIRECTED SPENDING ITEMS**
>
> The following table is submitted in compliance with clause 9 of rule XXI, and lists the congressional earmarks (as defined in paragraph (e) of clause 9 contained in the bill or in this report. Neither the bill nor the report contain any limited tax benefits or limited tariff benefits as defined in paragraphs (f) or (g) of clause 9 of rule XXI.[23]

Table 5.2 Congressional Earmarks in the 2009 House Appropriations subcommittee report on the Agriculture, Rural development, Food and Drug Administration, and Related Agencies Appropriations Act

2006	*2008*		*2009*		*2010 Committee*	
$ in millions	*#*	*$ in millions*	*#*	*$ in millions*	*#*	*$ in millions*
$865	623	$400	521	$380	322	$220

Following that is a list of the 322 earmarks in this appropriations bill. For each project certain information is listed: the federal agency that is to disburse the money and the particular account from which it is to be paid, the name and location of the recipient of the funding, the exact dollar amount of the grant, and the name or names of the MCs who requested the project.

Earmarks occasionally appear in the text of legislation itself. For example, the bill making appropriations for the Department of Homeland Security contains 173 earmarks. Those projects are also listed in a table in the conference committee report on that bill; they are called "Congressionally Directed Spending Items." Unlike the bill itself, that table contains the names of the MCs who requested the items.[24] For illustrative purposes, one page of those earmarks is contained in the Appendix.

The Fiscal Year 2010 Energy and Water Development appropriations bill offers yet another variation. That bill contains 939 earmarks. Like the Agriculture subcommittee report, the earmarks are listed by sponsor in a table at the end of the conference committee report, but the total amounts are referenced in the text of the legislation itself; for example,

> *of the amount appropriated in this paragraph, $292,135,000 shall be used for the projects specified in the table that appears under the heading "Congressionally Directed Energy Efficiency and Renewable Energy Projects" in the joint explanatory statement accompanying the conference report on this Act.*[25]

Where such wording exists in the text of legislation itself (a certain amount of money "shall be used"), the executive agency has no discretion.

Budget History and Structure

This section shows the distribution of earmarks in several ways: as a percentage of the federal budget, by substantive policy area, by party, and by state.[26] In presenting data on earmarks, it is preferable to use a definition that is consistent across subcommittees. The data used in this section are from CAGW; as their time series of data is longer by far than that of any other organization, including the government.[27]

Earmarks are controversial in the United States, but not because they account for a large share of the federal budget. They do not. Table 5.3 shows the total share of federal expenditures, or "outlays," in federal budget jargon, devoted to earmarks over the past five years (a subset of the data from Table 5.1) and calculates the cost as a proportion of total federal outlays. However, "total outlays" includes entitlement programs such as Social Security and Medicare. Such programs are funded by "direct spending" over which the appropriations committees have no control; instead, spending is controlled by the legislation that specifies eligibility criteria and formulas for the distribution of the funds. Therefore, it also makes sense to calculate appropriations for earmarks as a proportion of discretionary spending, the portion of the budget that is controlled by the annual appropriations process.[28]

As Table 5.3 shows, earmarks have typically constituted less than 1% of total federal spending; indeed, their share of spending (although not their total cost) has dropped by more than half over the past five years from 1% to less than one-half of 1%. Not surprisingly, earmarks are a larger, albeit declining, proportion of discretionary spending. The peak year for earmarking was fiscal year 2006; in that year, earmarks constituted nearly 3% of the discretionary budget; by 2010, earmarks made up a bit more than 1% of that portion of federal outlays. Note, however, that the number of earmarks did not decline significantly over that period, except for FY 2007, when earmarks were temporarily banned from the omnibus appropriations bill that funded most federal agencies. In fact, the number of earmarks actually grew as the cost declined from 2006 to 2008 (ignoring the anomalous year of 2007). Thus, Congress divided dollars into more discrete projects per dollar spent as spending declined, helping MCs to continue to help large numbers of recipients.

Table 5.4 reports on the earmarks in eleven appropriation bills for FY 2010. As can be seen, the number and cost of earmarks in these bills vary enormously. Small numbers do not necessarily entail a small cost, as the

Table 5.3 Earmarks as a Proportion of Federal Spending

*Fiscal Year**	*Number of Earmarks*	*Cost of Earmarks in Billions*	*Cost as a Proportion of Total Federal Spending**	*Cost as a Proportion of Discretionary Spending*
2006	9,963	29	0.01	0.029
2007	2,658	13.2	0.0048	0.013
2008	11,610	17.2	0.0058	0.015
2009	10,160	19.6	0.0056	0.016
2010 estimate	9,129	16.5	0.0044	0.012

*Data on federal spending taken from Office of Management and Budget Historical Tables.

Table 5.4 Earmarks in FY 2010 Appropriations Bills

Appropriations Bill	*Number of Earmarks*	*Cost of Earmarks*
Agriculture	475	396,453,000
Commerce	1,520	714,401,000
Defense	1,752	10,253,078,200
Energy and Water	939	1,174,523,000
Foreign Operations	7	209,440,000
Homeland Security	173	242,828,564
Interior	548	361,084,950
Labor/HHS/Education	1,789	813,753,000
Military Construction	182	1,100,086,000
Transportation	1,483	1,216,711,034

182 earmarks for Military Construction indicate. In the bill with the largest number of earmarks, the bill funding the departments of Labor/Health and Human Services, and Education, one of the largest earmarks is for Senator Thad Cochran (R-Miss.), the ranking minority member on both the full Senate Appropriations Committee and the Labor/HHS/Education subcommittee, which provided the earmark in question. The earmark is for $30 million, and is allocated for "Delta Health Alliance, Inc. to improve the delivery of public health services in the Mississippi Delta region under title III of the Public Health Service Act (HHS – HRSA)." Although this earmark is remarkable for its cost, it is not unusual for earmarks to be bestowed on local nonprofit service providers or local governments. An example of the latter is an earmark of $125,000 for Senator Mark Begich (D-Alas.) for "City of Anchorage, for facilities and equipment relating to public health (HHS - HRSA Health Facilities and Services)."

No set of examples of earmarks from each category can explain the variation in numbers and cost. But some obvious patterns can be explained. While Military Construction contains the fourth largest dollar amount of earmarks, it accounts for the third fewest in number. This is because construction projects are typically much more expensive than grants for service providers, which make up a great many earmarks in other areas. More broadly, the most costly sets of earmarks are in bills that fund capital projects such as, in addition to Military Construction, weapons systems (Defense), waterway and water treatment projects (Energy and Water), and highways (Transportation).

Table 5.5 breaks down earmarks by party for the years since Congress has required that earmark sponsors be identified. The data indicate that, not surprisingly, majority party members (the Democrats for all years reported) get more earmarks than the minority. As the final two columns show, the Democratic advantage in number of earmarks exceeds the advantage in the cost of earmarks. Nevertheless, with only one exception, Democrats got

Table 5.5 Earmarks by Party, FY 2008–2010

Fiscal Year	*Democrats**		*Republicans*		*Pct for Democrats*	
	Number	*Cost*	*Number*	*Cost*	*Number*	*Cost*
2008	5,213	5,459,246,219	3,408	4,383,647,314	61	51
2009	4,651	4,763,736,464	3,034	3,321,940,992	60	59
2010	5,070	5,062,152,123	2,207	2,639,932,600	70	61

*Includes two independent senators, Sanders (Vt.) and Lieberman (Conn.)

more earmarks by either measure than their proportion of seats in Congress would predict. For FYs 2008 and 2009, whose appropriations bills were passed in 2007 and 2008 respectively (the 110th Congress), Democrats held 53% of House seats and 51% of Senate seats. For FY 2010, they held 59% of House and Senate seats. Only with respect to the cost of earmarks for FY 2008 do the Democrats not enjoy a disproportionate advantage in earmarks.[29]

In Table 5.6, the cost of a state's earmarks is divided by the number of congressional districts in the state (an approximate indicator of population); states are then ranked from those with highest to the lowest earmark value. The most obvious pattern is evident in the first seven states in the list. All of those states are represented by senators with extraordinary power over the federal budget. Hawaii, the top state in the ranking, was represented by Daniel Inouye (D), who was the chairman of the Senate Appropriations Committee, which distributes earmarks. Thad Cochran (R), the committee's ranking minority member, represented Mississippi, the seventh ranking state. Taking states two through six on the list, Kent Conrad (D-N.D.) was chairman of the Senate Budget Committee; Max Baucus (D-Mont.) was chairman of the Senate Finance Committee; Lisa Murkowski (R-Alas.) was a member of the Appropriations Committee (and Ted Stevens of Alaska, barely defeated in 2008 by Democrat Mark Begich, was the former chairman of the committee); the late Robert Byrd (D-W.Va.), the self-styled "king of pork" was the former long-term chairman of the committee and most senior member of the Senate; Tim Johnson (D-S.D.) was a member of the Appropriations Committee and, more importantly, chairman of the lucrative Military Construction Subcommittee.

Notable in this list of top states is the absence of powerful House members. The chairman of the House Appropriations Committee, David Obey, represented Wisconsin, the 28th ranking state on the list; the ranking minority member of that committee, Jerry Lewis, is from California, the 40th-ranked state. It seems clear from the distribution of earmarked dollars, measured roughly according to population, that high-ranking senators have more clout

Table 5.6 Cost Ranked by State FY 2010

State	*Cost of Earmarks*	*# CDs*	*Cost/CD*
Haw.	326,099,850	2	163049925
N.D.	127,743,350	1	127743350
Mont.	102,400,450	1	102400450
Alas.	92,072,850	1	92072850
W.V.	265,728,000	3	88576000
S.D.	87,874,150	1	87874150
Miss.	321,643,000	4	80410750
Vt.	61,733,280	1	61733280
Nev.	154,616,675	3	51538892
Utah	151,300,000	3	50433333
Del.	44,169,900	1	44169900
N.M.	114,499,540	3	38166513
R.I.	71,937,000	2	35968500
Ala	242,252,000	7	34607429
Maine	66,239,000	2	33119500
Kentucky	196,222,250	6	32703708
Kan.	129,159,000	4	32289750
N.H.	61,213,000	2	30606500
Iowa	147,995,700	5	29599140
Wash.	261,367,600	9	29040844
Md.	223,315,400	8	27914425
Ark,	110,474,164	4	27618541
Idaho	47,738,000	2	23869000
Conn.	115,613,800	5	23122760
La.	150,400,000	7	21485714
N.J.	263,387,850	13	20260604
Mo.	179,962,000	9	19995778
Wisc.	152,580,210	8	19072526
Mass.	183,991,300	10	18399130
Penn.	330,541,000	18	18363389
Okla.	88,982,000	5	17796400
S.C.	106,527,000	6	17754500
Va.	181,271,500	11	16479227
Fla.	404,019,700	25	16160788
Ore.	71,790,164	5	14358033
Neb.	41,251,800	3	13750600
Ohio	236,120,200	18	13117789
Tex.	406,235,400	32	12694856
Mich.	190,396,400	15	12693093
Calif.	635,319,300	53	11987157
Ariz.	91,712,000	8	11464000
N.C.	144,384,900	13	11106531
Colo.	77,397,500	7	11056786
Ga.	143,307,000	13	11023615
Ind.	91,121,000	9	10124556
Ill.	191,646,800	19	10086674
Tenn.	90,545,000	9	10060556
N.Y.	282,983,165	29	9758040
Minn.	67,303,100	8	8412888
Wy.	6,686,000	1	6686000

States ranked by the mean value of earmarks per congressional district on state-wide appropriations than their House counterparts. That is not surprising, given that senators, unlike House members, represent the entire state.

Operations

Earmarks are normally initiated by organizations within members' constituencies. The requests come from a wide variety of sources: local governments, universities, nonprofit social service organizations such as hospitals or battered women's shelters, and businesses, especially defense contractors (or businesses that would like to attain that status). The request may come from the organization itself or, if it has the resources, from a lobbying firm acting as a go-between. Indeed, lobbying for earmarks has undergone an explosion in the past decade or so. The number of firms that reported lobbying Congress on budget and appropriations issues grew from 1,447 in 1998 to 4,013 in 2005. "Even that number is incomplete because lobbyists are exempt from filing disclosure forms for work done on behalf of state and local governments."[30] Many such lobbyists are former members of Congress or former key staffers, especially former staff members of the appropriations committees. Public Citizen reported that between 1998 and 2005, 43% of MCs who left Congress and were eligible to become lobbyists had done so.[31]

The initial steps in obtaining an earmark are best described by Scott Frisch and Sean Kelly, who interviewed a number of staffers responsible for processing earmark requests in the offices of House members and senators. Upon receiving a request, staff members apply an initial "smell test" to determine whether the earmark is something that the MC can defend if it is discovered by the news media or a watchdog group; if not, it may cause political problems for the MC and thus may be refused by the staff member in charge of vetting the requests. Frisch and Kelly quote one senior staff member as follows: "At the end of the day my boss is going to make a decision based on my recommendation, and it is my job on the line, and hers too. We have a rule of thumb and that is 'don't take actions that are going to land you on the front page of the *Washington Post* in a negative way.'"[32]

A project that passes the initial smell test then is evaluated by other criteria, such as whether it is likely to create jobs in the district, whether the MC supports the group and its cause, and whether the earmark fits the needs of the executive branch agency that will have to administer it.[33] That said, Frisch and Kelly note that many offices are reluctant to refuse any earmark request and simply forward them all to the Appropriations Committee.[34]

MCs submit the earmark requests to the appropriations subcommittee in their respective house of Congress with jurisdiction over the funding of the agency that would administer the earmark. In the House, MCs' offices submit those requests to an electronic database. The requests are first evaluated by subcommittee staff, mainly the subcommittee clerk (the traditional term for the staff director). There is no standardized procedure by which requests are handled here, but the major winnowing must necessarily come at this level. Based on my own interviews with subcommittee clerks as well as those of other scholars (for example, Frisch and Kelly 2011, 36), subcommittee clerks are extremely reluctant to discuss the details and criteria that govern the selection process; in fact, they are well-known for being highly protective of their subcommittees' internal procedures and overall reputations. Nevertheless, some clerks whom I interviewed indicated that they made final decisions on the smaller earmarks (taking care to do as the chairs would wish), but many earmarks were decided upon by the subcommittee chairs themselves.[35]

The subcommittee clerks also gave some indication of the priorities assigned to requests from different groups of MCs. Members of the subcommittee in question received high priority, as one of the purposes of distributing earmarks is to earn the firm support of subcommittee members on the broader appropriations bill to which the earmarks are attached. Other favored members are the chairs of the subcommittee and full committee as well as rank and file members of the full committee. In addition, of course, the leaders of the House and Senate are favored, given their ability to help or hurt the chances of appropriations bills. Finally, members of the majority party who appear to be in electoral danger receive preferential treatment.[36]

The papers of Ralph Regula, a Republican and former chair of the House Labor, Health, and Human Services Subcommittee outline that subcommittee's priorities for distributing earmarks for Fiscal Year 2006. In that case, MCs were divided into the following categories: the chair of the subcommittee distributing the earmarks, the Appropriations Committee chair and, roughly tied with the former, House leadership, other Appropriations subcommittee chairs, appropriations subcommittee members (presumably members of the subcommittee allocating the earmarks), [other] Appropriations Committee members, chairs of other House committees, members of the powerful Rules Committee, and finally, rank and file members. This appears to be an approximate, although not exact, priority ordering for the level of funding. In addition, as I found in my own interviews, vulnerable members were given more funding for earmarks. The amounts allocated by Regula to each of the categories of recipients ranged from $29,600,000 for his own district to $400,000 for rank-and-file members who were not electorally endangered.[37]

In addition to determining how much to allocate to each MC, subcommittee staff must determine whether an earmark is eligible for federal funding; some earmarks are rejected on that basis alone. Beyond this baseline, some subcommittees simply allocate a sum to a member and [apparently] allow the member's priority ranking to determine which earmarks are funded; others play a more active role, seeking to avoid the bad publicity that can come from funding bad earmarks.[38]

The earmarks that survive the winnowing process at the subcommittee level in the House or the Senate are included in the subcommittee bill, which is voted on in the full Appropriations Committee and on the floor of the House or Senate. Finally, earmarks that survive those stages (and most of those that appear in the subcommittee bill do survive) then go with that bill to the House-Senate conference committee that must resolve the differences between the two houses' versions of the appropriations bill. This committee must reach a compromise on the bill that includes a mutually acceptable accommodation of earmark requests. However, an additional wrinkle appears at this stage of the process: many new earmarks suddenly appear in the conference reports on appropriations bills. For example, at the end of 2007, when most of the individual appropriations bills were combined into one massive omnibus bill, 298 earmarks were added during conference, more than half of them for members of the Appropriations Committees or electorally vulnerable members.[39] Watchdog groups such as CAGW have bitterly criticized such "airdropped" earmarks on the grounds that they undergo even less scrutiny than earmarks added at the beginning of the legislative process.

Presidents have often condemned earmarks but have rarely gone so far as to veto bills that contain them. An exception was Ronald Reagan's veto of the 1987 highway reauthorization bill that contained 152 earmarks; not surprisingly, that veto was promptly overridden by Congress. President Obama has taken inconsistent positions over time, but in his 2011 State of the Union message, he vowed to veto any appropriations bills containing earmarks. That threat was politically less risky in the past, given that House Republicans had already pledged to ban earmarks and the Senate was well on its way to doing so.

Views on Earmarks: Politicians, Administrators, Citizens, and Groups

Politicians: Prior to the 2011 moratorium on earmarks, most members of Congress energetically asserted their constitutional right to earmark funds for local needs, framing their case in terms of Congress's constitutionally conferred power to make all appropriations, Congress's co-equal status relative to the executive branch, and Congress's superiority to the executive branch as a representative institution, one whose members are more knowledgeable about their constituents' needs than any "faceless, unelected bureaucrat."

Not surprisingly, the leaders of the House and Senate Appropriations Committees have been (until 2011) the most energetic defenders of the Congress's prerogative to earmark spending for individual MCs' districts. David Obey,

(D-Wisc.), the chairman of the House Appropriations Committee until his retirement at the end of the 2010, said, "A ban on earmarks greatly weakens the authority Congress has over spending, to the benefit of the executive branch."[40]

In the Senate, John McCain (R-Ariz.) has for many years railed against earmarks and highlighted his crusade against them in his unsuccessful 2008 presidential campaign. In his campaign for reelection to the Senate in 2010, in an evident effort to boost McCain's chances against primary challenger J.D. Hayworth, CAGW declared McCain a "taxpayer hero" for his efforts to end earmarks.[41] Similarly, Republican senator Tom Coburn (Okla.), and Democratic senators Claire McCaskill (Mo.) and Mark Udall (Colo.), among others, pressed for an earmark ban in the 112th Congress. Nevertheless, the vast majority of those who eventually opposed earmarks previously partook of them.

Opposition to earmarking by such members appears to be driven by the fact that earmarks have become symbols of waste in an era in which the federal budget deficit has become a major political issue. Although a few members acknowledge that eliminating earmarks may not reduce federal spending but will, instead, change the way in which money is allocated, many apparently felt irresistibly pressured to embrace a change that was already inevitable.

Administrators: Less vocal about earmarks are the administrators who must disburse the funds to local recipients. Not surprisingly, most are loathe to antagonize the very MCs who provide their agencies' funding. Thus, in the executive branch, public statements about earmarking are generally confined to the president and his appointees.

At the presidential level, James Savage's study of academic earmarking (1999) cites three presidents—Ronald Reagan, George H.W. Bush, and Bill Clinton—as opponents of academic earmarks. The arguments cited range from examples of projects that appear to be ridiculous. For example, a Clinton administration official cited a "$100,000 earmark for the University of Hawaii to study how beagles detect brown tree snakes as an instance of questionable spending."[42] However, from the eye of another beholder, this is a worthy earmark, as this non-native species of snake is a major threat to Hawaiian songbirds. Environmentalists undoubtedly supported a project that might lead to their detection and elimination. The main criticism of such earmarks (as with other types of earmarks) is that they circumvent the peer review process that is intended to ensure that the most meritorious research gains federal funding. In the years since Savage's study, Presidents George W. Bush and (ultimately) Barack Obama have also opposed earmarking to one degree or another.

In interviews conducted in 1990, a former head of the Federal Highway Administration strenuously opposed earmarks. He argued that they "preempt the professional administration of the program. Congress should be in policy-making only." He argued that earmarks caused state transportation departments to re-order their project priorities: "I don't think they [earmarks] are boondoggles; they are desirable, but not top priority." Moreover, he argued that earmarks are often under funded, with, for example, $2 million devoted to "seed money project planning, but the public [erroneously] thinks they are going to get a half-billion dollar project."

Asked about the executive branch's reaction to highway earmarks, a top analyst at the Department of Transportation said, "[earmarks] don't have enough merit or are too low-priority to get funded by the states; some aren't cost-effective. It also usurps state and local power under federalism for Congress to dictate what states will do. It's a waste of money." Supporting that interpretation, the Transportation Department's Inspector General recently issued a report stating that "many earmarked projects considered by the agencies as low priority are being funded over higher priority, non-earmarked projects."[43]

James Savage (2009) interviewed administration officials concerning earmarks in the budget of the US Navy's Office of Naval Research (ONR). Although Table 5.3 showed that earmarks constitute around 1% of the discretionary budget, distribution among agencies is uneven. Savage reports that in FY 2007, 25% of the ONR's budget was earmarked for a total of 250 earmarks in that budget. Moreover, he argues that the costs go beyond even these figures. The agency must bear the administrative costs of searching out information, negotiating and coordinating agreements among stakeholders, and monitoring projects that are often only sketchily described in the congressional conference committee report. These additional costs are considerable, but the ONR is prohibited by Congress from charging them to the earmarks. Instead, the office must shift personnel away from its normal duties to administer earmarks.

Savage's interviews indicated a plethora of other problems associated with implementing earmarks. The release of funds is often delayed because the ONR has trouble discovering the specific identity and content of some projects and must devote considerable staff time to doing so. Additionally, delays in spend-out can cause serious political problems with Congress, who sometimes retaliate by threatening the agency's funding. Moreover, earmark recipients (in this case, typically defense contractors) may be unfamiliar with the Navy's procedures because they bypassed the normal contract application process; thus, staff time must be devoted to trying to bring the contractors into compliance with regulations without antagonizing the contractor and the MC who sponsored the earmark. Finally, budgetary problems add to the Navy's woes in two ways: earmarks come out of their core budget (as is the case with nearly all earmarks) and some earmarks are underfunded, making it necessary for the ONR to take even more money out of their core budget to implement them.

Although this is only one case study, it is likely that other agencies face similar problems, given that many of the earmark characteristics that cause these problems for the ONR are common to other earmarks.

Ordinary Citizens: Members of Congress have engaged in earmarking because they believe that it helps their constituents and/or potential campaign contributors (although MCs do not own up to the latter motive). As noted above, scholarly research largely has found a connection (albeit in some cases a slight one) between federal benefits targeted to individual congressional districts and electoral support for incumbents, although it should be noted that there is little scholarly consensus on how district level federal spending should be measured.

Impressionistically, there have been two congressional elections in which earmarks seem either to have hurt or not helped incumbents, including Democrats. The first was 1994, an election in which pork barrel politics was a rallying cry for Republicans seeking successfully to take majority control of the House and Senate. A number of MCs who previously were thought to be invulnerable, partly on the basis of their ability to deliver federal money, lost their seats in that election. One prominent incumbent Democrat whose chief of staff I interviewed just before that election said, glumly, that for the first time, bringing federal money to the district seemed to be hurting more than helping. She was already packing up the office, even though the election was days away. Also defeated in that election was Texas Democrat Jack Brooks, who was well-known for his ability to bring home federal money and the economic development that accompanied it. Many of the pork barrelers who lost probably succumbed to a combination of a Republican wave election and the fact that their districts had trended more and more Republican over the years. Yet in the past, their ability to procure federal money had helped to insulate them from partisan change in their districts.

The second election in which earmarks failed to save members (even if they did not cause their defeat) was 2010. Earmarks were, if anything, even more of an issue in that election, in which the combination of a bad economy and ballooning federal deficits produced a budget-cutting fervor in the electorate, a combination of forces that clearly benefited Republicans. Among the casualties was the powerful Democratic chairman of the House Appropriations Committee, David Obey of Wisconsin, who apparently concluded that he could not win and chose to retire rather than face an ignominious defeat. Other high-profile pork barrelers were defeated; most prominent among them was the chair of the House Transportation and Infrastructure Committee, James Oberstar (D-Minn.), whose committee distributes thousands of transportation earmarks in its highway bills every six years.

Yet despite this apparent anti-earmark tide, there is survey evidence that even in the 2010 election, voters still favored earmarks as long as they came to their own districts or states. In a survey of 1,003 people in late July, 2010, the Pew Research Center asked how earmarks would affect one's inclination to vote for the incumbent. 53% of respondents said they would be *more* likely to vote for a candidate who had "a record of bringing government projects and money to [their] district." Only 12% said that such a record would make them less likely to vote for such a candidate, and 33% said it would make no difference.[44] Such findings suggest that the electoral losses of particular pork barreling members may have had little to do with the benefits that they had brought home. Rather, as in 1994, they may simply have been casualties of midterm defeats for the party of the president, a trend that is substantially influenced by the state of the economy, which worked against Democrats in that election.

Indeed, some news reports indicate considerable distress among organizations that stand to lose essential funding as a result of the ban on earmarks. For example, in a series of stories between the end of December, 2009, and early February, 2010, National Public Radio interviewed a number of beneficiaries of current earmarks. Those people voiced fears that the earmark ban would, for example, endanger the restoration of the Everglades in Florida and deprive east coast states of the funding needed to expand their ports to accept the large container ships that will soon be able to traverse the expanded Panama Canal.[45] Alaska has been particularly reliant on earmarks for its economic health; the late Sen. Ted Stevens (R), who served for years as chair or ranking minority member of the Appropriations Committee, secured massive earmark funding for that state. As Sen. Lisa Murkowski said, "the ban is 'going to be a real kick in the gut for many of our communities.' She said it will do nothing to put a dent in the federal debt and amounts to the legislative branch 'abdicating' its power to appropriate and handing it to federal agencies."[46]

Oversight

Normally, oversight is thought of as a process carried out by Congress over the executive and is aimed at ensuring that an agency is carrying out the intent of Congress. However, there is no process for the oversight of congressional earmarks that is standardized, routine, and comprehensive. It is well known that there is little incentive for Congress to carry out "police patrol" oversight, in which "at its own initiative, Congress examines a sample of executive-agency activities, with the aim of detecting and remedying any violations of legislative goals and, by its surveillance, discouraging such violation."[47] Nevertheless, with regard to earmarks, the members who requested them and congressional subcommittees that granted them have an incentive to respond to the intended recipients of earmarks when the latter complain about their administration. This is a version of "fire alarm" oversight which McCubbins and Schwartz define as follows: "a system of rules, procedures, and informal practices that enable individual citizens and organized interest groups to examine administrative decisions (sometimes in prospect), to charge executive agencies with violating congressional goals, and to seek remedies from agencies, courts, and Congress itself."[48] "Informal practices" could include earmark beneficiaries' complaints which trigger pressure on the administering agency from the member of Congress (and possibly the appropriations subcommittee) who requested the earmark. As noted earlier, agencies fear exactly this type of oversight, as failure to satisfy those who complain could result in retaliation at budget time next year.

However if what is meant by oversight is some sort of systematic surveillance of earmarks by a body that is charged with ensuring that they are administered honestly, the main compliance method likely resides in the White House's Office of Management and Budget (OMB), which is charged with, among other things, overseeing the administration of the federal budget. That office requires audits of state and local governments and nonprofit organizations that administer federal awards of $500,000 or more; presumably, this includes earmarks.[49] The extent to which earmarks are revoked due to malfeasance is unknown, but very few such problems ever come to light.

Challenges

The current moratorium on earmarks was imposed only when the practice became part of a broader narrative of out-of-control government spending put forth by conservative groups and a few crusading members of Congress such as John McCain and Jeff Flake. Indeed, the preceding analysis suggests that earmarks pose many challenges and problems.

A major criticism of earmarks is that the practice circumvents the normal competitive process by which grants are awarded by the executive branch and related agencies. Academic earmarks are particularly vulnerable to this criticism. Many in the scientific community oppose these earmarks, as they are intended to avoid the normal peer review process, which is designed to award federal scientific research grants strictly on the merits of the project and the qualifications of the researchers. As noted above, *Science Magazine* was among the most vocal in arguing that such earmarks weaken the scientific enterprise. Such critics note that too much of the money allocated to academic earmarks does not go to research at all; an official of the Department of Energy noted that in the FY 1987 legislation funding its operations, all of the earmarked projects were for construction, thus diverting to "bricks and mortar" money that otherwise would have been devoted to research.[50]

However, many members of Congress argue that the peer-review process is unfairly biased toward a relatively few elite universities in a small number of states, while the rest of the nation's academic institutions are effectively excluded. Those members argue that they are merely seeking their state's fair share of scientific funding, which is thought to bring considerable economic benefit to their states. As such defenders intended, the result is that money for scientific research and the facilities in which to conduct it is spread out among universities large and small, known and relatively unknown, around the country.

Second, earmarks have negative implications for congressional and administrative oversight of the 99% of the budget that is not devoted to earmarks. Prior to the earmark moratorium, relatively small appropriations subcommittee staffs had to process, in many cases, thousands of earmark requests, typically in a period of two months. The Senate's Defense Appropriations Subcommittee staff reported spending half of its time processing earmarks.[51] Frisch and Kelly, who did extensive interviews with appropriations staffers, argue that the large numbers of earmark requests "overwhelmed the capacity" of appropriations staff to evaluate those project requests and took time that they should have devoted to evaluating the funding of major programs.[52]

Based on data compiled by the Stabile Center for Investigative Journalism at Columbia University and the Sunlight Foundation, *USA Today* reports that "almost 1 in 3 highway dollars earmarked since 1991—about $13 billion—remains unspent."[53] By law, money for specific earmarks must remain available in the Highway Trust Fund (derived from fuel taxes) indefinitely. Reasons for the inability to spend earmarked funds are numerous: the projects may be shelved for various reasons, money is left over from completed projects (such as the Atlanta Olympics), the project may previously have been started, in which case earmarked funds cannot be spent on it, or the location of the project is incorrectly identified (as US Route 31 instead of state road 31). In other cases, the earmark may fund a study of a new road that the state does not have the money or the desire to build.

Finally, as lobbying firms increasingly have become involved in seeking earmarks for their clients, corruption and the appearance of corruption have magnified concerns about earmarking among watchdog groups and others. Although relatively few cases of earmark buying have been proved in court, it is apparently increasingly common for a lobbyist to successfully request an earmark for a client and for that client subsequently to make a donation to the sponsoring MC's reelection campaign. Adding to those concerns is the fact that former members of Congress and Appropriations Committee staffers frequently are employed by such lobbying firms soon after their departure from government, typically earning many times more than they did in their former occupations. Although former members are enjoined from directly lobbying their former colleagues for a period of two years, they still can smooth the path for other members of the firm to the appropriate people. The possibility of obtaining such a job offers obvious incentives to be accommodating to the lobbying firms that request earmarks for their clients.

Some of these connections between lobbyists and members of Congress have resulted in high-profile scandals, if few prosecutions. A recent one was an investigation of the PMA Group, which lobbied Congress for lucrative defense-related earmarks, typically for weapons systems. The CEO of PMA, a former top staffer of the House Appropriations Committee, was indicted in August, 2010 and pled guilty in September of that year to charges of making more than $300,000 in illegal campaign contributions. It was widely speculated that these contributions were intended to provide access to MCs who could help PMA's clients obtain earmarks.[54] Although the Office of Congressional Ethics investigated seven House appropriators in connection with the scandal, in the end, it took action against none of them.[55]

Among the earliest earmarking scandals to emerge was that involving Rep. Randy "Duke" Cunningham (R-Calif.), who resigned his seat in Congress and pled guilty in 2005 to taking $2.4 million in bribes, among other inducements, from defense contractors in return for earmarks.[56] Other members of Congress have been implicated, but not charged, in similar scandals.[57]

Learning from the negative impact of the scandals that emerged while Republicans were in control of the House. However, lawmakers quickly found a way around the ban. Numerous reports from around the country indicated that for-profit entities formed partnerships with non-profits; earmarks were won for the non-profits and passed on to their corporate partners. For example, the Syracuse *Post-Standard* reported that Rep. Dan Maffei (D-N.Y.) requested an earmark for the Manufacturers Association of Central New York to develop and build devices to detect trace explosives; that money would be passed to Inficon, a company that would actually get most of the earmark and perform the research and development.[58]

Similarly, the total moratorium on earmarking implemented in 2011 has not stopped other practices designed to gain funds for such projects. Two common practices are "lettermarking" and "phonemarking," where MCs either write to or call an agency directly to request financing for a project, thus making an end-run around the legislative process altogether and around the new transparency imposed on earmarking in 2007. Agencies have the same incentive to grant such requests, especially to appropriators, as they do with earmarks. As a former Senate appropriations staffer said in a recent *New York Times* article, "When you have people who control your budget, that you have to appear before on an annual basis to ask for funding, you listen to what they have to say."[59]

Lessons Learned/Best Practices

Best practices for earmark policy would include complete transparency, serious controls on earmarking for for-profit entities to address the potential for corruption; systematic oversight of earmarks transmitted to the executive branch; reprogramming to other purposes of funds appropriated for "orphan" earmarks, and restriction of the proportion of a program's overall funding that can be devoted to earmarks.

Congress has already taken important steps to impose greater transparency in the earmarking process. As noted above, beginning in 2007, Congress enacted a series of reforms to the appropriations process intended to shine the light of day on congressional earmarks. Those changes include rules changes in both the House and Senate that required that each earmark be accompanied by the name of the member or members of Congress who had requested it. In the House, the rules also required that earmark requests include justifications (a practice that was already common) and that members or their spouses would not financially benefit; moreover, leaders were prohibited from promising earmarks in exchange for members' votes on legislation, a measure that was likely intended to address the fears that committee leaders were using earmarks to buy MCs' votes for more costly appropriations bills than they otherwise would support.[60]

In early 2009, the chairs of both the House and Senate appropriations committees went further. Responding to pressures from anti-earmark groups, they required members to post on their own Web sites a list of all of their earmark requests at the time they transmitted them, explain the earmark's purpose, and justify each earmark's value to taxpayers.[61]

These reforms make it possible to hold MCs accountable for several things: for their requests (for example, are they by some measure excessive?); for their priorities as indicated by the earmarks actually funded by the subcommittees (which they typically base on the members' priorities); for possible linkages between their earmarks and campaign contributions. In addition, several groups—including Taxpayers for Common Sense (TCS), Citizens for Responsibility and Ethics in Washington (CREW), CAGW, and Public Citizen—have advocated for a central database of congressional earmarks. Some of those groups provide such databases themselves but argue that this task is the responsibility of Congress.[62]

Those four advocacy groups—TCS, CREW, CAGW, and Public Citizen—formed a bipartisan coalition that also included four lobbyists, one of whom was a former MC, to make recommendations for a series of earmark reforms. Their whole list of recommendations follows:

1. In order to cut the cord between earmarks and campaign contributions, Congress should limit earmarks directed to campaign contributors.
2. To eliminate any connection between legislation and campaign contributions, legislative staff should be barred from participating in fundraising activities.
3. To increase transparency, Congress should create a new database of all congressional earmarks.
4. To ensure taxpayer money has been spent appropriately, the Government Accountability Office should randomly audit earmarks.
5. To promote congressional responsibility without stifling innovation, members of Congress should certify that earmark recipients are qualified to handle the project.[63]

However, the first and last recommendations above, while addressing serious problems, are either too vague (the first) or likely to be ineffective (the fifth). The connection between earmarks and campaign contributions should be addressed more directly than the first recommendation would do. Federal law already prohibits government contractors from making contributions and other expenditures in federal elections.[64] Although this restriction would presumably apply to an earmark recipient once the earmark was awarded, it does not prohibit those seeking earmarks from contributing to campaigns prior to the award of the earmark. To truly address this problem, such a prohibition should be imposed, perhaps during the election cycle in which a corporation seeks an earmark and the previous cycle as well.

With respect to the qualifications of earmark recipients to handle their projects, it is doubtful that MCs are generally qualified to make such certifications. It would be much more desirable to require that such certifications be made by the agency that would administer the earmark and has the expertise to determine a contractor's qualifications.

However, the latter recommendation conflicts with an evident need to reduce the burden that earmarks impose on the executive branch agencies that must administer them, a burden that in some cases appears to impair the agencies' ability to perform the tasks for which Congress designed them. By definition, earmarks put local interests ahead of broad national policy goals. It therefore would make sense for Congress to make an explicit allocation of total funding for earmarks, an allocation that would, in addition, impose a limit on the proportion of any agency's budget that can be directed to earmarks. Such a limit should apply to the specific offices administering earmarks, such as the Office of Naval Research. As Savage found, 25% of ONR's FY 2007 budget was devoted to earmarks, a total that would necessarily impair its ability to carry out its legislatively mandated mission.

Rather than recommend a specific proportion of federal appropriations or of an agency's budget that should be devoted to earmarks, I suggest that Congress do so because it would force that body to transparently balance national needs against local needs as it makes spending decisions. Of course, this might not be popular with individual members of Congress, but they might like it better than banning earmarks altogether.

Finally, as noted above, some earmarked funds are never spent, isolating those funds and depriving programs of monies that otherwise could be used. Efforts by the Department of Transportation to persuade Congress to free such "orphan" earmarks for redistribution were fruitless, but *USA Today* reported that President Obama's proposed 2011 budget would cancel earmarks that are more than twenty years old, a proposal that would free \$263 million.[65] Congress itself should set a specific time limit for the initiation of a project and if the time limit were exceeded, release the earmarked funds to the agency or state for which they were appropriated.

GLOSSARY OF KEY TERMS

CREW – Citizens for Responsibility and Ethics in Washington
CAGW – Citizens Against Government Waste
CDF – Constituency Development Funds
MCs – Member of Congress
OMB – Office of Management and Budget
TCS – Taxpayers for Common Sense
ONR – US Navy's Office of Naval Research

NOTES

1. Mayhew 1974, 53.
2. Mayhew 1974, 53–54.
3. Citizens Against Government Waste 2011.
4. US Senate Committee on Appropriations Feb. 1, 2011
5. Remarks by the President in the State of the Union Address 2011
6. Shepsle and Weingast 1981, 96.
7. See Frisch and Kelly 2011; Skocpol 1992; Maass 1951; Evans 2004; and Lee 2002.
8. Fenno 1966, 627.

9. Definitions of earmarks vary; as a result, tallies vary as well. The Congressional Research Service (2006) reported earmarks for even-numbered years between 1994 and 2004. Due to different definitions of earmarks, their totals were considerably higher than those appearing in Table 5.1. Totals compiled by Taxpayers for Common Sense, another advocacy group, are different yet (http://www.taxpayer.net), as are those complied by the White House Office of Management and Budget (http://earmarks.omb.gov/earmarks-public/).

10. Frisch and Kelly 2011.

11. Evans 2004.

12. Balla, Lawrence, Maltzman and Sigelman 2002.

13. Evans 2004.

14. Mervis 2010.

15. See Fiorina 1977; 1981; Johannes and McAdams 1981; Evans Yiannakis 1981; Cain, Ferejohn and Fiorina 1987; Stein and Bickers 1994, 1995; Alvarez and Saving 1997; and Lazarus and Reilly 2010.

16. Starkey 2010.

17. Stanton 2010a.

18. Rucker and Kane 2010.

19. Stanton 2010b.

20. Remarks by the President on Earmark Reform 2009.

21 The Legislative Transparency and Accountability Act of 2007 (P.L. 110-81) required identification the sponsors of all earmarks in spending and tax bills. In addition, H.R. 4921 (adopted by the House on June 18, 2007) created a point of order when a conference report contains "air-dropped earmarks" (that is, earmarks that did not appear in the original House or Senate bills that are the subject of the conference).

22. Arnold 1979.

23. Agriculture Subcommittee Report 111–181, 2009, 74–75.

24. Committee on Appropriations H. Rpt. 111–298, 2009, 136–146.

25. Committee on Appropriations, H. Rpt. 111–278, 2009, 18; italics in the original

26. The data must be offered with a caveat: prior to 2007, when earmarks were unambiguously identified by Congress for the first time, there was no generally agreed-upon definition of earmarks. Indeed, even the subcommittees of the House and Senate appropriations committees differed among themselves on the definition, according to a 2006 report by the Congressional Research Service, and the White House Office of Management and Budget employs its own definition. Thus, in their 2006 report, the CRS tabulated earmarks for each subcommittee, using that subcommittee's own definition, regardless of the fact that those definitions were inconsistent with each other (CRS 2006, CRS-3). Outside groups that collect such data also used different definitions prior to 2007, although they were consistent across subcommittees. Most definitions share this characteristic: an earmark is a directive to a federal agency to fund "individual projects, locations, or institutions" (CRS 2006, CRS-2) in members' districts or states.

27. CAGW uses the following definition: "a 'pork' project is a line-item in an appropriations bill that designatestax dollars for a specific purpose in circumvention

of established budgetary procedures." A project is pork if it meets one of the following criteria: it is requested by only one chamber of Congress; it is not specifically authorized; it is not competitively awarded; it is not requested by the President; it greatly exceeds the President's budget request or the previous year's funding; it is not the subject of congressional hearings; or it serves only a local or special interest.

28. Schick 2007, 57.

29. The total number of earmarks in Table 5.5 is lower than the totals in the previous tables. This is because some earmarks were sponsored by members of both parties; those were omitted from Table 5.5.

30. Finnigan 2007, 9.

31. Public Citizen 2005.

32. Frisch and Kelly 2011, 34.

33. Although most earmarks are vetted and approved for transmittal to the appropriations committees by MCs' staff, the MCs themselves have the final say on which earmarks are requested.

34. Frisch and Kelly 2011, 34–35.

35. Evans 2004, 173.

36. Ibid, 173–174.

37. Frisch and Kelly 2011, 36–37.

38. Ibid, 37.

39. Stanton and Singer 2007.

40. PolitiFact Wisconsin.

41. "Taxpayer Watchdog Group . . ." 2010.

42. Savage 1999, 183.

43. Department of Transportation 2007.

44. "Earmarks Could Help Candidates . . ." 2010.

45. Allen 2010.

46. "In Alaska, Reluctance to Accept the End of Earmarks" 2010.

47. McCubbins and Schwartz 1984.

48. Ibid, 166.

49. Office of Management and Budget 2010.

50. Norman 1986, 617.

51. Savage 2009, 452.

52. Frisch and Kelly 2011, 145.

53. Podkul and Korte 2011.

54. "Paul Magliocchetti Pleads Guilty" 2010.

55. Palmer 2010.

56. Finnigan 2007, 11.

57. For a list as of 2007, see Finnigan 2007.

58. Weiner 2010.

59. Nixon 2010.

60. Dennis 2007.

61. Dennis and Newmyer 2009.

62. "Bipartisan Coalition of Lobbyists . . . ." 2010.

63. Ibid.

64. http://www.fec.gov/pages/brochures/fecfeca.shtml#anchor257909
65. Podkul and Korte 2011.

REFERENCES

"2008 Republican Platform." http://www.gop.com/2008Platform/2008platform.pdf. 2/28/11.

"A Taxpayer Victory! Thank You!" 2011. Taxpayers for Common Sense. http://taxpayer.net/search_by_tag.php?action=view&proj_id=4296&tag=earmark%20reform&type=Project. 2/28/11.

Allen, Greg. 2010. "To Defenders, Some Earmarks are Sound Politics." *Morning Edition.* NPR. http://www.npr.org/2010/12/22/132205569/to-defenders-some-earmarks-are-sound-politics. 2/21/11.

Alvarez, R. Michael and Jason L. Saving. 1997. "Deficits, Democrats, and Distributive Benefits: Congressional Elections and the Pork Barrel in the 1980s". *Political Research Quarterly* 50: 809–831.

Arnold, R. Douglas. 1979. *Congress and the Bureaucracy: A Theory of Influence.* New Haven: Yale University Press.

Balla, S. J., E Lawrence, F Maltzman and L Sigelman. 2002. "Partisanship, Blame Avoidance, and the Distribution of Legislative Pork." *American Journal of Political Science* 46: 515–25.

"Bipartisan Coalition of Lobbyists and Advocates Announces Common Sense Earmark Reform Principles." *Taxpayers for Common Sense.* http://www.taxpayer.net/search_by_tag.php?action=view&proj_id=3775&tag=transparency&type=Project#PR. 2/27/11.

Cain, Bruce, John Ferejohn and Morris Fiorina. 1987. *The Personal Vote: Constituency Service and Electoral Independence.* Cambridge: Harvard University Press.

Citizens Against Government Waste. 2011. "Mission/History." http://www.cagw.org/about-us/missionhistory.html. 2/28/11.

Congresssional Research Service. 2006. "Memorandum: Earmarks in Appropriations Acts: by 1994, FY 1996, FY 1998, FY 2000, FY 2002, FY 2004, FY 2005." Congressional Research Service, Washington, D.C.

Dennis, Steven T. 2007 (January 8). "House Adopts Budget, Earmark Rules." *CQ Weekly.* http://library.cqpress.com/cqweekly/document.php?id=weekly report110-000002424026&. 2/21/07.

———. 2010 (March 10). "Obey Announces Partial Ban on Earmarks," *Roll Call.* http://www.rollcall.com/news/44039-1.html?type=printer_friendly. 3/10/10.

——— and Tory Newmyer. 2009. "Earmark Changes Unveiled." *Roll Call.* Jan. 7. http://www.rollcall.com/issues/54_68/-31099-1.html?zkPrintable=true. Accessed 2/19/11.

Department of Transportation. 2007. "Review of Congress Earmarks Within Department of Transportation Funds." Office of the Inspector General Report Number AV-2007-066, September 7.

"Earmark Reform." 2011. Public Citizen. http://www.citizen.org/Page.aspx?pid=4668. 2/28/11.

"Earmarks Could Help Candidates in Midterms; Palin and Tea Party Connections Could Hurt." 2010, August 2. Pew Research Center. http://people-press.org/report/642/. 2/21/11.

Engstrom, Erick J. and Georg Vanberg. 2010. "Assessing the Allocation of Pork: Evidence from Congressional Earmarks." *American Politics Research* 38:959–985.

Evans, Diana. 2004. *Greasing the Wheels: Using Pork Barrel Projects to Build Majority Coalitions in Congress.* New York: Cambridge University Press.

———. 2011 (forthcoming). "Pork Barrel Politics." *The Oxford Handbook of Congress.* Oxford University Press.

Feldman, Paul and James Jondrow. 1984. "Congressional Elections and Local Federal Spending." American *Journal of Political Science* 28(1): 147–165.

Fenno, Richard F., Jr. 1966. *The Power of the Purse: Appropriations Politics in Congress.* Boston: Little, Brown.

Finnigan, Tom. 2007. "All About Pork: The Abuse of Earmarks and the Needed Reforms." Citizens Against Government Waste. Http://www.cagw.org, accessed 2/16/11.

Fiorina, Morris P. 1977. "An Outline for a Model of Party Choice." American *Journal of Political Science* 21(3): 601–686.

Fiorina, Morris P. 1981. "Some Problems in Studying the Effects of Resource Allocation in Congressional Elections." *American Journal of Political Science* 25: 543–567.

Frisch, Scott A. 1998. *The Politics of Pork: A Study of Congressional Appropriation Earmarks.* NY: Garland.

——— and Sean Q. Kelly. 2011. *Cheese Factories on the Moon: Why Earmarks Are Good for American Democracy.* Boulder, CO: Paradigm Books.

Hulse, Carl. 2010 (February 7). "Spending Cuts Meet Selective Support." *New York Times.* http://www.nytimes.com/2010/02/07/us/politics/07spend.html?_r=1&scp=1&sq=%22Spending%20Cuts%20meet%20selective%20support%22&st=cse. 2/28/11.

"In Alaska, Reluctance to Accept the End of Earmarks." 2010, February 3. NPR. http://www.npr.org/templates/story/story.php?storyId=133449349. 2/21/11.

Inhofe, James M. 2010. "Eliminating Earmarks is a Phony Issue." *National Review Online.* November 12. http://www.nationalreview.com/corner/253159/eliminating-earmarks-phony-issue-james-m-inhofe. 2/19/11.

Johannes, John R. and John C. McAdams. 1981. "The Congressional Incumbency Effect: Is it Casework, Policy Compatibility, or Something Else? An Examination of the 1978 Election." American *Journal of Political Science* 25(3): 512–542.

Kasdin, PAR, http://onlinelibrary.wiley.com/doi/10.1111/j.1540-6210.2010.02154.x/pdf 2/2/11.

Kirk, Robert S., William J. Mallett and David Randall Peterman. 2011. "Transportation Spending Under an Earmark Ban." Washington, D.C.: Congressional Research Service.

Lazarus, Jeffrey. 2010. "Giving the People What they Want? The Distribution of Earmarks in the U.S. Hosue of Representatives." *American Journal of Political Science* 54:338–353.

Lazarus, Jeffrey and Shauna Reilly. 2010. "The Electoral Benefits of Distributive Spending." *Political Research Quarterly* 62(2):343–355.

Lee, Frances E. 2003. "Geographic Politics in the U.S. House of Representatives: Coalition Building and Distribution of Benefits." *American Journal of Political Science* 47(4): 714–28.

LegisStorm. http://www.legistorm.com/earmarks.html. Accessed 2.9/11.

Lewis-Beck, Michael S. and Richard Nadeau. 2009. "Obama and the Economy in 2008." *PS: Political Science and Politics* 42: 479–483.

Maass, Arthur A. 1951. *Muddy Waters: The Army Engineers and the Nation's Rivers.* Cambridge: Harvard University Press.

Mayhew, David R. 1974. *Congress: The Electoral Connection.* New Haven: Yale University Press.

McCain 2010. "Fighting for a More Effective Government." http://www.johnmccain.com/issues/post/fighting-for-a-more-effective-government/. 2/28/11.

McCubbins, Mathew D. and Thomas Schwartz. 1984. "Congressional Oversight Overlooked: Police Patrols vs. Fire Alarms." *American Journal of Political Science* 28:1, 165–179.

Melcher, Joan. 2008. "The Un-Bear-Able Irony of Earmarks." *Miller-McCune.* (October 9). http://www.miller-mccune.com/blogs/news-blog/the-un-bear-able-irony-of-earmarks-4190. 3/5/11.

Mervis, Jeffrey. 2010 (August 20). "Senator Builds His Legacy with University of Alabama Earmarks." *Science Magazine.* Accessed at http://www.sciencemag.org/content/329/5994/893.full?sid=6eadc534-54c5-41f9-a734-e3f1b1ab3dd0, 1/27/11.

Nixon, Ron. 2010 (December 28). "Earmarks Ban May Loom, but Lawmakers Find Ways to Finance Pet Projects." *The New York Times.* P. A11.

Norman, Colin. 1986. AHouse Endorses Pork Barrel Funding.@ *Science* 233:616–617.

Office of Management and Budget. 2010. "OMB Circular A-133 Compliance Supplement 2010." http://www.whitehouse.gov/omb/circulars/a133_compliance_supplement_2010. 2/23/11.

Office of Management and Budget. 2011. "Historical Tables, Budget of the U.S. Government, Fiscal Year 2011." http://www.gpoaccess.gov/usbudget/fy11/pdf/hist.pdf. 2/9/11.

Palmer, Anna. 2010 (August 9). "Indictment May Mark End of PMA Scandal." *Roll Call.* http://www.rollcall.com/issues/56_19/-49103-1.html?zkPrintable=true. 2/26/11.

"Paul Magliocchetti Pleads Guilty." 2010 (September 24). *Politico.com.* http://www.politico.com/news/stories/0910/42690.html 2/27/11.

Podkul, Cezary and Gregory Korte. 2011 (January 5). "'Earmarks' to Nowhere." *USA Today,* p. 1A.

PolitiFact Wisconsin. http://ucsdcalrev.wordpress.com/2011/01/16/the-ban-on-earmarks/. 2/19/11.

Public Citizen. 2005. "Congressional Revolving Doors: The Journey From Congress to K Street." http://www.citizen.org/publications/index.cfm?sectionID=108&start=31&maxrows=10. 3/5/11.

"The Promise Audit: Tracking President Obama's Progress on Campaign Promises." 2011. *The National Journal.* http://promises.nationaljournal.com/government-spending/restore-earmark-spending-to-pre-1994-levels/. 2/28/11.

Remarks by the President on Earmark Reform. 2009. The White House. Accessed at http://www.whitehouse.gov/the_press_office/Remarks-by-the-president.

Remarks by the President in the State of the Union Address. 2011. The White House. Accessed at http://www.whitehouse.gov/the-press-office/2011/01/25/remarks-president-state-union-address.

"Renewing America's Promise: The 2008 Democratic National Platform." 2008. http://www.democrats.org/about/party_platform. 2/28/11.

Rucker, Philip and Paul Kane. 2010 (December 15). "Senate Spending Bill contains Thousands of Earmarks." *Washington Post.* http://www.washingtonpost.com/wp-dyn/content/article/2010/12/14. 12/15/10.

Savage, James D. 2009. "The Administrative Costs of Congressional Earmarking: The Case of the Office of Naval Research." *Public Administration Review.* 69:448–457.

Savage, James D. 1999. *Funding Science in America.* New York: Cambridge University Press.

Schick, Allen. 2007. *The Federal Budget: Politics, Policy, Process.* Washington: Brookings Institution Press.

Seelye, Katharine Q. 2010. "Stand Against Earmarks Grows Lonely as Home State Sees a Need." *New York Times.* A12.

Sellers, Patrick J. 1997. A Fiscal Consistency and Federal District Spending.@ *American Journal of Political Science* 41:1024–1041.

Shepsle, Kenneth A. and Barry R. Weingast. 1981. A Political Preferences for the Pork Barrel.@ *American Journal of Political Science* 25:96–111.

Skocpol, Theda. 1992. *Protecting Soldiers and Mothers.* Cambridge: Belknap Press of Harvard University Press.

Stanton, John. 2010a. "Tea Party Activists Join Call for Earmark Ban." *Roll Call.* November 10. Accessed at http://www.rollcall.com/news/-200422-1.html.

———. 2010b. "In Backing Earmark Ban, McConnell Won't Cede Credit to DeMint." *Roll Call.* November 15. http://www.rollcall.com/news/-200547-1.html. 11/16/10.

Stanton, John and Paul Singer. 2007. "Airdrops for the Vulnerable." *Roll Call.* December 19. Accessed at http://www.rollcall.com/issues/53_74/-21445-1.html?zkPrintable=true. 2/19/11.

Starkey, Melanie. 2010. "DeMint Expects GOP Senators to Adopt Earmarks Ban." *Roll Call.* November 14. Accessed at http://www.rollcall.com/news/-200534-1.html.

Stein, Robert M. and Kenneth N. Bickers. 1994. "Congressional Elections and the Pork Barrel." *Journal of Politics* 56: 377–399.

———. 1995. *Perpetuating the Pork Barrel: Policy Subsystems and American Democracy.* New York: Cambridge University Press.

Sulzberger, A.G. 2010 (November 23). "Defenders of Earmarks Point to Urgent Needs That Would Not Be Met." *New York Times.* A17.

"Taxpayer Watchdog Group Names Sen. John McCain 'Taxpayer Hero'." Citizens Against Government Waste. http://mccain.senate.gov/public/index.cfm?FuseAction=Files.View&FileStore_id=5a02a975-c460-4814-9db7-6a4b90a0b47c. 2/19/11.

U.S. Congress. House of Representatives. Committee on Appropriations, Agriculture, Rural Development, Food and Drug Administration, and Related Agencies Appropriations Act, 2010. 111th Congress, 1st Sess., H. Rpt. 111–181. http://web.lexis-nexis.com/congcomp/document?_m=53c60110272955ae1715f139906488b0&wchp=dGLzVzb-zSkSA&_md5=0b3882cdca6772f63443931104d1779b (February 2, 2011).

U.S. Congress. House of Representatives. Committee on Appropriations, Energy and Water Development and Related Agencies Appropriations Act. 2010. 111th Congress, 1st Sess., H. Rpt. 111–278. http://www.gpo.gov/fdsys/pkg/CRPT-111hrpt278/pdf/CRPT-111hrpt278.pdf. Accessed 2/5/11.

U.S. Congress. House of Representatives. Committee on Appropriations, Department of Homeland Security Appropriations Act, 2010 . 111th Congress, 1st Sess., H. Rpt. 111–298. http://www.gpo.gov/fdsys/pkg/CRPT-111hrpt298/pdf/CRPT-111hrpt298.pdf. Accessed 2/5/11.

U.S. Congress. Senate. Committee on Appropriations. 2011, February 1. "Committee Announces Earmark Moratorium." http://appropriations.senate.gov/news/cfm?method=news.view&id, (February 2, 2011).

Weiner, Mark. 2010 (May 16). "Local 'earmarks' run a stop sign." *The Post-Standard.* http://blog.syracuse.com/news/print.html?entry;/2010/05.localearmarks. 5/24/10.

Yiannakis, Diana Evans. 1981. "The Grateful Electorate: Casework and Congressional Elections." *American Journal of Political Science* 25(3): 568–580.

APPENDIX

Agency	*Account*	*Project*	*Amount*	*Requester(s)*
DHS	Office of the Under Secretary lot Management	Center of Excellence in Logistics and Technology (LOGTECH). Institute for Defense and Business. The University of North Carolina, Chapel Hill, NC	$1,000,000	David Price
CBP	Salaries & Expenses	Portable Solar Charging Rechargeable Battery System, Global Solar, AZ	$800,000	Ed Pastor
CBP	Construction and Facilities Management	Advanced Training Center. WV	$39,700,000	Robert Byrd
CBP	Construction and Facilities Management	Hangar and Offices for US Customs and Border Protection, City of El Paso, TX	$3,500,000	Silvestre Reyes
TSA	Aviation Security	Transportation Security Research and Training Center, National Safe Skies Alliance. TN	$1,250,000	John Duncan Jr.
CG	Operating Expenses	Operations Systems Center, WV	$3,600,000	Robert Byrd
CG	Acquisition, Construction, and Improvements	Coast Guard Academy Pier, CT	$300,000	Christopher Dodd
CG	Acquisition, Construction, and Improvements	Coast Guard Station Cleveland Harbor, OH	$16,800,000	George Voinovich
CG	Alteration ot Bridges	Fort Madison. IA	$4,000,000	Tom Harkin; David Loebsack
NPPD	Infrastructure Protection and Information Security	National Infrastructure Simulation and Analysis Center, NM	$4,000,000	Jeff Bingaman; Tom Udall
NPPD	Infrastructure Protection and Information Security	Philadelphia Buffer Zone Protection Video Surveillance Expansion Project, City ol Philadelphia, PA	$1,000,000	Chaka Fattah
NPPD	Infrastructure Protection and Information Security	Slate and Local Cyber Security Training, University of Texas, San Antonio, TX	$3,500,000	Ciro Rodriguez
NPPD	Infrastructure Protection and Information Security	Power and Cyber Systems Protection, Analysis, and Testing Program at the Idaho National Laboratory. Idaho National Laboratory, ID	$3,000,000	Michael Simpson; Mike Crapo; James Risch

Source: U.S. Congress. House of Representatives. Committee on Appropriations. 2009. 111th Congress, 1st sess., H. Rpt. 111–298.

Chapter 6

Drug Dons and the Development of Executive Driven Bi-Partisan CDFs in Jamaica

Horace Bartilow

INTRODUCTION

The ruling Jamaica Labor Party in its 2007 electoral campaign promised to establish the Constituency Development Fund (CDF) to provide Members of Parliament (MPs) with financial resources to execute approved social and economic projects within their constituencies. The CDF was given the legal mandate to fund welfare projects and activities, economic enablement projects and small infrastructure projects. The main focus of the CDF was to promote human and infrastructure development that originate from Jamaica's communities, with the goal of increasing the level of self-reliance among these communities and political constituencies. Other objectives of the CDF included increasing the effectiveness of MPs' welfare activities and projects within their constituencies, which ultimately strengthens the relationship between government and the people.[1]

The analysis of the CDF in Jamaica must be understood in terms of the clientelistic political context that preceded its formal introduction in financial year 2008–2009. Political clientelism, which has characterized much of Jamaica's political history, created the sociopolitical conditions that gave rise to garrison communities and the power of the "Don"—the strongman community leader whose financial and political power would ultimately challenge the authority of MPs in some constituencies and ultimately undermine the very notion of representative democracy. In an attempt to break with the country's clientelistic past and more importantly to strengthen MPs' relationships with their constituency by making them more responsive to the needs of the community, various forms of monitoring mechanisms have been built into the design of the CDF to ensure a high degree of accountability and transparency.

This chapter is organized as follows. The first section discusses the political context of the CDF in Jamaica with an emphasis on the clientelistic nature of the Jamaican party system and the emergence of the "Don"—the crime boss who has become an important feature in the life of some communities in Jamaica. The next section discusses the predecessors to the CDFs—the Local Development Program (LDP), the Social and Economic Support Program (SESP) and the Lift Up Jamaica Program (LUJ). The third section discusses the funding and operational structure of the CDF. This is followed by a discussion of the politics of the CDF and a comprehensive treatment of the alleged political corruption that some members of the Jamaican media claim to characterize the operations of the CDF. After a discussion of the role of civil society groups in the implementation of CDF projects, the chapter concludes with a discussion of the challenges and constraints in the administration of the CDF and identifies areas for further research.

Political Context of the CDF

The traditional perspective of political clientelism defines the practice as the exchange of economic and social favors to a poor and socially fragmented population in return for party support. The essential element of the patron-clientelistic relationship is the state's provision of economic and social benefits to the lower classes in exchange for their electoral support.[2] Students of comparative politics have long identified patron clientelism as the leading mechanism through which political parties in much of the developing world organize the political support of the masses.[3]

However, while the traditional perspective of clientelism is correct, Stone points out that it lacks a theoretical understanding of the processes that are involved in the institutionalization of clientelism. According to Stone, the traditional perspective of political clientelism places emphasis on the exchange of political party support for material benefits while ignoring the larger mechanisms through which clientelism shapes the structure of political power. Stone argues that clientelism in many developing countries, like Jamaica, is more than a system to win votes, but a mechanism to institutionalize a power structure that is significantly different from the nature of interest or class-based politics that is typical of liberal democracies in advanced industrial countries. And in this regard, Stone considers Jamaica to be the prototype clientelistic democratic state.[4]

This more complex view of clientelism is reflected in the recent work of Nicholas van de Walle who argues that clientelism is and will remain a pervasive feature of politics in the developing world even under conditions of increasing democratization. He argues that the important theoretical question is not whether democratization in the developing world will decrease or increase clientelism, but rather how will democratization modify the continued practices of clientelism.[5] Like Stone, van de Walle defines clientelism in terms of its institutional features. Political clientelism, he argues is characteristic of a "web of clientelistic relationships that structure the relationship between state and citizen."[6]

In his view there are several processes that structure the institutionalization of clientelism. These include the nature of the political regime. The more democratic a political system is, the larger the number of people who receive patronage and the more distributive the system becomes. The location of political decision-making also conditions the institutionalization of clientelism. He argues that the emergence of competitive elections is likely to shift the locus of clientelism away from the executive branch towards political parties and the legislatures. The fiscal resources that are available to the state will also shape the institutionalization of clientelism. As the Jamaican case will demonstrate, debt-laden states cannot afford the widespread level of patronage that is often found in rich advanced industrial states.[7]

Jamaica as a prototypical clientelistic democratic state exhibits characteristics that are consistent with van de Walle's notion of how clientelism is structured and institutionalized. Jamaica's democracy, social structure and the competitive nature of its electoral politics have, in past years, increased the number of people who benefit from patronage and placed the locus of clientelism on the political parties. In Jamaica, the system of patronage resulted in the integration of the lower classes into the two dominant political parties—the Peoples National Party (PNP) and the Jamaica Labor Party (JLP)—forging loyalty to the party and not the sociopolitical system as a whole. In his analysis of political behavior and attitudes in Jamaica during the 1970s, Carl Stone showed that 36% of the working class and 70% of the lower class sought patronage in the corporate area of Kingston and St. Andrew.[8]

Clientelism is institutionalized in a hierarchical social structure in Jamaica. On top of this structure sits the party bosses and the top leadership of both political parties. Below the party bosses and leadership are the brokers or the intermediaries, which include party activists, organizers, businessmen, journalists, educators, administrators and community notables, referred to here as Dons, who provide points of contact between party leadership and clients in the distribution and allocation of material and social benefits. Brokers are drawn into the clientelistic network because they provide material benefits from which they can exchange information, money, skills, and contracts with politically beneficial clients. From independence to the late 1980s, all the essential aspects of national political life in Jamaica were largely integrated into a clientelistic network in which individual political actors function as brokers or clients of the parties' leadership and bosses. Brokers and clients were largely recruited from outside the formal apparatus of the parties as they brought crucial resources that strengthened the power of the parties' leadership and bosses.[9]

By the 1970s, financial crisis besieged the parties' clientelistic mechanism for allocating and distributing economic and social benefits to the lower classes in exchange for their political support. The cumulative effects of the oil shocks of the 1970s exploded the country's balance of payment and fiscal deficits. The collapse of the bauxite market, an important source of foreign exchange revenue, and the recessionary effects of the various austerity programs of the International Monetary Fund (IMF) to stabilize the Jamaican economy created the conditions for a greater demand for patronage while providing no economic surplus from which the political parties could meet this demand.[10] Table 6.1, chronicles Jamaica's growing balance of payments deficits since the early 1970s. All indicators show that exports consistently lagged behind imports that culminated in a chronic balance of trade deficit whereby the current account deficit amounted to 15% of the country's GDP by 1985. The government's fiscal deficits, as shown in Table 6.2, grew simultaneously with the growth in the country's balance of payments deficits. By 1985 the public sector deficit accounted for 18% of the country's GDP.

Table 6.1 Jamaica: Balance of Payments (millions of US dollars)

Year	*Exports*	*Imports*	*Trade Balance*	*Current Account Deficit*	*GDP*	*Current Account Deficit/GDP*
1969	206.1	363.3	−157.2	124	992.6	10.38%
1970	279.1	437.8	−158.7	153	1,170.6	10.88%
1971	275.2	459.8	−184.6	172	1,282.4	11.18%
1972	292.3	489.3	−197.0	197	1,439.1	10.49%
1973	347.8	615.1	−267.3	248	1,719.9	13.09%
1974	630.8	850.8	−220.0	92	2,159.2	3.87%
1975	733.0	1,021.4	−288.4	283	2,600.6	9.89%
1976	560.9	829.8	−268.9	303	2,696.4	10.20%
1977	711.2	746.9	−35.7	42	2,954.3	1.30%
1978	772.2	864.7	−92.5	50	3,737.4	1.89%
1979	806.3	1,002.8	−196.5	139	4,274.6	5.73%
1980	935.5	1,173.8	−238.3	166	4,750.1	6.23%
1981	966.2	1,467.1	−500.9	337	5,267.2	11.39%
1982	746.7	1,375.9	−629.2	403	5,841.9	12.30%
1983	673.1	1,280.9	−607.8	355	6,897.0	9.95%
1984	687.9	1,183.2	−495.3	332	9,381.0	13.96%
1985	535.1	1,143.6	−608.5	301	11,263.1	14.88%

Source: International Financial Statistics Year Book (IFS) 1987, pp. 422–243; and IFS, January 1988, p. 292.

Table 6.2 Jamaica: Fiscal Deficit (Millions of Jamaican Dollars)

Year	*Fiscal Deficit*	*GDP*	*Fiscal Deficit/GDP*
1969	20.5	992.6	2.07%
1970	31.7	1,170.6	2.71%
1971	47.8	1,282.4	3.73%
1972	59.4	1,439.1	4.13%
1973	90.5	1,719.9	5.26%
1974*	167.9	2,159.2	7.78%
1975	206.0	2,600.6	7.92%
1976	418.3	2,696.4	15.51%
1977	428.2	2,954.3	14.49%
1978	625.0	3,737.4	16.72%
1979	655.8	4,274.6	15.34%
1980	986.0	4,750.1	20.76%
1981	874.9	5,267.2	16.61%
1982	896.2	5,841.9	15.34%
1983	941.2	6,897.0	13.65%
1984	1,287.1	9,381.0	13.72%
1985	2,002.5	11,263.1	17.78%

Source: International Financial Statistics Year Book (IFS) 1987, pp. 422–243; and IFS, January 1988, p. 292.

These mounting deficits placed significant constraints on the ability of the political parties to finance patronage to the lower classes in exchange for their political support. Consequently, the parties' clientelistic structure of power eroded significantly as some intermediaries, especially community notables or Dons, no longer sought upward mobility within the political party structure; rather, they sought to establish a domain of power through organized crime that was independent of the parties' traditional system of clientelism. In some communities in Jamaica, the financial proceeds from organized crime has allowed Dons to distribute and allocate financial and social benefits to members of their community in ways that far exceed the financial capabilities of both political parties.[11] What has now emerged in Jamaica, is a crime-induced clientelistic-patronage system. In this system, Dons have become informal bosses who are loosely associated with the leadership of the political parties but operate independent of them in the distribution of benefits to the community in exchange for the community's acquiescence with organized crime as well as its support and protection from local law enforcement.[12] Consequently, the traditional relevance and the power of the political parties to integrate the lower classes into the party apparatus via patronage has been severely weakened as they increasingly look to Dons to distribute crime-induced patronage and in the process tolerate organized criminal networks that operate within their communities.[13]

Interviews in Jamaica,[14] during November 2010, confirmed that an important political implication of the CDF is its potential to erode the power of Dons, reassert the relevance of MPs within their constituencies and reduce crime in certain communities. In a focus group interview with the Westmoreland Parish council, members believe that since the CDF provide social and economic assistance to communities its sustained expenditure would weaken the power of Dons in certain communities in Jamaica.[15] In a similar focused group interview with the Manchester Parish Council, members also claim that since CDF projects help provide employment in various communities in the restoration of schools, housing and infrastructure it exerts a reductive effect on crime.[16]

Individual interviews[17] conducted with MPs from both political parties revealed similar perceptions of the political effects of CDF projects on crime and the power of Dons in some communities. In an interview with PNP opposition MP, Robert Pickersgill, it was noted that Jamaica's protracted budgetary constraints have made MPs financially impotent in responding to the needs of their constituencies, which has subsequently tarnished their credibility. Pickersgill argued that since there has been an absence of public expenditure in various communities in Jamaica, Dons develop and criminal gangs move in to fill the vacuum left by the state. Therefore, according to MP Pickersgill, an important political implication of the CDF, is the potential weakening of the power of Dons in certain communities and the reassertion of the political credibility and relevance of MPs in the lives of their constituencies.[18]

It is within this political context that the design, the operations, and the implementation process of the CDF must be understood. The CDF in Jamaica is in part a reaction to MPs' increasing marginalization from the life of their constituencies. Individual interviews with Jamaican MPs on both sides of the political aisle revealed that in the absence of the CDF MPs were unable to respond to the social and welfare needs of their constituencies. Consequently, they believe that their financial impotence, relative to the financial power of Dons in some communities, made them marginal to the lives of members in their constituencies who increasingly sought the assistance of the community Don to provide for their social and welfare needs.

The existing literature on the role of legislatures in developing countries speaks in part to this phenomenon. Barkan argues that legislatures in emerging democracies and in Africa in particular, perform four core and unique functions that distinguish them from other political institutions and explains why legislatures are an essential component of democracy. The first is that legislatures provide the institutional mechanism that makes representative governance meaningful and practical. The legislature provides the institutional forum in which competing interests are articulated and their objectives advanced through the policy making process. The second is that legislatures legislate. A legislature passes laws and in some instances is no more than a rubber stamp for the executive. In other instances, legislatures working either in partnership with or independent of the executive craft legislation and shape public policy. The third is that the legislature exercises oversight of the executive branch and ensures that laws that are passed are actually implemented by the state. The fourth is that the legislature provides constituency service, which Barkan argues is the legislators' principal task. Constituency service allows the legislature to act as individuals rather than as part of a collective institutional body.[19] Barkan suggests that there are two types of constituency service. The first is akin to Richard Fenno's home style politics where legislators make regular visits to their home districts to offer assistance to individuals in their constituency.[20] The second is akin to the CDF where legislators provide financial support for community development projects that provide members of their constituency with roads, water systems, schools and health services.[21]

Barkan acknowledges that these core functions of the legislature exist in tension with each other and this tension is a defining and essential feature of the legislature as an institution. Representation requires legislators to become advocates for the particular concerns and interests of their respective constituencies, while legislating requires making bargains and compromises across these interests. There is also tension between legislating and constituency service. Legislating seeks to make decisions that serve the broader interests of the nation, while constituency service seeks to serve the particular interests of a subset in the nation.[22]

While recent studies of legislatures in developing countries accurately describe the inherent tension among the core functions of the legislature, these studies fail to consider the role and the effect that the underground economy has on the traditional functions of the legislature. Specifically, recent legislative scholarship does not consider the inherent tension between community powers such as the Don and the legislator as it relates to the provision of constituency service. The financial power of Dons allows them to respond to the needs of the community in ways that dwarf legislators' ability to provide service to their constituencies. In the Jamaican case, legislators believe that their financial impotence, relative to the financial power of Dons made them marginal to the lives of members in their constituencies who increasingly look to the community Don to provide constituency service, an important function of the legislature that in some communities is hijacked by the Don. These realities strongly suggest that the illicit and the underground crime networks must be factored into our understanding of the conditions under which the legislature operates in the developing world.

In a meaningful sense, the CDF is partly an attempt to maintain party clientelism but one that is based on transparency and representative democracy. In Jamaica, the design and operation of the CDF represents an attempt to redeem the country's democratic future from a crime-induced patronage system.[23]

The Predecessors of the CDF

Floyd Morris, the former Minister of State, argued that the role of legislators, in the Jamaican context, has never been confined to making law and the formulation of public policy. Morris argued that over the years legislators had to respond to the growing needs of their constituencies for economic and social assistance or what Barkan describes as constituency service. The Local Development Program (LDP) was established in 1978 to provide funds that would allow MPs to respond to emergencies in their constituencies. These would include the restoration of roads and the clearing of roadways due to natural disasters like hurricanes.[24] However, according to Morris, by 1990 the cumulative effects of the IMF's structural adjustment policies, which drastically devalued the Jamaican dollar, forced drastic cuts in public sector expenditures, and removed price controls and government subsidies. This caused mounting pressures on MPs to provide assistance to their constituencies to cushion the pain of economic liberalization. And since the LDP was designed to respond to emergencies there were no funding programs available that would allow MPs to respond to the negative social and economic externalities of structural adjustment that was borne within their constituencies.[25] Consequently, the Social and Economic Support Program (SESP) was established in October 1990 with a view to reduce the number of persons living below the poverty line, by instituting social and economic support programs that could improve the quality of life for such persons. The SESP was also aimed at alleviating the economic and social hardships being experienced by students attending secondary and tertiary educational institutions. The SESP was administered by the Office of the Prime Minister and provided funds to communities for infrastructure projects, as well as some individual benefits for school materials, funerals, housing for the indigent, and in support of entrepreneurial activity.[26] Under the SESP each MP received an allocation of JA$3.5 million, which was a significant increase over the LDP where MPs received JA$500,000.[27]

While the SESP allowed MPs to provide assistance to their constituencies it was not intended to address the larger problem of growing unemployment that was also a by-product of structural adjustment. On June 1, 1999, then PNP Prime Minister P.J. Patterson launched the island-wide public work program, Lift Up Jamaica (LUJ).[28] The LUJ targeted some 40,000 unemployed youths between the ages of 18 to 30 at an estimated cost of JA$2.5 billion. The program focused on two main areas, which included:

- Reforestation that used timber trees of 2,500 hectares of crown land.
- The rehabilitation, repair and upgrading of physical assets within communities such as drainage, basic schools, parks and sanitary conveniences.

The implementing agency for the forestry component of LUJ was the Forestry Department (FD). The Urban Development Corporation (UDC) was given the responsibility for the island-wide coordination of the LUJ program. The collaborative effort of several government agencies was essential for the implementation of the program.[29] The implementation process worked as follows:

- The regional staff of the FD was given the responsibility of identifying work projects. The FD's LUJ coordinator would review project proposals and then send them to the UDC for approval.
- Once the work projects have been approved, the Social Development Commission (SDC) who was given the responsibility for sensitizing the communities from which workers were employed is notified.
- When the selection of workers to be employed is complete they are sent to the Human Employment and Resource Training Trust (HEART) who was responsible for organizing a three-day training seminar that orientated the workers with regards to standard protocols and appropriate work attitudes.[30]

When the JLP administration of Bruce Golding assumed power after the party's electoral victory in 2007, resources that funded the LDP, SESP and LUJ were collapsed into one fund to establish the CDF.[31] The Golding government's motive for creating the CDF was shaped by the growing need to reassert the relevance of MPs within their constituencies and to bring government closer to the people by encouraging constituency involvement in the selection and design of CDF projects. And while there is no evidence to suggest that Mr. Golding's creation of the CDF was directly motivated to counter the power of Dons, it is important to note that one of Jamaica's most powerful Dons—Christopher Dudus Coke operated from within Mr. Golding's constituency of Tivoli Gardens. All MPs and Parish Council members who were interviewed for this report noted that an indirect political consequence of the CDF is that it empowers communities in ways that over time could limit their dependence on the financial resources of Dons, encourage democratic governance at the constituency level and ultimately strengthen the credibility of the MP within his/her constituency. And in the words of MP Pearnel Charles "if there is such a thing as a Don in the constituency the MP should be the only legitimate Don."[32]

The sociopolitical context that proceeded the CDF's introduction in Jamaica largely explains the stringent and robust levels of monitoring that is built into the ways in which the CDF is administered and how its resources are allocated. In other words, if it is true that the unintended political consequence of the CDF is that over time it can reduce communities' financial dependence on Dons, then the probability of achieving this outcome is only possible if the administration of the CDF provides high levels of transparency and accountability and severely limits the opportunity for political corruption in the administration of CDF resources.

The Funding and Operational Structure of the CDF

The CDF, which became operational during fiscal year 2008–09, is funded from the national budget. In the first year of its operation it allocated JA$40 million per constituency [US $396,000] which was a tremendous increase in expenditure relative to its predecessors. However, budgetary constraints in the second year reduced the Fund's allocation to JA$20 million per constituency, which is still a significant increase compared to the SESP where each MP received an allocation of JA$3.5 million and the LDP where MPs received JA$500,000.[33] Moreover, under the terms of the CDF, 5% of the annual allocation of the Fund is reserved to respond to Welfare and Emergency needs, while another 5% is intended to address Social Housing needs of MPs' constituencies.[34] Table 6.3, below provides the general structure of Jamaica's CDF allocation since it was established.

During the 2008–2009 fiscal year, all 60 MPs claimed to have made full use of the JA$40 million allocated to each of them, and, of the total amount disbursed, JA$695 million (29%) went to Human and Social Development

Table 6.3 Allocation Structure of CDF

Fiscal Year	*Total CDF Budget*	*Percentage of Total National Budget*	*Amount per Constituency (60 in Total)*
2008–2009[1]	JA$2.46 billion	0.5%	JA$40 million (US$461,000)
2009–2010[2]	JA$1.26 billion	0.23%	JA$20 million (US$231,000)
2010–2011[3]	Approx. JA$1.22 billion	0.24%	JA$20 million (US$231,000)

[1]Jamaica Gleaner. (2008). MPs rue reduced development fund. Available from: http://www.jamaica-gleaner.com/gleaner/20080330/lead/lead5.html. Retrieved on July 25, 2010.

[2]Jamaica Labour Party. (2009). CDF cut almost in half—MPs to get $20 million to spend in their constituencies this year. Available from: http://www.jamaicalabourparty.com/base/content/cdf-cut-almost-half-mps-get-20-million-spend-their-constituencies-year. Retrieved on July 25, 2010.

[3]Total national budget for fiscal year 2010–2011 is $503.97 billion, which is available from: http://www.mof.gov.jm/budget/fsre/FY%202010-2011.

projects, JA$189 million (8%) to economic enablement, JA$109.5 million (4.6%) to disaster mitigation and JA$1.4 billion (58%) to physical infrastructure projects.[35] Funded areas included: road repairs, economic enablement, water projects, rural electrification, sports development, education/scholarship grants, assistance in purchasing school books, general upgrading of bridges and other facilities, construction of computer laboratories and homework centers, as well as rehabilitation of community centers.[36]

Figure 6.1 describes the operational structure of the CDF, which emphasizes its robust levels of accountability, transparency and the involvement of MPs' constituencies in the design and initiation of community projects. The major agencies that are involved in the administration and monitoring of the CDF include: the Office of the Prime Minister (OPM) who is given the responsibility for the management and the disbursement of the fund; the Constituency Development Fund Local Committee (CDFLC) whose main responsibility is to identify the needs of the community and design local project proposals that would address those needs; the Constituency Development Fund Program Management Unit (CDFPMU) which has the responsibility to review project proposals as well as monitor the implementation of approved CDF projects; the Office of the Contractor General (OCG) whose main responsibility is to monitor and audit all CDF projects and the agencies that administer CDF resources; and the Constituency Development Fund Parliamentary Committee (CDFPC) who has the responsibility to give the final review and approval of all CDF projects.

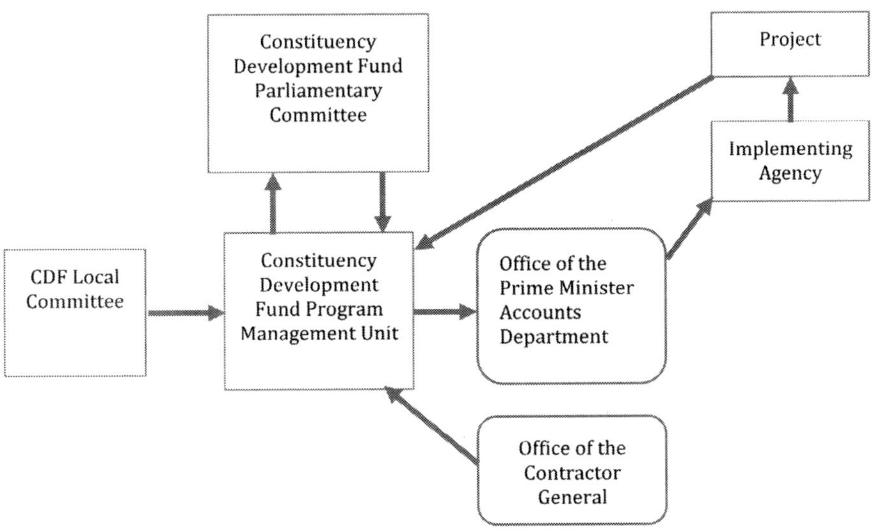

Figure 6.1

The CDF is structured along the line of multiple levels of accountability and transparency. The OPM is given the responsibility for the management and disbursement of the Fund and to ensure that it operates along lines of transparency and accountability to ensure that local communities become stakeholders in their own development. To this end the CDFLC, which is chaired by the constituencies' MP is mandated to develop local project proposals and to guide and monitor the use of CDF resources. The CDFLC is comprised of:

- The MP.
- The constituency caretakers for the two major political parties.
- Religious leaders from the constituency.
- Business community leaders from the constituency.
- Citizen association representatives.
- And other community leaders.

The CDFLC is responsible for identifying projects to be undertaken, areas of pressing community needs as well as individuals in need of special social assistance. The CDFLC meets periodically to ensure fairness in the selection of local project proposals, the efficient and effective execution of CDF-funded projects and that projects are compliant with stipulated policies that govern procurement procedures.

Project proposals are submitted to the CDFPMU which is responsible for reviewing projects to ensure that they satisfy all the criteria to receive funding and that the overall CDF annual budget is not exceeded. The CDFPMU also provides technical assistance to the CDFLC in the development of project proposals and liaises with the relevant government agencies to ensure that proposed projects conform to the procurement standards and practices of the government. The CDFPMU also monitors the implementation of all CDF projects and activities to ensure that projects are managed properly and that they achieve their objectives within the proposed time and budget. A central component of the monitoring process is that government agencies that are given the responsibility of implementing CDF projects are required to submit monthly progress reports on the performance of all projects and activities to the CDFPMU. The operations of the CDFPMU itself is also monitored and audited by the OCG. In 2009, the OCG audited two hundred projects with an associated aggregated approved disbursed sum that valued approximately JA$447,742,859.82.[37] It is important to note that in its 2009 audit of the CDFPMU the OCG found no evidence of political corruption in the administration of the CDF nor was there any evidence of the misuse of the CDF funds. The OCG, however, found that there were several procedural inconsistencies in the practice of the CDF process. These included the following:

1. Misunderstandings of the role and responsibilities of the implementing agencies with respect to the disbursement of the funds and the overall CDF process.
2. There were also conflicting project status reports of the CDF, which were received from the CDFPMU and the implementing agencies.
3. Project status reports that were received from the CDFPMU were at times found to be vague, especially in respect to projects that were classified as "Physical Infrastructure" projects.
4. The OCG found that the CDFPMU at times was not operating in accordance with the CDF Operational Manual, which was used as a guide in the OCG's monitoring exercise.
5. The CDFPMU at times failed to respond to the OCG's formal requisition request in a timely manner.[38]

However, while the OCG acknowledged that these procedural inconsistencies were largely a function of the fact that the "CDFPMU operates as a Secretariat with marginal resources," it was of the opinion that the CDFPMU was not "operating effectively and efficiently in accordance with the provisions which are outlined in its Operational Procedures and that the CDFPMU has indicated that the project document is to be revised."[39]

Project proposals that are vetted by the CDFPMU are submitted to the CDFPC—a subcommittee of the House of Representatives that is comprised of government and opposition MPs who are responsible for the final review and approval of all CDF projects.

Once projects have been approved by the CDFPC, the CDFPMU makes a request to the OPM's Finance and Accounts Branch (FAB) for the funding of the project. The Finance and Accounts Branch of the OPM disburse funds directly to the implementing agencies whether they are government agencies or Parish Councils. It is important to note that no cash that is intended to finance CDF projects goes directly or indirectly to the MP or to individuals within the MP's constituency. Funds for approved projects are electronically transferred from the OPM's Finance and Accounts Branch to the bank accounts of the government agencies or the Parish Councils that are responsible for the implementation of the project. In instances where CDF resources are used in MPs constituencies to make repairs to homes or used to pay tuition fees, no cash goes directly to the MP or to the individual homeowner or to the parents of students. Instead, CDF monies are used to purchase the approved supplies from the hardware store that offers the lowest cost for the supplies. The Parish Council then instructs the homeowner to retrieve the supplies from the hardware store. When CDF resources are used to fund tuition fees these resources go directly to the schools where the students are enrolled.

The OPM's Finance and Accounts Branch also monitors the implementing agencies to ensure that all funds disbursed to them are properly managed and applied to the approved projects. Therefore, allegations among some members of the media, specifically the *Jamaica Gleaner*, that the CDF is just another form of "Pork-Barrel" political corruption is uninformed about the ways in which the CDF is structured and organized.

Figures 6.2.1 through 6.2.4 show a small sample of CDF projects that range from the funding of an advanced adult math class in the urban constituency of Southern St. Andrew, to the construction of an agricultural green house and the proposed rehabilitation of the Linstead hospital in the respective rural constituencies of Eastern Portland and North Western St. Catherine.

The Politics of the CDF

The administration of the CDF in Jamaica is driven by the executive branch of government and is similar to the administration of political earmarks as practiced in the United States and Kenya. The CDF in Jamaica was created to bring government closer to the people and could potentially erode the power

Figure 6.2.1 CDF Funded Adult Advanced Math Class at Charley Smith High School MP Dr. Omar Lloyd Davis (Constituency: St. Andrew Southern).

Figure 6.2.2 CDF & Canadian Development Corporation Funded Agricultural Green House MP Dr. Patrick Harris (Constituency: Trelawny Northern).

Figure 6.2.3 Proposed Rehabilitation of the Linstead Hospital using CDF Funds MP Mr. Robert Dixon Pickersgill (Constituency: St. Catherine North Western).

Figure 6.2.4 Proposed Rehabilitation of the Linstead Hospital using CDF Funds MP Mr. Robert Dixon Pickersgill (Constituency: St. Catherine North Western).

of Dons. Interviews with Jamaican MPs on both sides of the political aisle revealed that they do not see the CDF as government resources that solidify the base of their political support. To the contrary, Jamaican MPs view the CDF as a way to enhance the delivery of service to their constituencies and as such are held electorally accountable for the quality of such service.

The Perception of Political Corruption and the CDF

The comparison between the CDF in Jamaica and the "system" of pork barrel politics as practiced in US national and state governments has fed the public perception that the CDF is simply another form of government corruption. Perceptions of corruption raise questions about the effectiveness of the state's delivery of services, the extent to which the delivery of state services is transparent and accountable and the extent to which the participation of civil society groups in shaping public policy is meaningful. In Jamaica, many of these concerns and perceptions of government corruption have largely come from the editorials pages of the *Gleaner*, the Island's most influential newspaper. Editorials have called for the immediate dismantling of the CDF, arguing that the program is merely the personal slush fund for MPs and is devoid of any monitoring mechanisms to ensure accountability and transparency in the expenditure of public resources.[40]

While the editorials have been highly critical of the CDF, they have been quite limited in their ability to provide any compelling systematic evidence of political corruption in their administration. One editorial claimed to have uncovered evidence, albeit anecdotal, of political corruption in the use of the CDF. An article entitled "Natalie's Million Dollar Secret: What MPs were hiding in Constituency Development Talks" reported that in 2008 PNP MP Natalie Neita-Headley breached the rules of the CDF by going ahead with a JA$1.3 million roadwork project without first securing approval for the project from the CDFPMU and CDFPC.[41] However, far from proving pork barrel corruption the episode of "Natalie's Million Dollar Secret" proved quite the opposite and highlighted an instance of procedural error, not calculated corruption, that was caught and remedied by the various monitoring mechanisms that has been built into the design and structure of the CDF.[42]

One cannot claim that political corruption is not a problem in Jamaica or that it is not pervasive in some agencies of government or that some agencies may be more vulnerable to corruption than others.[43] In the case of CDFs, the structure of the CDF's implementation process provides no opportunity for MPs or individuals in MPs' constituencies to come into direct or indirect contact with CDF cash. This suggests that the various editorial claims by the Gleaner of pork barrel corruption in the administration of CDF resources is simply uninformed about the ways in which the CDF is structured and organized.[44]

The Role of Civil Society Groups in the Implementation of the CDF

An important proxy for the pervasiveness of corruption in government agencies is the absence of civil society groups in the policy-making process.[45] This is because civil society involvement in policy-making increases the probability that the operations of government will be transparent and accountable to societal interests that extend beyond the formal apparatus of the state. The implementation of the CDF's social welfare projects has increasingly involved the active participation of the Adventist Relief Developmental Agency (ADRA)—a nongovernmental organization that is affiliated with the Adventist church in Jamaica. In a focus group interview with the Manchester Parish Council, members noted that ADRA has provided additional assistance to CDF clients as well as to other residents in the community. In the rural communities of South Manchester ADRA is involved in housing development and repairs and plays a vital role in implementing the social welfare projects of the CDF. In many instances, ADRA has completed housing projects started with CDF resources by provide the necessary labor. Moreover, at the level of the CDFLC, ADRA interfaces with the MP in the development of project proposals that address the social welfare needs of the community. The CDFLC in Southwest Manchester developed a proposal to assist the constituency's poor by building toilets and providing assistance for housing development. In conjunction with the CDF, ADRA has taken on three housing projects by providing the labor while the resources from the CDF are used to secure the materials. ADRA's role in the implementation of CDF projects is not limited to the provision of labor. In some instances ADRA has purchased water storage tanks and has provided additional funding to complete housing projects that were started with CDF financing.[46]

While civil society groups like ADRA plays no role in the oversight of CDF projects, they are largely involved in the delivery of services and the implementation of social welfare projects that are labor intensive. Hence, their participation in the development and implementation of CDF projects strengthens a core objective of the CDF, which is to bring government and the people close together.

In a similar manner, CDFs often serve as a catalyst to trigger additional resources from international developmental donor countries and agencies who along with the CDF funds agricultural and animal husbandry projects in some rural constituencies in Jamaica.[47] For example, in the constituency of Northern Trelawney, CDF funding has been instrumental in triggering additional financing from the Canadian International Development Agency (CIDA) to stock and breed animal farms with a specialized breed of pigs and the building of greenhouses that produce vegetables. The use of CDF resources in these ways mitigates the burden of continued operating expenditures that has often been a problem for CDF-funded projects. However, the use of CDF funding as a trigger for additional resources is not routinely replicated and is only possible where the funding objectives of the CDF is congruent with the objectives of external donors like the CIDA. In this instance the CDF project in Northern Trelawney was consistent with CIDA's Canada Fund for Local Initiatives (CFLI). The CFLI is designed to provide funding for small projects that are implemented by local organizations in Jamaica that offer direct social, economic, or technical assistance to local populations. Priority is normally given to projects that increase the self-reliance of local communities and organizations so that gains can be sustained after project funding ends.[48] These are all priorities that are consistent with the policy objectives of the CDF, which along with other objectives is designed to promote human and infrastructure development that originate from local communities and increase the self-reliance of these communities.

The Challenges and Constraints of the CDF

In the wake of the global economic recession, talks between the Golden government and the IMF to secure financing to manage the country's large balance of payments deficit increases the likelihood that in the coming fiscal year the budget for the CDF will be significantly reduced from levels seen in fiscal year 2008–2009. Budgetary cuts not only threaten to drastically reduce much needed funding for community development but also weakens the effective administrative monitoring of the CDF. For example, major cuts to the staff of CDFPMU have already made it difficult for the CDFPMU to respond to the OCG's formal requests for information that is needed to effectively monitor the CDF.[49]

The Need for Further Research

Interviews with MPs from both political parties, the staff of the CDFPMU, the Chairman of the CDFPC and implementing agencies such as the National Works Agency, the Rural Electrification Program, the Manchester and Westmoreland Parish Councils all believe that the CDF exerts a reductive effect on crime while exerting a positive effect on various aspects of development such as agricultural production, employment and education. To better assess the developmental impact of the CDF future research should supplement the qualitative information that this report presents by employing quantitative statistical techniques to generate systematic estimates of the effects of CDF resources on constituency-level measures of development in Jamaica and elsewhere in the developing world. It would be worthwhile to empirically test the following hypotheses:

1. Is an increase in CDF funding likely to increase constituencies' per capita income?
2. Is an increase in CDF funding likely to increase constituencies' agricultural output?
3. Is an increase in CDF funding likely to increase constituencies' level of employment?
4. Is an increase in CDF funding likely to increase constituencies' educational achievement?
5. Is an increase in CDF funding likely to increase constituencies' literacy rates?
6. Is an increase in CDF funding likely to increase constituencies' access to health care?
7. Is an increase in CDF funding likely to improve constituencies' overall health?
8. Is an increase in CDF funding likely to reduce the level of crime and violence in constituencies?

GLOSSARY OF KEY TERMS

ADRA – Adventist Relief Developmental Agency
CDF – Constituency Development Fund
CDFLC – Constituency Development Fund Local committee
CDFPMU – Constituency Development Fund Program Management Unit
CDFPC – Constituency Development Fund Parliamentary Committee
CIDA – Canadian International Development Agency
FAB – Finance and Accounts Branch
IMF – International Monetary Fund
LDP – Local Development Program
LUJ – Lift Up Jamaica Program
OPM – Office of the Prime Minister
OCG – Office of the Contractor General
SESP – Social and Economic Support Program

NOTES

1. Ministry of Finance and the Public Service, 2011, 44; and Ministry of Financing and Planning, 2008.
2. Scott, 1972.
3. Stephens and Stephens, 1986.
4. Stone, 1973, 93.
5. van de Walle. 2009.
6. Ibid., 3.
7. Ibid., 4.
8. Stone, 80.
9. Stone, 1980, 97–103.
10. Bartilow, 1997.
11. Interview with JLP MP Pearnel Patroe Charles, 2010.
12. USAID. 2008, 6.
13. Ibid., 19.
14. Focused group interviews in Jamaica were conducted with eight members of the Westmoreland Parish Council and 10 members of the Manchester Parish Council. Ms Moveta Monroe, head of the Constituency Development Fund Program Management Unit was present at the interviews and facilitated this researcher's access to the Parish Council members. In both instances the interviews lasted approximately one hour and forty-five minutes. Parish Council members responded to the following questions: (1) describe the process of implementing CDF projects at the level of Parish Council? (2) What effect, do you believe, that CDF projects have on crime in communities where such projects are implemented? (3) Do CDF projects erode the power of Dons while reasserting the political credibility and relevance of MPs within communities where CDF projects are implemented?

15. Interview with the Westmoreland Parish Council.

16. Interview with the Manchester Parish Council.

17. Individual interviews were conducted with PNP MP Robert Pickersgill; JLP MP Pernel Patroe Charles; PNP MP Dr. Omar Davis; JLP MP and Chairman of the Constituency Development Fund Parliamentary committee, Everald Warmington; and PNP MP Dr. Patrick Harris. These interviews lasted for one hour and MPs were asked the following questions: (1) describe your role as an MP in the design and implementation of CDF projects in your constituency? (2) What effect, do you believe, that CDF projects have on crime in communities where such projects are implemented? (3) From your perspective, do CDF projects erode the power of Dons while reasserting the political credibility and relevance of MPs within communities where such projects are implemented?

18. Interview with PNP MP Robert Pickersgill.

19. Barkan, 2008, 124–137.

20. Fenno, Jr. 2002.

21. Ibid., 126.

22. Barkan 2008, 126 and Barkan, 2009, 6–8.

23. Henry, February 2, 2008.

24. Interview with Floyd Morris.

25. Ibid.

26. Inter-American Development Bank. 2005, 12.

27. Interview with Floyd Morris.

28. Ministry of Finance. 1999.

29. Urban Development Corporation. 1999.

30. Ibid.

31. Interview with Floyd Morris.

32. Interview with JLP MP Pearnel Patroe Charles.

33. Interview with Floyd Morris.

34. Office of the Contractor General. *Contractor General's Annual Report*, 2009, 103.

35. Jamaica Observer, 2009, *MPs make full use of constituency funds.*

36. Jamaica Labour Party. 2008, *Work Commences On Projects Under CDF.*

37. Office of the Contractor General. *Contractor General's Annual Report*, 2009, 103.

38. Office of the Contractor General. *Contractor General's Annual Report*, 2009, 108.

39. Office of the Contractor General. *Contractor General's Annual Report*, 2009, 108.

40. See Gleaner Editorial. 2008. "Mr. Golding's Barrel of Pork."; ———. 2009. "May the CDF Go in Peace."; ———. 2009. "Let the CDF trough go dry."; ———. 2009. "Foregoing constituency pork."; ———. 2010. "MPs should spurn CDF."; ———. 2010. "Another Case Against CDF Pork."; ———. 2010. "Dismantle the 'creng creng'."; and ———. 2010. "The Ascendancy of Political Pork."

41. Reid, 2010. "Natalie's Million Dollar Secret: What the MPs were hiding in Constituency Development Fund Talks."

42. See Interview with CDFPC Chairman JLP MP Everald Warmington; and Interview with PNP MP Robert Pickersgill.

43. USAID, 10 & 17.

44. Interviews with Ms. Moveta Monroe, head of the CDFPMU and Ms Pauline Scott Blair, Project Development Specialist of the CDFMU and MP Everald Warmington, Chairman of the CDFPC, revealed that the Gleaner has never sought information from the Office of the Prime Minister, the Cabinet Office, the CDFPC or the Ministry of Finance and the Public Service on the policies and/operational guidelines and procedures of the CDF.

45. USAID, 4.

46. Interview with the Manchester Parish Council.

47. Interview with PNP MP Dr. Patrick Harris.

48. Canadian International Development Agency, 2011.

49. Office of the Contractor General. *Contractor General's Annual Report*, 2009, 108.

REFERENCES

Barkan, Joel D. 2008. "Progress and Retreat in Africa: Legislatures on the Rise?" *Journal of Democracy* 19 (2): 124–137.

———, ed. 2009. "Legislative Power in Emerging African Democracies." In *Legislative Power in Emerging African Democracies*. Bolder: Lynne Rienner Publisher. 1–31.

Bartilow, Horace A. 1997. *The debt dilemma: IMF Negotiations in Jamaica, Grenada and Guyana*. of *Warwick University Caribbean studies*. London: Caribbean.

Canadian International Development Agency. 2011. "Project Profile for Canada Fund for Local Initiatives (CFLI) - Jamaica - 2011–2012." http://www.acdi-cida.gc.ca/CIDAWEB/cpo.nsf/vWebCSAZEn/80C699E9B9DE65028525787F003718B0.

Eggen, Dan. 2010. "U.S.-Jamaica Relations Tested by Lobbying Dispute." In *The Washington Post*. Washington D.C.

Gleaner Editorial. 2008. "Mr. Golding's Barrel of Pork." In *The Gleaner*. Kingston: The Gleaner.

———. 2009a. "May the CDF Go in Peace." In *The Gleaner*. Kingston.

———. 2009b. "Let the CDF trough go dry." In *The Gleaner*. Kingston.

———. 2009c. "Foregoing constituency pork." In *The Gleaner*. Kingston.

———. 2010a. "MPs should spurn CDF." In *The Gleaner*. Kingston.

———. 2010b. "Another Case Against CDF Pork." In *The Gleaner*. Kingston.

———. 2010c. "Dismantle the 'creng creng'." In *The Gleaner*. Kingston.

———. 2010d. "The Ascendancy of Political Pork." In *The Gleaner*. Kingston.

Henry, Martin. February 2, 2008. "The Constituency Development Fund." In *Jamaica Gleaner*. Kingston.

Inter-American Development Bank. 2005. "Jamaica Social Safety Net Reform." In. Washington, D.C: Inter-American Development Bank. 12.

Interview with CDFPC Chairman JLP MP Everald Warmington. November 12, 2010.

Interview with Floyd Morris former Minister of State. November 10, 2010.
Interview with JLP MP Pearnel Patroe Charles. November 19 2010.
Interview with PNP MP Dr. Patrick Harris. November 23, 2010.
Interview with PNP MP Robert Pickersgill. November 11, 2010.
Interview with the Manchester Parish Council. November 18, 2010.
Interview with the Westmoreland Parish Council. November 19, 2010.
Ministry of Finance. 1978. "The Local Development Program." In. Kingston, Jamaica: Government of Jamaica.
———. 1992. "The Social and Economic Support Program." In. Kingston, Jamaica: Government of Jamaica.
———. 1999. "Lift Up Jamaica Program." In. Kingston, Jamaica: Government of Jamaica.
Ministry of Finance and the Public Service. 2011. "Revised Constituency Development Fund (CDF): Operational Procedures." In. Kingston, Jamaica: Miniatry of Finance and the Public Service. 44.
Ministry of Financing and Planning. 2008. *Constituency Development Fund Operational Procedures.*
Nicholas van de Walle. 2009. "The Democratization of Political Clientelism in Sub-Saharan Africa." Presented at the 3rd European Conference on African Studies, Leipzig, Germany.
Office of the Contractor General. 2009. *Contractor General's Annual Report.*
———. 2009. *Monitoring of the Constituency Development Fund.*
Reid, Tony. 2010. "Natalie's Million Dollar Secret: What the MPs were Hiding in Constituency Development Fund Talks." In *The Gleaner*. Kingston: The Gleaner.
Richard F. Fenno, Jr. 2002. *Home Style: House Members in the Districts.* New York: Longman.
Scott, James. 1972. *Comparative Political Corruption.* New Jersey: Prentice Hall.
Stephens, Evelyne Huber and John D. Stephens. 1986. *Democratic Socialism in Jamaica: The Political and Social Transformation in Dependent Capitalism.* New Jeresy: Princeton University Press.
Stone, Carl. 1973. "Class, Race and Political Behavior in Urban Jamaica." In. Mona: Institute for Social and Economic Research, University of the West Indies.
———. 1980. *Democracy and clientelism in Jamaica.* New Brunswick, N.J.: Transaction Books.
Urban Development Corporation. 1999. "The UDC and the Coordination of the Lift Up Jamaica Program." In. Kingston, Jamaica: Social Development Commission.
USAID. 2008. "Corruption Assessment for Jamaica." In, ed. Margaret O'Donnell and Trevor Munroe Corbin Lyday, Management Systems International. Washington, DC USAID.

Chapter 7

Constituency Needs, Constitutional Propriety and Clientelist Patronage

Constituency Development Funds in India

Harry Blair

INTRODUCTION

Among the constituency development fund (CDF) programs adopted in many countries, particularly in the British Commonwealth, India's is by far the largest and most complex, and perhaps the oldest as well. Since 1993, India has had in place a CDF which at the time of my research in 2010 was allocating some US $465,000 annually to each member of its upper and lower houses of parliament (MPs), and which they in turn designate to local infrastructural projects averaging around US $8500 each.[1] Known as the Member of Parliament Local Area Development Scheme (MPLADS), the program has become fundamental to MPs' efforts to maintain ongoing connections to their constituencies. Most of the states in India's federal system, as well as a good number of urban governments, have similar provisions. Given the country's lively civil society and a freewheeling media over this period—amplified recently by a Right to Information law—these Local Area Development Schemes (LADS) have been analyzed and critiqued in considerable depth, both positively and negatively.

On the positive side, it is argued that the LADS system allows MPs to fill in some of the developmental gaps inevitably left by the bureaucracy at all levels and strengthens the linkages between representative and constituency that are critical to democratic governance. On the negative side, two separate kinds of arguments have emerged. The first asserts that LADS has simply provided new paths for manipulation, patronage and graft in a polity that has been plagued by all three problems for decades and indeed centuries. The second holds that by giving MPs authority to allocate funds to specific public projects, LADS violates the constitutional authority of the executive branch of government: legislators should make policy and enact laws, not build culverts and schoolhouses. All three perspectives will be discussed here in some detail.

BACKGROUND AND ORIGINS

Up to the early 1970s, or in other words for roughly the first quarter century of India's independence, national and state elections were held simultaneously, meaning that MPs and members of each state's Legislative Assembly (MLAs) campaigned at the same time. MLA seats have always been nested within parliamentary constituencies, such that each MP has between five and eight MLA seats contained within his own. In contrast with the American experience, in which candidates for lower-level offices are often perceived to "ride on the coattails" of those for higher positions, Indian coattails have stretched in the opposite direction. Local elections, even down to the village level, have tended to excite more interest than higher level contests,[2] such that MP candidates could to a considerable extent coast along in the wake created by MLA contestants. This system significantly helped the Indian National Congress retain electoral majorities at both state and national levels in the country's first several elections by using MLA candidates as intermediaries to mobilize votes for the MP on the same party ticket. In 1971, however, instead of waiting for Parliament's full five-year term to end, Prime Minister Indira Gandhi called a snap election at the national level, meaning that MP contestants had to run for office without the aid of MLA candidates running parallel campaigns. In other words, bereft of their beaters on the hunt for votes, MP hopefuls had to flush out potential game with their own efforts.[3]

In India as elsewhere, politicians have long had a good number of ways to maintain linkages with voters. Networks of intermediaries, local bosses, camp followers, brokers, enforcers, and "vote banks," all maintained through ties of kinship and patron-client connections based on landholdings, have been the principal ones historically, with moneys siphoned from government-funded development programs furnishing extra lubrication in the post-independence era. But as the nonagricultural economy expanded, labor became more mobile, urbanization increased, and voters came to expect more from their political leaders than occasional forays in search of votes at election time, new mechanisms to connect political leaders with their constituencies became more desirable, especially after MP and MLA elections were "delinked."

One such mechanism first emerged in the Bombay Municipal Corporation (the city's elected governing body) in the mid-1970s, when each council member (known as a "corporator") was allotted Rs 50,000 annually to devote at his own discretion to municipal works in his ward, with the corporation undertaking the works so designated. By the mid-1990s, these funds had been increased to Rs 900,000 annually per corporator. In the mid-1980s, the program was taken up by Maharashtra state (of which Bombay was the capital), with a discretionary program for each MLA. Introduced at Rs 1 million, the allocations had grown to Rs 4 million by the early 1990s. Several other states followed suit, including Uttar Pradesh, the country's largest.[4]

Inspired by these state-level developments, MPs at the center in New Delhi began demanding a similar nationwide fund for themselves. Spearheaded by an MP from Bombay, Ram Naik, they prevailed upon then-Prime Minister Narasimha Rao to support their request. Thus in December 1993, an MPLADS was created by the Parliament, with a Rs 5 million allocation for each MP, raised the next year to 10 million (Rs "1 crore" in South Asian terms) annually for each MP. Five years later, the annual allocation was increased to Rs 20 million, where it stayed until 2011.[5]

These allowances are available to members of both the lower house (Lok Sabha) and the upper house (Rajya Sabha). The present paper will deal principally with the Lok Sabha MPs, who are directly elected in individual constituencies using the first-past-the-post system widespread in Westminster-style democracies. Accordingly, the acronym "MP" will refer to Lok Sabha members unless otherwise indicated.[6] Lok Sabha members must allocate their LADS funds within their constituency, while Rajya Sabha can direct their funds anywhere within their state.

HOW THE PROGRAM WORKS

As MPLADS went on, its regulations expanded. Its first set of Guidelines setting out the brand new program comprised only seven pages (and that included two cover pages!), but as experience accumulated, the rules governing it expanded, partly in response to criticisms and partly as the ministry administering the program crafted new rules to make the system more effective. A fourth edition of the *Guidelines* (now taking up fully 38 pages) appeared in 2005, and a fifth edition was expected to appear in 2011.[7]

The rules for MPLADS are spelled out in an official *Guidelines* publication issued by the Ministry of Statistics and Programme Implementation in New Delhi (MOSPI), which is charged with oversight of the program. As of 2010, the major features of MPLADS were these:

- Funds must be used to create "durable assets," in particular ones enhancing drinking water, education, public health, sanitation and roads; some works are specifically prohibited, such as private, commercial or religious structures, land acquisition, maintenance of any kind, and buildings intended for central or state governments (buildings intended for local governments are permitted).

- A specified proportion of each MP's fund must go to works benefiting Scheduled Caste (Dalit, or formerly Untouchable) and Scheduled Tribe (Adivasi) populations.[8]
- MPLADS projects are approved and monitored by the chief administrative officer (designated for this purpose as the "District Authority") of the district within which they are to take place.[9] This District Authority determines whether a project is technically feasible and whether it comes within the parameters set out in the *Guidelines*.
- The agency actually implementing each MPLADS project is selected by the District Authority. In general Panchayati Raj (local government units at village, township and district level) bodies are expected to undertake this work, but the District Authority can select a government agency or a capable nongovernmental organization (NGO) instead. Commercial contractors are prohibited.
- The District Authority is required to inspect at least 10% of all the works under implementation each year.
- MPLADS funds can be pooled with those provided by government agencies at any level, so long as the latter are used first and the former leads to completion of the work. In other words, MPs can use their funds as matching grants to leverage state investments in infrastructure.
- MPLADS funds are "non-lapsable," meaning that unlike most government allocations, they do not revert back to their source if unused during the fiscal year. Instead, they accumulate from year to year, even over an election, so that the MP (or his successor) can spend them in the following term.
- Under the national Right to Information Act of 2005 any citizen has the right to obtain information on any aspect of MPLADS and the work undertaken by it.
- A stone or metal plaque identifying the sponsoring MP is to be "permanently erected" for each completed project.

THE SIZE AND IMPACT OF LADS

In December 2010 Rs 20 million allocation for each MP equaled approximately US $465,000 for a constituency averaging around 2.2 million in population. If we use the UNDP's measure Purchasing Power Parity (PPP) dollars as a multiplier,[10] that Rs 20 million amounted to roughly PPP$ 1.3 million at an MP's command, or about PPP$ 0.60 per citizen per year. The sum seems small when compared with per capita income, which in 2010 was reckoned at PPP$ 3176. Nor is it very large when viewed against total government spending, which runs around Rs 1 billion per district, an area roughly equivalent to an MP constituency.

In terms of local impact, however, LADS wields a considerably larger footprint. To begin with, about 60% of that Rs 1 billion district budget goes to "establishment" (i.e., personnel) costs, and of the remaining 40% that goes to investment, only around 14% or Rs 140 million is discretionary. In other words, at Rs 20 million, the MPLADS allotment represents a sum equivalent to about one-seventh of what all local governments can invest on a discretionary basis. State-level MLAs generally have proportionally larger funds to spend. In Karnataka, each MLA receives an annual LADS allotment of Rs 10 million, and there are six MLA seats within each MP constituency. Thus the six MLAs collectively have Rs 60 million to invest, or three times as much as the MP, a sum equivalent to three sevenths of the state funding available for local investment purposes. Taken together, then, the MP (Rs 20m) plus the MLAs (Rs 60m) can invest Rs 80m, or more than half as much as the entire governmental apparatus has at its discretionary disposal for investment within the boundaries of the average MP constituency.

In addition to MPs and MLAs, elected council members in some municipal corporations also receive LADS allotments. Thus Hyderabad, a city of some four million inhabitants in southern India, has 150 corporators, each of whom gets Rs 4m in LADS funds every year. This would mean each corporator receives about Rs 160 per constituent, which would be a bit less than US $4, or in PPP terms would be just over $10. Collectively, the MPs, MLAs and corporators can spend about PPP$ 14.50 per citizen in Hyderabad—a great deal more than the PPP$ 0.60 available to an MP alone. LADS is definitely a complex program.

ADMINISTRATIVE BOUNDARIES AND TIERS OF GOVERNANCE

India has 626 administrative districts and 543 parliamentary constituencies, and the boundaries of these two types of units only sometimes coincide exactly. Thus an MP's seat often includes parts of two or more districts, while a district can frequently be split between two or more constituencies. It follows then that an individual MP can have to deal with multiple District Authorities, and a single District Authority can have several MPs allocating their LADS money within his/her territory. Given the huge demands on this officer's time because of his responsibility for almost all government administrative activity within his district (with an average population approaching two million), it is not surprising that supervision of the MPLADS program may not be as comprehensive as one might hope. Thus there have been problems with meeting the 10% project inspection rule, even given that the District Authority is permitted to assign the task to subordinates. In short, placing the responsibility for implementing and monitoring MPLADS on a District Authority has not proven a very effective way to manage the program.

India's multiple tiers of governance add another measure of complexity, albeit one that can have synergistic effects at times. When an MP and MLA are of the same political party, they can combine their funds or extend them in coordination across a larger number of projects than either could do alone. For instance, if an MP has 3 MLAs of his own party within his constituency and each MLA has a LADS fund of Rs 10 million, then together they have Rs 50 million that they can deploy in discrete projects across their area, which collectively (they can hope) will motivate voters to support them in the next election. But where an MP and his MLAs are of a different party, it is likely that the political impact of any projects he initiates will be neutralized by those launched by MLAs. In urban areas with municipal corporations that have LADS programs for their corporators, the problem is intensified one step further.

In sum, the structural aspects of this huge country with its multiple tiers of governance and overlapping boundaries between electoral and administrative units make for considerable confusion and even contradiction. Legislators often have to deal with several different administrators, while administrative officers frequently find themselves having to handle the differing demands of national and state level representatives (and sometime city corporators as well). In some places, the legislators can act in synergistic concert with elected party members at different levels, but probably more often in this highly competitive and vigorously contested polity, they find themselves confronting elected officials of other parties in other governance tiers. The multiplicity of legislative tiers and divided administrative units also makes it much more difficult to assess the extent to which the various LADS programs have individually or collectively had any actual impact on development. Balanced against this confusion, one could argue that on the other hand it is the voters who stand to benefit from multiple legislators bringing infrastructural assets to their constituencies.

ASSESSING LADS IMPACT

The Legislators' View of LADS Programs

When interviewed, most legislators at both national and state levels thought very highly of their LADS programs. Most frequently mentioned was the thought that "When voters ask me what have I done for them, what could I say if it were not for MPLADS?" This was accompanied by the observation that voters are not impressed by contributions to macro-level policy or foreign affairs or participation in important international conferences, but rather are concerned with their own day-to-day existence, and LADS gives a legislator the opportunity to accomplish something demonstrable in his constituency.

Some legislators complained that LADS actually constituted something of a burden in that, while constituent demands for projects was huge, funds to meet the demands were quite limited. Consequently, for every village that received streetlights or drinking water facilities, there were other villages that had to be disappointed. To be sure, this is a grumble heard from elected officeholders everywhere, but the very existence of LADS means that Indian legislators cannot credibly blame the bureaucracy for repeated failure to meet public demand for infrastructural investment. When constituents know that their representative has at least some command over how state resources are directed, they can reproach him or her for not directing some of those resources their way. Nonetheless, most legislators believe that the benefits of LADS far outweigh the discomforts arising from constituent unhappiness.

How Legislators Have Allocated their LADS Funds

Legislators allocated their funds to a wide variety of projects. Here are some examples:

- **Roads.** Road construction remains a popular activity, amounting to almost one-third of all MPLADS works supported and 37% of all funds expended so far, more than any other sector, as is evident in Table 7.1.
- **Electrification.** Even today, something like 15% of India's almost 600,000 villages remain unelectrified, meaning that MPs from rural areas face serious demands for expanding the power grid. To make up part of the gap, one MP plans to spend much of his MPLADS fund on solar-powered lamps that girls would bring to school each day to get recharged from a solar generator, thereby increasing school attendance and at the same time providing a great improvement over the kerosene lanterns that have been the main source of lighting in village homes. Ten percent of his annual fund would buy about 1200 such lamps. Another MP has been putting solar street lights in unelectrified villages (a hundred of them would take about 10% of his annual LADS fund).
- **Drinking water.** Safe drinking water has become a serious problem in many areas, because of salinization due to overused irrigation systems and arsenic in the water table. One MP is trying to move some of his LADS fund into water purification machines, though he is having trouble because the program won't support equipment rentals (they would not be

"durable assets"), while another is promoting deep wells that would bore beneath arsenic-tainted layers in the water table.

- **Public buildings.** This category can cover a wide variety of structures (though they cannot be intended for government use). Examples would be storm protection shelters, orphanages, libraries, hostels and old age centers. One prominent category is the "community hall," which sounds like a neighborhood meeting hall, but which is often a building intended for a particular ethnic group like a caste, which would be improper under the MPLADS guidelines.
- **Bigger projects.** One MP, who was able to coordinate with several MLAs of the same party in his urban constituency, devoted all his fund in one year to rebuilding a railroad overpass at a critical intersection, while his MLA counterparts invested their allotments in smaller and more dispersed projects. Another MP spent his entire allotment on a hospital.

Data have now been compiled and released for a bit more than 40% of the moneys spent so far on MPLADS, as presented in Table 7.1. Here it will be

Table 7.1 Sectoral Distribution of Works Sanctioned by MPLADS, 1994–2009

	No. of Works Sanctioned	*% of Works Sanctioned*	*Cost of Works Sanctioned (Rs millions)*	*% of Total Allocations*	*Average Cost per Project (Rs millions)*
Roads, Pathways and Bridges	155080	32.0%	30060.38	37.2%	0.19
Other Public Facilities	137380	28.3%	19767.69	24.5%	0.14
Education	79002	16.3%	14283.91	17.7%	0.18
Drinking Water Facility	52615	10.8%	5328.20	6.6%	0.10
Sanitation and Public Health	18203	3.8%	2810.67	3.5%	0.15
Electricity Facility	17724	3.7%	2484.98	3.1%	0.14
Health and Family Welfare	5982	1.2%	2161.88	2.7%	0.36
Irrigation	8600	1.8%	2042.61	2.5%	0.24
Sports	8026	1.7%	1475.32	1.8%	0.18
Animal Care	2170	0.4%	273.48	0.3%	0.13
Non-conventional Energy Sources	324	0.1%	65.43	0.1%	0.20
Total	**485106**	**100.0%**	**80754.54**	**100.0%**	**0.17**

Note: These figures represent works over the entire history of MPLADS (1994–2009), "culled from the data so far uploaded on the software, which can be considered a sample of the total number of works sanctioned under the scheme." The total expenditure shown here (Rs 80.754 billion) constitutes about 42% of the grand total amount expended altogether under MPLADS as of March 2009. (GOI 2010: 16, 22). It is not possible to ascertain the extent to which this "sample" is representative of the whole universe of works undertaken or their cost.

seen that roadworks are the largest category, with "other public facilities" second followed by education. A 2001 outside review of more than 17,000 MPLADS projects in 57 sample constituencies found that some 46% of completed projects over the 1994–1998 period cost less than Rs 50,000 (around US $1600 in the mid-1990s and about US $1350 in 2001) and 67% cost less than Rs 100,000.[11] It concluded that far too many of the works were

> so small that one may classify [them] as petty works. The roads thus constructed are often *kachcha* [unpaved] and of short length because of inadequate funds . . . .This perhaps is not in conformity with the objective of creating durable assets.[12]

In more recent years, project size has increased markedly. In 2008–09 (the latest year available), cost per completed project in the two states for which I gathered data (all-India data were not available as such) came to Rs 345,000 (just over $8600 as of 2009).[13] Even though the sectoral priorities (roads vs. education, etc.) have remained essentially the same over the life of MPLADS, it is clear that larger projects were being undertaken. What had been a desire to spread activity around as many villages as possible had at least to some extent become a desire to create fewer, larger and hopefully more durable (as well as more visible to constituents) assets.

A closer look at a single state reveals a pattern of MPLADS priorities similar to that observed at the national level, as can be seen in Table 7.2, which breaks down the four largest spending sectors into subcategories for Karnataka over the same 1994–2009 period.[14] As for the country as a whole, here also "Roads, Pathways and Bridges" and "Other Public Facilities" have been the lead sectors, though in this case the latter takes first place. Interestingly, the biggest single subcategory in terms of actual projects has been "Community Centers," which account for almost 30% of all projects initiated thus far in the state. A very large proportion of these centers are surely the "community halls" mentioned by almost all the people I interviewed in Bangalore—buildings intended for specific communities of voters, generally local caste groups. Structures for particular caste communities are not specifically prohibited in Guidelines, but from the first edition these instructions have proscribed "works belonging to . . . private institutions," a wording that in the most recent version is rendered as "works belonging to private, cooperative and commercial organizations"—language that clearly rules out any building intended for the use of one caste group to the exclusion of all others.[15]

One suspects that "Buildings for cultural activities" at 4.5% of projects includes similar structures as well as religious buildings (also mentioned by a number of my respondents). A strict interpretation of the official guidelines

Table 7.2 Karnataka Summary of Works for MPLADS Program, 1994–2009 (Reported as of 29 January 2011)

S.No.	*Sector and Sub-sector*	*Total Sanctioned Cost of Works (Rs)*	*Total Number of Works*	*Percent of Funds*	*Percent of Works*	*Avg. Cost of Each Work (Rs)*
OTHER PUBLIC FACILITIES						
1	Battery operated buses for Government agencies	37,739,527	166	1.12%	0.76%	227,347
2	Boundary walls for buildings permissible in the scheme	41,205,450	354	1.22%	1.63%	116,400
3	Buildings for cultural activities	139,623,314	981	4.13%	4.51%	142,328
4	Common work sheds for artisans	1,870,000	12	0.06%	0.06%	155,833
5	Bus-sheds/stops for public transport passengers	60,535,147	668	1.79%	3.07%	90,621
6	Construction of common shelters for old and handicapped	4,350,000	20	0.13%	0.09%	217,500
7	Construction of community centers	886,701,744	6,464	26.20%	29.71%	137,175
8	Construction of public libraries & reading rooms	31,224,988	222	0.92%	1.02%	140,653
9	Crematoriums and structures on burial/cremation ground	25,442,024	174	0.75%	0.80%	146,219
10	Other public works not covered elsewhere	86,627,454	557	2.56%	2.56%	155,525
11	Public parks	6,559,012	64	0.19%	0.29%	102,485
12	Purchase of motor boats for flood and cyclone prone areas	2,557,151	17	0.08%	0.08%	150,421
Subtotal Other Public Facilities		**1,324,435,811**	**9,699**	**39.14%**	**44.58%**	**136,554**
ROADS, PATHWAYS & BRIDGES						
1	Construction of culverts and bridges	175,276,900	675	5.18%	3.10%	259,669
2	Construction of footpaths	14,237,500	87	0.42%	0.40%	163,649
3	Construction of roads, approach roads, link roads, pathways	886,479,249	5,467	26.20%	25.13%	162,151
4	Level crossing at unmanned railway crossing	4,173,910	10	0.12%	0.05%	417,391
Subtotal Roads, Pathways & Bridges		**1,080,167,559**	**6,239**	**31.92%**	**28.68%**	**173,132**

EDUCATION						
1	Building for Government educational institutions	172,316,957	785	5.09%	3.61%	219,512
2	Buildings for Government aided & unaided education institutions	198,676,663	766	5.87%	3.52%	259,369
3	Computers for Government and Government aided education institutions	28,406,299	111	0.84%	0.51%	255,913
4	Other projects for educational institutions	74,256,864	417	2.19%	1.92%	178,074
Subtotal Education		**473,656,783**	**2,079**	**14.00%**	**9.56%**	**227,829**
SPORTS						
1	Buildings for multi-gym	4,473,000	41	0.13%	0.19%	109,098
2	Buildings for physical training institutions	1,455,000	10	0.04%	0.05%	145,500
3	Buildings for sports activities	127,121,017	856	3.76%	3.93%	148,506
4	Fixed (immoveable) sport equipment	1,350,000	12	0.04%	0.06%	112,500
5	Other public projects for sport activities	12,418,016	70	0.37%	0.32%	177,400
Subtotal Sports		**146,817,033**	**989**	**4.34%**	**4.55%**	**148,450**
Drinking Water Facility		127,566,450	874	3.77%	4.02%	145,957
Sanitation & Public Health		85,317,426	877	2.52%	4.03%	97,283
Irrigation		69,284,955	487	2.05%	2.24%	142,269
Health & Family Welfare		48,873,437	263	1.44%	1.21%	185,831
Electricity Facility		14,503,570	169	0.43%	0.78%	85,820
Animal Care		8,361,008	57	0.25%	0.26%	146,684
Non-Conventional Energy Sources		4,802,368	22	0.14%	0.10%	218,289
GRAND TOTAL		**3,383,786,400**	**21,755**	**100.00%**	**100.00%**	**155,541**

prohibits both kinds of projects, but while temples and mosques are relatively easy to identify and reject on the part of the District Authority, "community halls" could very well be neighborhood social centers that are used by multiple groups rather than buildings intended to be used by only a single ethnic group. For example, the central government's MPLADS report for 2008–09 includes a picture of a "community hall" in Karnataka (see Figure 7.1).[16] The building is topped with a large image of the Hindu deity Hanuman, and although the edifice is not strictly speaking a religious temple, it does exude a religious aura that would discourage non-Hindus from entering it. So the line is fuzzy at best between what is legitimate and what is prohibited.

A second subcategory of interest here is the item labeled "Construction of roads, approach roads, link roads, pathways," which included almost 5,500 projects during the period. These efforts, costing on average just over Rs 160,000, fit more clearly within the MPLADS guidelines, as did two of the major subcategories in Education (Buildings for government educational institutions) and Sports (Buildings for sports activities). The remaining major subcategory (Buildings for Government aided & unaided educational institutions, at 5.87% of total MPLADS spending) represents a widening of the Guidelines in 1999, presumably to provide MPs more scope to meet community needs, but also allowing more latitude to favor "partymen"[17] and specific communities.

Figure 7.1 Community Hall Constructed with MPLADS Funding, Bagalkot District, Karnataka State, 2008–09. *Source*: GOI (2010: 90).

To move the discussion closer to the MP's interest, the bottom row showing 21,755 projects undertaken over MPLADS' 15 years implies an average of 777 projects for each of the state's 28 parliamentary constituencies with more than 200 of them devoted to "community centers" and almost 200 focusing on "roads, approach roads, link roads and pathways." Such a system allowed MPs to spread projects liberally around their constituencies to meet local needs, and presumably to build recognition and support for the next election.

TARGETING CONSTITUENCIES

Two World Bank researchers, Philip Keefer and Stuti Khemani, have looked at the political history of constituencies and party incumbencies as a factor motivating MPLADS spending.[18] They found that the more consistently voters in a constituency have supported a particular party, the less their MPs tended to spend their MPLADS funds, i.e., where politicians could take voter support for granted, they had less incentive to devote any effort to doling out these funds. Such a pattern would make sense when voter attachment is programmatic, for example poor voters supporting a leftist party committed to land reform or lower caste voters backing a party promising increased job or educational opportunities for "backward castes." But the story would likely be rather different where the relationship between politicians and voters is essentially clientelistic, such that lower-level patrons and bosses providing support to a party in return for promised material benefits, which would give the incumbent incentive to deploy MPLADS funds as patronage. In this second case, attachment to the party would continue only so long as material benefits were forthcoming from higher level; if they were to dry up, local bosses along with their followers would desert the party, or new brokers and fixers would move in and entice the followers to a different party, leaving the old operatives adrift without a base.

In a variant on this approach, several researchers have speculated that politicians would use funds like MPLADS to focus on marginal voters to draw them to their party while ignoring those who were already safely in the party fold.[19] Again this makes good sense on the spending side (put the money where it will bring the highest return in the form of votes) but perhaps somewhat less on the withholding side (disregarding the need to grease the patronage machinery to maintain voter allegiance among those already committed to the party).

In all these studies, the central motivation for directing MPLADS funds to certain areas makes good political sense in terms of rational choice (i.e., spend the money where it will bring the highest return), but the concomitant incentive to eschew spending in areas where support can be taken for granted fits less well into a political calculus. Loyalist "vote banks" will hold together in the short run on inertial momentum, but over the longer (or even middle) run, can political leaders count on clients continuing to provide their support after the patronage begins to run out? Program-based party loyalty can endure for long periods, these analyses assert, and some areas in India illustrate this, in particular West Bengal, where the land reform and pro-small farmer agendas of the Communist Party of India-Marxist (CPI[M]) contributed greatly to its hold on state power through successive elections for decades and to its MP delegation to New Delhi. In recent years, however, the CPM's sway has begun to crumble as its voters have defected, indicating that even deep programmatic party loyalties do not last indefinitely, especially when left unlubricated with LADS moneys.[20]

A POLITICAL BUSINESS CYCLE?

The fact that MPLADS funds are non-lapsable over an MP's normal 5-year term of office would appear to offer a strong incentive to parliamentarians (and their counterparts at state and municipal levels) to engage in "political business cycles"—to hoard their funds during the earlier years of the five-year cycle and then spend the surplus in the final year or two in order to make the maximum impression on voters for the upcoming election. Certainly political business cycles do exist at the macro level in a number of countries for parties in power facing election, though evidence is somewhat mixed.[21] And the opportunity to engage in such behavior at the individual legislator level in the Indian system would be tempting.

One study does find a statistically significant pattern along these lines, with MPs tending to spend less than their allotment during the first half and more of the 14th Lok Sabha (the national parliament over the 2004–2009 term of office) and presumably spending the surplus during the last couple of years before the election.[22] This holding back correlated in particular with age (older MPs spent less in the early years), the political spectrum (MPs on the left spent more evenly than those in the political center, while those on the right tended to hoard more than the centrists), constituent education (higher school attendance meant more even spending), and reported crime (lower crime rates matched with more even spending).

The Comptroller and Auditor General's (CAG) report issued in March 2011 appears to confirm a political business cycle, finding MPLADS expenditures to have risen by roughly 50% in the election years 2004–05 and 2008–09 in comparison with a trough in 2006–07 between elections, although MOSPI itself finds a somewhat different pattern, as appears in Figure 7.2.[23]

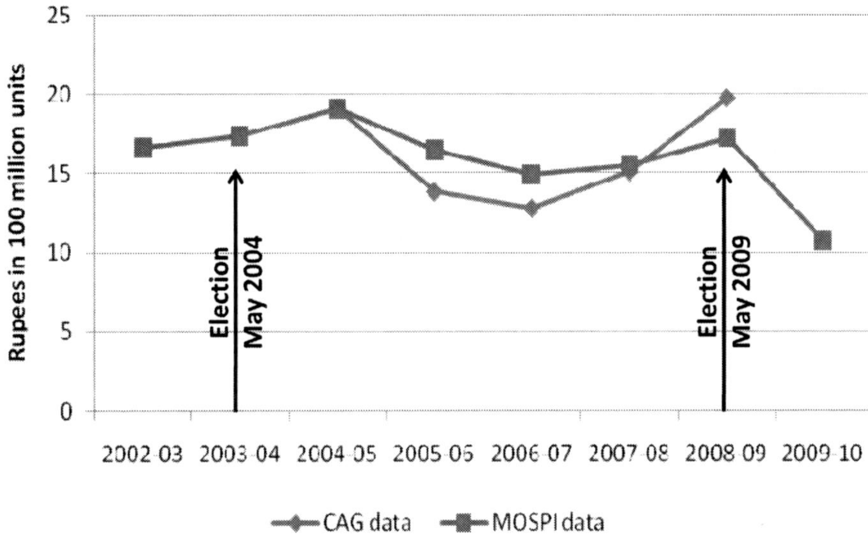

Figure 7.2

But while a case can be made for some sort of political business cycle, a better question would ask how well it works: Does more MPLADS spending toward the end of a five-year Lok Sabha term help an incumbent get reelected? I found some evidence that such spending does help with reelection in what I have been able to piece together concerning the Lok Sabha contest of May 2009, but the picture is quite mixed, in part because of the Indian electoral system, specifically the new set of boundaries put into place in 2008. In particular, the delimitation of constituencies for state legislative assembly and national parliamentary seats established by the Election Commission in the early 1970s and left in place almost 40 years changed significantly in November 2008 when a new delimitation was promulgated.

Given the changes in electoral boundaries, the data in Table 7.4 should be taken as suggestive rather than definitive. The data show MPLADS spending patterns for the 28 Karnataka MPs during their last year of office for the 14th Lok Sabha. The 18 MPs who did not get reelected requested on average that Rs 10.8 million be allocated ("released" in Table 7.4) to specific projects, only a bit more than half of the Rs 20 million they were entitled to for the year, while those who were reelected asked for an average of Rs 28.3 million (i.e., they had saved up at least 8.3 million from previous years, which they could add to the 20 million coming to them in 2008–09). In other words, those returning to office requested 2.6 times more money than those who did not. In their recommendations, the MPs who would return to office recommended 2.7 times more projects (average 201 compared with 75).

Table 7.3 Karnataka: Delimitation of Seats in Parliament and State Assembly before and after 2009 Change

		Delimitation in Place before 2009			*Delimitation in Place for 2009*		
Elected Body	*Total Seats*	*General Seats*	*Reserved for Scheduled Castes*	*Reserved for Scheduled Tribes*	*General Seats*	*Reserved for Scheduled Castes*	*Reserved for Scheduled Tribes*
Lok Sabha	28	24	4	0	21	5	2
State Assembly	224	189	33	2	173	36	15

Note: In addition to the overall increase in reserved seats, some previously reserved seats became general, while some previously general seats became reserved.
Source: GOI (2008).

Table 7.4 Karnataka MPLADS Activities and Election Results during 2008–09

	Rs (million) Released by MP	*Rs (million) Expended on Projects*	*Projects Recommended by MP*	*Projects Sanctioned by District Authority*	*Projects Completed*
Total for MPs re-elected (n = 10)	282.5	287.8	2013	1687	986
Total for MPs not reelected (n = 18)	194.5	179.6	1356	1415	654
Average for MPs reelected	28.3	28.8	201	169	99
Average for MPs not reelected	10.8	10.0	75	79	36

An average of 94 of their projects were completed during the period, again 2.7 times more than the average 36 reported for the MPs not getting reelected in May 2009. And finally, in completing their total of 986 projects, the District Authorities spent almost three times as much money (average 28.8 million) as they did in completing projects for the non-returning MPs (average 10.0 million).[24]

At first glance, then, Karnataka appears to give some striking evidence of a political business cycle at work: MPs who got reelected recommended many more projects and completed many more than those who did not return to office. On the other hand,

- The new district boundaries took away many voters from some constituencies while replacing them with new voters, so the citizens casting ballots in May 2009 may not have been affected at all by the MPs spending patterns previously.

Table 7.5 Maharashtra MPLADS Activities and Election Results during 2008–09

	Rs (million) Released by MP	*Rs (million) Expended on Projects*	*Projects Recommended by MP*	*Projects Sanctioned by District Authority*	*Projects Completed*
Total for MPs reelected (n = 21)	492.6	456.4	2719	1396	1148
Total for MPs not reelected (n = 28)	593.6	684.2	2659	1928	1868
Average for MPs reelected	23.5	21.7	129.5	66.5	54.7
Average for MPs not reelected	22.0	25.3	98.5	71.4	69.2

- Some MPs were denied the chance to run again when their seats were redesignated from general to reserved or vice versa.
- Some MPs who could have run again may have chosen not to do so.

A look at another state—Maharashtra—sheds some doubt on the political business cycle idea. The figures provided in Table 7.5 indicate that while winning MPs asked on average for slightly more funds (Rs 23.5m as against 22.0m from MPs who did not return) and for quite a few more projects (130 vs. 99), their constituencies saw fewer projects completed (average 55 vs. 69 for the non-returning MPs) and less money spent (Rs 21.7m vs. 25.3m). In terms of political business cycles, we could say that the winners tried to spend about the same amount of money in their final year as those who did not return to Parliament, but they saw significantly less money actually spent and fewer projects completed, so that whatever impact MPLADS projects might have made on constituents was less than for those MPs who did not get reelected. Taking the two states together, the case for a political business cycle stands at best unproven, so far as can be ascertained from the data at hand.

The real surprise here is that more evidence of targeting and political business cycles has not emerged. Either the legislators have been more upright and less cynical in their behavior than they are commonly given credit for, or they were unaware of the possibilities for targeting and cycling, or they had indeed considered all these options but concluded that the redelimitation would render such maneuvers fruitless.

Further insights are provided by a novel study of the 2008 Delhi assembly elections. Abhijit Banerjee and his MIT team conducted a controlled experiment in ten MLA constituencies, in which candidate information was disseminated through a door-to-door information pamphlet distribution, newspaper supplements in Hindi and English delivered to the target area, and focus group discussions that covered 5–10% of a locality's households. The candidate profiles were developed by a Delhi-based NGO, Satark Nagarik Sangathan (SNS, or Citizens Vigilance Association). SNS used the Indian Right to Information (RTI) Act (passed in 2005) to obtain data on incumbents' assembly attendance and participation records, their participation in legislative committee activity, and finally their allocation of MLA-LADS, which in the Delhi case amounted to Rs 20 million a year (10 times per capita the funds MPs had available). Thus LADS data comprised one of three kinds of incumbent information disseminated in three ways to the "treatment group" of voters, while the "control group" received no information in the experiment.

The English language *Times of India* published an illustrative report card from SNS that profiled two MLAs, who spent the great majority of their LADS money on "roads and footpaths," which SNS found in many cases amounted to fake projects in which money was spent but nothing was actually built, implying considerable leakage. The data uncovered by SNS through using the RTI act showed that the average incumbent in the sample frame spent only about half the available amount (Rs 50 million as against the total Rs 100 million that each MLA could have spent over the five years, or about Rs 250 per constituent out of a possible Rs 500). But spending overall appears to have had little effect; the experimenters found that the total amount of LADS spending had no statistical impact on voter support for incumbents. Parsing their results further, however, the team found that spending LADS funds in slum areas did increase voter support for incumbents by about 2%—statistically significant and potentially critical in a tight contest, but not what could be called a major impact on voter behavior. Other factors like wealth, education and attendance at legislative committees affected candidate vote share more than LADS spending patterns. The information campaign did enhance voter turnout in the treatment areas by 3.6% as compared with the control localities, but the increase did not favor incumbents or candidates of any particular party. So while more candidate information may be good for voter participation, knowing more about LADS spending doesn't appear to translate into increased (or decreased) vote share for incumbents.

THE CONSTITUTIONAL CRITIQUE

This line of criticism is essentially philosophical, holding that the program is unconstitutional.[25] One approach holds that the constitutional function of a legislator is to enact laws and to monitor their implementation, i.e., to deal with policymaking and oversight, but implementation itself belongs to the executive branch and its bureaucracy. The legislature should decide how much to spend on drinking water programs, for example, and perhaps also as to general criteria for locating them (e.g., in neighborhoods where average income is below the official poverty line), but the executive should decide exactly where to situate the new facilities. MPLADS gives MPs the right to assume this second function in addition to the first.

A second approach points to the fact that the Indian Constitution of 1950, like the American one, assigns particular powers to the union and other powers to the states. In this division, virtually everything that could be classed as a "durable asset" at the local level comes under the state heading. Then the 73rd and 74th Amendments to the Constitution specifically assigns most local public functions like providing drinking water, sanitation, and local roads to local government bodies, which in India means the Panchayati Raj institutions operating at district, block and village level,[26] as well as the municipal corporations in larger urban settlements. It follows that MPs and MLAs in making LADS allocations are engaging in what constitutionally has been assigned to lower level institutions of governance.

These arguments led to a writ petition filed in 1999, charging that the national government had acted *ultra vires* of the Constitution in creating and implementing MPLADS. Eventually, in May 2010, the Supreme Court, in *Bhim Singh vs. Union of India & Others* rejected the first argument by asserting that "the constitutional principle of separation of powers will only be violated if an essential function of one branch is taken over by another branch, leading to a removal of checks and balances."[27] In the case of MPLADS, the court wrote:

> Even though MPs have been given a seemingly executive function, their role is limited to "recommending" works and actual implementation is done by the local authorities. There is no removal of checks and balances since these are duly provided and have to be strictly adhered to by the guidelines of the Scheme and the Parliament. Therefore, the Scheme does not violate the separation of powers.[28]

The Court also rejected the second argument by writing:

> Panchayat Raj Institutions, Municipalities as well as local bodies have also not been denuded of their role or jurisdiction by the Scheme as due place has been accorded to them by the guidelines, in the implementation of the Scheme.[29]

THE GENERAL CRITIQUE: MPLADS AS AN AVENUE FOR ABUSES

As with any program involving political leaders and allocation of state funds, especially one in a country like India with its uninhibited media, there have been many stories, allegations and rumors of LADS abuses at all levels, including corruption of various kinds. Five more or less distinct themes have emerged along these lines.

Leveraging state funds with LADS. Actually this practice is not only permitted but even encouraged in the official Guidelines, which state that MPLADS "can be converged with the Central and State Government schemes provided such works are eligible under MPLADS." The Guidelines go on to give MPLADS a topping-up role, saying that "Wherever such pooling is done, funds from other scheme sources should be used first and the MPLADS funds should be released later, so that MPLADS fund results in completion of the work."[30]

More cynically, one might suppose an MP could arrange to contribute the last 5% of an extensive program to erect drinking facilities throughout half his constituency, which would bring him wide recognition (through the project plaques if nothing else) throughout a large area at little cost. And certainly this provision in the Guidelines offers the potential for MPs to seriously compromise the prerogative of a state or local government to decide its own priorities by dangling matching grants in front of them. A municipality that objectively should be involved in malaria eradication to deal with a serious epidemic could be distracted into building bus stands or football fields, for example.

Interestingly, I heard few complaints that MPLADS funds were distorting local priorities through matching grants, though there did seem a widespread feeling that pooling funds was a shady practice at best. A number of legislators asserted that they themselves did not practice pooling, but that they knew that others did, with the implication that such behavior indicated a lower moral standard.

Targeting infrastructure to specific groups. While the MPs and MLAs interviewed reported uniformly that they adhered to the Guidelines in allocating LADS funds to projects, a number observed that "other legislators" often skirted the rules by building structures benefiting a particular community. A favorite selection seems to be the "community hall," which as earlier noted could be a multipurpose building available to all residents of a neighborhood, but it could also be (and apparently very often is) a building designated for a particular caste community, which is prohibited under the Guidelines. There were also allegations that some legislators used the LADS program to construct religious buildings, a practice directly proscribed by the Guidelines. More subtle skirting of the Guidelines occurs when LADS funds go to constructing something like a drinking water facility, public toilet or street lighting in a locality inhabited only by an ethnic group that the officeholder wants to target for its voters. While not strictly illegal, such uses of LADS moneys would seem to violate the spirit of the program.

Compliant District Authorities. A principal enabling factor in LADS abuses lies in the District Authorities system for vetting, approving, implementing and monitoring projects. These officers can simply give a blanket approval to all LADS proposals, invite the legislator to pick the implementing agency, and neglect to monitor the results. Some indirect evidence comes in memoranda sent out by MOSPI in New Delhi complaining that the 10% inspection rule is not being followed,[31] though this official grousing from above does not per se show the incidence of infraction.

In any case it is not hard to imagine that an overworked and understaffed district collector would find it easier to grant a blank check to an MP demanding the expenditure of relatively small sums, or at least to acquiesce in each new request as it came in than it would be to scrutinize each project with the care it should be getting according to the Guidelines. So it is not surprising that one GOI study found the practice to be widespread indeed.[32]

Political patronage. A more serious issue that has been exacerbated by inadequate official supervision has been the use of MPLADS funds for political patronage. The Guidelines specify that while elected local governance institutions like Panchayats are to be preferred as the implementing agencies for projects,

> the District Authority may choose either Government Department unit or Government agency or reputed NGO as capable of implementing the works satisfactorily as Implementing Agencies.[33]

"Reputed NGOs" has evidently proven to be a term sufficiently flexible to allow significant numbers of organizations staffed with "partymen" to become MPLADS implementers. Thus all manner of local party loyalists and camp followers emerge as program beneficiaries, and projects turn into short-term employment providers for the party faithful (or people the party hopes will support the party in future). To this extent, then, MPLADS can lubricate the party machine and help perpetuate a political system based on neo-patrimonialism.

Outright corruption. Although MPLADS might appear to offer a good number of opportunities for speculation and venality, in fact little hard evidence of outright corruption has appeared since the program's beginnings. The only real scandal has resulted from a sting operation orchestrated by a television station in late 2005, in the course of which seven MPs (five from the Lok Sabha and two from the Rajya Sabha) were caught on camera accepting "commissions" to steer MPLADS projects into particular hands. The scandal came just on the heels of a slightly bigger disgrace in the Parliament occasioned by eleven MPs taking payoffs to raise queries during the Question Hour in the Lok Sabha, and disappeared fairly quickly. Compared to other scandals at the central level, this one was fairly minor. All things considered, the mischief emerging from MPLADS relates more to the use of funds for fueling patronage machines than actual corruption.

COMPREHENSIVE MPLADS EVALUATIONS

In addition to the more narrowly focused research discussed above, several major studies of MPLADS as a program have appeared so far, mainly from government watchdog agencies. A 2011 report from the CAG focused on District Authority offices rather than MP constituencies choosing its sample of 128 among India's 626 administrative districts. Some of the findings:

- Discrepancies in issuing Utilization Certificates meant that in 12 districts only about two-thirds of reported expenditures on projects had actually taken place, implying that the remainder had been lost through leakage.[34]
- Monitoring continued to fall far short of requirements. In fully 86 districts that were audited, no inspections of completed works had been conducted, while in many others despite DA claims at having conducted them, no records were available.[35]
- Contrary to MPLADS guidelines, MPs were found to have recommended the implementing agency for projects, which in many cases turned out to be the user agency itself (e.g., an NGO was both implementer in constructing a work and the user of the completed work), a practice offering much opportunities for siphoning funds.[36]
- Regulations proscribing construction of commercial, private and religious buildings continued to be ignored. In Karnataka, for example, some 94 works for religious purposes were undertaken, costing Rs 18.4 million.[37]

These irregularities and excesses may in fact have been less serious than the CAG reports indicated. Rather like the General Accountability Office of the US government, the CAG sees its charge as ferreting out instances of malfeasance, waste and irregularities in public sector activities. It is much less interested in ascertaining the relative prevalence of problems. Thus as noted above its investigators found 94 cases in which MPLADS funds were used on works for religious purposes in Karnataka, which were among the 163 projects involving officially prohibited kinds of works among the six districts checked on in the state; the cost here was Rs 32.4 million. The grand total of such works in the 100 districts included in the 29 states and union territories examined in this component of the study came to 2340, estimated to cost Rs 737.6 million.

The figures do seem large and the negative thrust of CAG's 2011 report, like its predecessors, generated considerable coverage in the media, but a short accounting exercise will put them into perspective.[38] In the final year of CAG's five-year time period surveyed, Karnataka state saw 3610 MPLADS projects sanctioned at a cost of Rs 623 million. The six districts chosen for the CAG study were about one-fifth of the state's total 29 districts, so we might then think of 722 projects (one-fifth of 3610) as the universe being sampled. If we multiply that by 5 to get the full five-year period, we are back to 3610, of which 163 were found improper, or a bit more than 4% of the total. Admittedly this is very rough calculation, but the point should be clear that while there was some misuse of the funds, the problems were relatively small. Similar exercises could be undertaken with most of the remaining CAG findings. In the end, CAG has abundantly shown that MPLADS has demonstrated any number of problems, but with the exception of the 10% monitoring requirement (which appears basically not to have been done most of the time), its shortcomings have not been as serious as would appear at first glance.

The **Programme Evaluation Office (PEO) of the Planning Commission** conducted a narrower but more in-depth study of 57 MP constituencies over the 1994–99 period, issuing its report in 2001.[39] The study team interviewed more than 4000 people, including MPs, District Authorities, "development functionaries" (civil engineers, local development officers), elected local government council members and a large sample of citizens for each constituency.

In addition to confirming some of the CAG findings, the PEO also found some other shortcomings in MPLADS administration:

- The proliferation of small projects meagerly funded as noted above fed into many other problems. Projects were often either not completed or poor in quality. Even when finished, the new assets tended to be badly maintained. And with so many projects, District Authorities rarely (only 4 out of 103 interviewed) visited the required 10% of projects each year.
- Despite the requirement to obtain cost estimates for each recommended project before allocating MPLADS funds for it, most of the time the funding is allocated directly when the recommendation is made.
- Rather than select implementers themselves as per the Guidelines, e.g., through some kind of tendering process, a majority of District Authorities asked for guidance from the MPs on choosing an implementer. And despite the injunction against using private contractors, almost half of the "development functionaries" interviewed said that project work had been executed by a private firm rather than local government units or "reputed NGOs" as specified in the Guidelines.
- Local elite capture would have been hard to prove in an assessment like the PEO's, but the study team evidently felt that MPLADS posed a serious risk of such distortion. The report observed that

> Locally felt needs perhaps vary across socio economic groups comprising the Society. A small group having easy access to the MP at times may impress upon him to recommend works according to *their* felt needs. Consequently the felt needs of many others may get overlooked.[40]

It is not difficult to see from these findings how MPs choosing to do so could steer project implementation contracts to "partymen" and thereby use the MPLADS funds to grease their local patronage machines.

The PEO report was not entirely negative. More than 60% of ordinary citizen respondents thought the assets created by MPLADS were "good" in quality, while less than 6% thought they were "poor." And 95% of local citizens said the assets had met their "felt needs," while 83% thought the new facilities had improved their quality of life.[41] The general population, then, seemed quite satisfied with the program.

Era Sezhiyan's 2005 study has been by far the most comprehensive assessment of MPLADS since its inception. In his book of 174 large size, double-columned pages, Sezhiyan (himself an MP for 22 years) incorporates virtually all the criticisms that have been launched against the program, reinforcing them with his own observations. In addition to the behavioral shortcomings he details, he expands on the legal and philosophical critique, concluding that MPLADS amounts to an "assault on the Constitution," centering his case on the conflict of interest and constitutional responsibility when MPs charged with guiding and evaluating the executive take on an executive role for themselves. Moreover, he charges, the program inhibits electoral competition by providing incumbent MPs an unfair advantage with its allocations.[42]

In response to the CAG and PEO complaints concerning inadequate monitoring, MOSPI itself has launched a fourth study of the program, conducted by the consultancy service of the National Bank for Agriculture and Rural Development (NABCONS). The NABCONS study began by examining closely about 50 projects in each of 30 districts covered in 2007–08, another 43 districts covered in 2008–09 and then 60 more in 2009–10.[43] The study was finished by summer 2010, and it has been reviewed both favorably and less favorably.[44]

CONCLUSIONS

India's many LADS programs have now been in place for almost two decades and over that time have become an integral part of the country's political fabric, certainly in the minds of their creators, which is to say the MPs at the center and their counterparts at state and local levels. Legislators see LADS as a key mechanism through which they maintain contact with their constituents, and indeed the program does give them some meaningful voice in setting priorities for local investment. As we have seen, an MP's annual LADS fund equals about one-seventh of the discretionary moneys government has available for investment in a typical parliamentary constituency, and when MLA-LADS funds are added in, the total comes to something more than half of what the state has at its disposal. It is scarcely surprising, then, that legislators think highly of the program, despite the headaches it can generate when funds available fall far short of constituent demand for new infrastructure.

Criticism of the program has been intense since its beginning. The full range of complaints include allocating LADS funds for prohibited purposes, squirreling away funds during the early years of an election cycle in order to unleash a burst of spending in the run-up to the following election, directing funds to fictitious "projects" that never get constructed, using compliant District Authorities to award contracts to party camp followers instead of using open bidding practices, using LADS to grease patronage machines, and even accepting bribes to steer funds into particular hands. And finally, these disparagements are topped off with the accusation that the LADS programs are unconstitutional in the first place, violating the separation of powers and center-state division of responsibilities set out in the Indian Constitution.

Some of the charges carry more weight than others, but collectively they make for a serious indictment of the program. Several calls have come for its elimination,[45] and in fact one chief minister has moved to eliminate it in his state and replace it with a new program (to be called the Chief Minister's Local Area Development Scheme or CMLADS), which would double the size of the erstwhile MLALADS but at the same time decentralize it to the district level, where MLAs will have a role in recommending projects, though local elected council leaders will evidently have a greater role in allocating the new funds.[46] His rationale to the MLAs for the reform is worth quoting:

> Your life is no more being made a hell by the local people who either wanted schemes for their favorite places or allotment of works to them or their kin . . . . You can now breathe easy and in [the] public eye your dignity has gone up.[47]

But given the popularity the programs enjoy among legislators (who would have to enact the abolition) along with the fact that the constitutionality of LADS programs has been affirmed with the 2010 Supreme Court decision, it is most unlikely that many if any LADS programs at all will be eradicated. Indeed, movement has been in the opposite direction at the national level, as the finance minister in New Delhi announced an increase in the MPLADS annual allocations from Rs 20 million to 50 million—a 150% jump—in March 2011.[48] This will be the equivalent of about 35% of the discretionary funds available to government bodies for promoting development at district level. And if one adds in the MLALADS funds available in most states, the total money available through CDFs will come to roughly 80% as much as government sources provide.[49]

Unlike the American system of "earmarks" with its secretive, arbitrary and uneven dispensation of state largess to legislative districts, LADS offers a much more (if not completely) transparent system in which every member of the legislative body receives an equal allotment of funds to spend on his constituency. The LADS program with its unlapsable allotments may encourage political business cycles and spending targeted on swing groups of voters, though there is not as yet any convincing evidence that such practices give an unfair advantage to incumbents. The program could be tightened up, to be sure, by demanding that District Authorities enforce guidelines on selecting project implementers instead of enabling legislators to grease their political machines by choosing contractors, and that these same Authorities engage in more rigorous monitoring (in particular, enforcing the 10% inspection requirement). Further, NGOs like SNS can continue and increase their use of the RTI law to find out and publicize how legislators have used their LADS allocations.[50] And the media could make greater efforts to transmit such information to voters.

Amid this context of legislators favoring a program that benefits both themselves and their constituents (albeit perhaps all too often small groups of constituents "having easy access to the MP" in the words of one official evaluation[51]), can LADS be justified? If we take it as a precept that in a legislative system with single-member districts, elected representatives need and should have ways to connect with their constituents beyond the rhetorical, then LADS is perhaps not a bad mechanism for facilitating this. It can certainly be argued that voters in a modern democracy, after all, should be entitled to ask their elected representatives, "What have you done for me (or my neighborhood/village/city) during your time office to improve public service delivery?"

Given a modest dose of political will at the top, these transparency safeguards and monitoring procedures should not be difficult to stiffen and enforce. And the combination of skillful and determined NGOs with a vigorous and autonomous media that India has developed in recent decades, now fortified with a RTI law that appears to be highly successful, should be able to ensure that LADS becomes a responsible and accountable system for nurturing a critical connection between elected representatives and their constituents, despite the imperfections that are sure to remain. And the 150% increase just recently bestowed on MPs means that in combination with MLALADS funding, legislators potentially could have a powerful impact on development at the local level in India.

GLOSSARY OF KEY TERMS

CAG – Comptroller and Auditor General
CPM – Communist Party of India-Marxist
LADS – Local Area Development Schemes
MPLADS – Member of Parliament Local Area Development Scheme
MLA – Member of Legislative Assembly
MOSPI – Ministry of Statistics and Programme Implementation in New Delhi
NABCONS – National Bank for Agriculture and Rural Development
NGO – Non-Governmental Organization
PEO – Programme Evaluation Office
PPP – Purchasing Power Parity
RTI – Indian Right to Information
SNS – (Satark Nagarik Sangathan Citizens Vigilance Association)

NOTES

1. In 2011 the yearly allocation was increased by two-and-a-half times to about $2.5 million. The present paper focuses on the program in place at the time of my research, however.

2. Election turnout, for instance, tends to be significantly higher in contests held at lower levels.

3. I am indebted for this interpretation to A. Surya Prakash, interviewed in November 2010.

4. This paragraph is based on Prakash 1995, 118.

5. Sezhiyan 2005, 14–24, gives a detailed account of the MPLADS launching in Parliament.

6. The Rajya Sabha MPs are elected indirectly for the most part, with state legislatures choosing 238 of the body's 250 members, generally by party in proportion to each party's strength in the state-level assembly.

7. Government of India 2005.

8. The Guidelines require that at least 15% of an MP's LADS fund be allocated to "areas inhabited by the Scheduled Caste population and 7.5% for areas inhabited by the Scheduled Tribe population." Where there are no Scheduled Tribes, the entire 22.5% may be spent for Schedule Caste areas and vice versa. See Government of India, 2005, 2–3. The 15% and 7.5% levels are roughly equivalent to the shares of these two groups in India's total population.

9. Generally this means the District Magistrate (in some states called the District Collector or Deputy Commissioner). S/he is an officer of the Indian Administrative Service, a centrally appointed civil servant charged with superintending and coordinating all national and state governmental activity within his/her district. A district is roughly the size of an MP constituency (around two million population), but their boundaries do not necessarily coincide.

10. The PPP attempts to measure the actual purchasing power of a similar basket of goods in different countries in comparison with the nominal exchange rate for currencies. Thus a haircut or an hour of an electrician's time in India would cost much less than the exchange rate between dollars and rupees would indicate. The PPP has become a standard unit of comparison for the World Bank, UNDP and other organizations.

11. Government of India 2001.

12. Ibid., vii.

13. Data from Government of India 2010. I have incorporated then-current rates of exchange in the dollar figures given in this paragraph and the preceding one.

14. The data shown in Table 7.2 are based on data provided by the Ministry of Statistics and Programme Implementation as "Priority Sector Reports" (mplads.nic.in/sslapps/mpladsworks/a.asp—accessed 30 Jan 2011), with the caveat that they are provided by District Authorities and that the Ministry is not responsible for their accuracy. The Ministry's own data for Karnataka are quite similar in proportion (though showing about 10% less spending and 10% fewer projects); however, they don't provide the subcategories depicted here in Table 7.2.

15. See Government of India 1994; and Government of India 2005, 21.

16. Government of India 2010, 90.

17. This commonly used term is analogous to such American expressions as party hacks, ward heelers, operatives, or handlers—vaguely shady but not necessarily criminal characters who deal in patronage and turn out voters at election time.

18. Keefer and Khemani 2009, 99–112.

19. See Devarajan, Khemani, and Shah 2010.

20. In the state's May 2011 election, the CPM lost control of the West Bengal Assembly, after more than 30 years in power (Polgreen 2011), though absent a detailed analysis the party's defeat cannot be attributed to LADS spending patterns.

21. Alesina et al, 1997 is the classic study on this topic.

22. Pal, and Das 2010, 63. Pal and Das were apparently unable to gather data for the last half of the 2004–2009 Lok Sabha term.

23. The two reports agree exactly on expenditures for only one year (2004–05) in Figure 7.2; reasons for the discrepancy are unclear.

24. Presumably the projects for the returning MPs were larger both as recommendations and as works completed, for in each case they amounted to spending almost three times as much money to provide around 50% more projects. In addition, it will be noted that in a number of cases, more money was spent than recommended, and more projects were "sanctioned" (approved by the District Authority) than were recommended, or were completed than approved. The apparent anomalies can be accounted for as projects recommended or sanctioned the previous year but not completed until the current year—which should help the incumbent, in that projects would become more visible to voters at a time closer to the election.

25. The case presented in the next two paragraphs is based largely on Aiyar (2009, 2010) and Sivaramakrishnan (2010), to both of whom I am also indebted for expanding their views in interviews. See also Kapur and Mehta (2006) and Ghosh (2010). The constitutional argument is an old one, first emerging at the beginning of the program in 1994 (Oomen and Pal 1994).

26. The Panchayati Raj structure of local government comprises elected councils at these three levels. Districts correspond more or less to American counties (though they tend to be much larger in population) in being creatures of the state, which can create them or merge them. Blocks (also called thanas, tehsils or taluqs in various parts of India) correspond to American townships, and villages to American habitations also called villages.

27. *Bhim Singh v. Union of India & Others,* Writ Petition (Civil) No. 21 of 1999.

28. Ibid., 84.

29. Ibidem.

30. Government of India 2005, 7.

31. See for instance Choudhary (2010). The MOSPI website for MPLADS (http://mplads.nic.in) contains *inter alia* some 43 circulars addressing various aspects of the program, dated from 2008 through the end of 2010.

32. Government of India 2001.

33. Government of India 2005, para 2.11.

34. Government of India, Comptroller and Auditor General of India 2011, 37, 102.

35. Ibid., 54.

36. Ibid., 19–20, 84–85.

37. Ibid., 11–14, 72–74.

38. See HT Correspondent, "MP development fund plan not doing well: CAG," *Hindustan Times,* March 18, 2011; and ENS Economic Bureau,. "Almost 50% of MPLAD corpus unspent, says CAG," *Indian Express*, March 19, 2011.

39. Government of India, *Report of the Comptroller and Auditor General on MPLADS* 2001.

40. The examples are taken from Government of India, *Report of the Comptroller and Auditor General on MPLADS* and the quotation is from page vi (see also Government of India, *Report of the Comptroller and Auditor General on MPLADS,* 58). Again as with the CAG studies, Sezhiyan, 2005, 86–92 devotes a whole chapter to the PEO report.

41. Government of India, *Report of the Comptroller and Auditor General on MPLADS*, 2001, 63–65.

42. Sezhiyan 2005.

43. Government of India, Comptroller and Auditor General of India, 2011, 209.

44. See Government of India, Comptroller and Auditor General of India 2011, 209–212; and Chauhan 2010.

45. For example the report of the Second Administrative Reforms Commission in 2007, which demanded that both MPLADS and MLALADS programs be abolished (Government in India 2007, 38–39, 41, 176). See also Sezhiyan. 2007.

46. This was Nitish Kumar, reelected with a huge majority as a reform chief minister of Bihar in November 2010 (Banerjee 2010; Singh 2010; Ahmad 2011; Our Special Correspondent 2011). MLAs will be compensated with increased salaries and allowances (Mishra 2011), but the new benefits will scarcely make up for the loss of patronage opportunities.

47. Ahmad 2011.

48. Chauhan 2011; and Iyer 2011.

49. The total will depend on how much LADS funding is available to each MLA and how many MLA seats are nested within each MP constituency. See the discussion above on page 6. The 80% figure represents my calculation for Karnataka.

50. SNS has experimented with employing its Delhi Vidhan Sabha techniques to state elections in Jharkhand and Bihar states in 2008 and 2010, despite the formidable logistics involved.

51. Government of India *Report of the Comptroller and Auditor General on MPLADS,* vi, 58.

REFERENCES

Ahmad, Faizan. 2011. "Bihar Doubles Allocation for New Avatar of MLA Fund." *Times of India* (27 February).

Aiyar, Yamini. 2009. "Confused Accountability." IndianExpress.com website, 20 June.

———. 2010. "SC Upholds the MPLADs Scheme: A Questionable Judgement?" (New Delhi: Accountability Initiative, Centre for Policy Research, 5 July), accessed at www.acccountabilityindia.in 3 November 2010.

Alesina, Alberto, Nouriel Roubini and Gerald D. Cohen. 1997. *Political Cycles and the Macroeconomy* (Cambridge, MA: MIT Press).

Arun, S. S. 2005. "Kickbacks Sting Members of Parliament." *Deccan Herald*, 22 December.

Bamzai, Sandeep. 2010. "A king's ransom." *India Today*, 29 November.

Banerjee, Abhijit V., Selvan Kumar, Rohini Pande and Felix Su. 2010. "Do informed voters make better choices? Experimental evidence from urban India." (Cambridge, MA: MIT Poverty Action Lab, 10 March). Accessed at http://www.povertyaction-lab.org/node/2764, 21 January 2011.

Banerjee, Shoumojit. 2010. "Bihar Scraps MLA Fund: Bid to Nip Corruption in Bud." *The Hindu*, 15 December .

Bhattacharjya, Satarujpa. 2006. "House in Turmoil." *India Today*, 2 January.

Blair, Harry. 2010. "Citizens, Politicians and Accountability for Public Service Delivery in India" (Paper for Symposium on Promoting Social Inclusion in South Asia: Policies, Pitfalls and Analysis of Welfare/Insecurity Regimes, Centre for Development Studies, University of Bath, 12–14 September.

Chauhan, Chetan. 2010. "Govt Study Finds Misuse of MPLAD Scheme; Centre to Seek Recovery of Money Spent Wrongly." *Hindustan Times*, 15 August.

Chauhan, Chetan. 2011. "MPs get 150% Hike in Funds." *Hindustan Times*, 11 March.

Choudhary, Anil Kumar. 2010. Letter on "Mandatory Inspection of MPLADS Works and Maintenance of Inspection Register." No. C/24/2008-MPLADS (GOI, MOSPI, 20 August), accessed at http://mplads.nic.in/circular20082010.pdf, 9 February 2011.

Deccan Herald. 2005. "Scrap the Scheme: The Sting Only Highlights Irregularities in the MPLADS." editorial, *Deccan Herald*, 22 December.

Devarajan, Shantayanan, Stuti Khemani and Shekhar Shah. 2007. "The Politics of Partial Decentralization." World Bank draft paper, November.

ENS Economic Bureau. 2011. "Almost 50% of MPLAD Corpus Unspent, says CAG." *Indian Express* (19 March).

Ghosh, Buddhabeb. 2010. "Decentralization: A Constitutional Mandate or Rhetoric?" *Economic and Political Weekly* 45, 38 (18 September), 83–84.

GOI 1994. Ministry of Programme Implementation. "Member of Parliament Local Area Development Scheme, Guidelines on Scheme Concept, Implementation and Monitoring." (New Delhi: GOI, December).

——— 1999. Ministry of Planning and Programme Implementation. "Guidelines on Member of Parliament Local Area Development Scheme." (New Delhi: GOI, September).

——— 2001a. Programme Evaluation Office, "Evaluation report on Member of Parliament Local Area Development Scheme." (New Delhi: GOI, Planning Commission).

——— 2001b. "Report of the Comptroller and Auditor General on MPLADS." (New Delhi). Accessed at www.cag.in/reports/civil/2001_book3a/mplads.pdf and at www.cag.in/reports/civil/2001_book3a/annexures.pdf, 13 December 2010.

——— 2002. Ministry of Planning and Programme Implementation. "Guidelines on Member of Parliament Local Area Development Scheme." (New Delhi: GOI, April).

——— 2005. Ministry of Statistics and Programme Implementation, "Guidelines on Member of Parliament Local Area Development Scheme (MPLADS)." (New Delhi: GOI, November). Accessed at www.mplads.nic.in, 15 January 2011.

——— 2007. Second Administrative Reforms Commission. *Ethics in Government*, Fourth Report (New Delhi: GOI, January).

——— 2008. Election Commission of India, "Delimitation of Parliamentary and Assembly Constituencies Order, 2008." (New Delhi: Election Commission, 28 November).

——— 2010. Ministry of Statistics and Programme Implementation, *Member of Parliament Local Area Development Scheme (Annual Report) 2008–09* (New Delhi: GOI).

——— 2011a. Ministry of Statistics and Programme Implementation, *Member of Parliament Local Area Development Scheme (Annual Report) 2009–10* (New Delhi: GOI).

——— 2011b. Comptroller and Auditor General of India, Performance Audit of Member of Parliament Local Area Development Scheme, Report No. 31 (New Delhi: GOI). Accessed at at http://saiindia.gov.in/cag/union-audit/report-no-31-performance-audit-member-parliament-local-area-development-scheme on 15 May 2011.

HT Correspondent. 2011. "MP Development Fund Plan not Doing Well: CAG." *Hindustan Times* (18 March).

Iyer, P. Vaidyanathan. 2011. "Plan Panel Overruled, MPLAD Corpus Hiked to Rs 5 cr." *Indian Express*, 12 March.

Kapur, Devesh and Pratap Bhanu Mehta. 2006. "The Indian Parliament as an Institution of Accountability." Democracy, Governance and Human Rights Programme Paper No. 23 (Geneva: United Nations Research Institute for Social Development, January).

Keefer, Philip, and Stuti Khemani. 2009. "When Do Legislators Pass on Pork? The Role of Political Parties in Determining Legislator Effort." *American Political Science Review* 103, 1 (February), 99–112.

Khemani, Stuti. 2010. "Political Capture of Decentralization: Vote-buying through Grants-financed Local Jurisdictions." Policy Research Working Paper 5350 (Washington: June).

Malhotra, Paras and Priyank Jain. 2009. "MLA-LADS: A Look into the Loopholes and Contradictions." Working Paper No. 225 (New Delhi: Centre for Civil Society). Accessed at www.ccsindia/downloads/intern-papers-09/mla-lads-225.pdf 5 November 2010.

Mishra, Ashok. 2011. "Bihar MLAs to get Rs 1 Lakh Salary." *Hindustan Times* (30 March).

Mohanty, Siba Sankar. 2004. "Rhetoric and Reality of MPLADS." (New Delhi: Centre for Budget and Governance Accountability

Nair, Meena, K. Prabhakar and Prarthana Rao. 2010. "A Mirror to the Police: A Bottom-up Assessment of the Karnataka Police." (Bangalore: Public Affairs Centre).

Oomen, M. A. and Mahi Pal. 1994. "MP's Local Area Development Scheme: A Dangerous Portent." *Economic and Political Weekly* 29, 5 (29 January), 223–225.

Our Special Correspondent. 2011. "Scramble for Seats of Power." Telegraph (Kolkata daily, 19 April). Accessed at www.telegraphindia.com/1110419/jsp/bihar/story_13871371.jsp 18 May 2011.

Pal, Rupayan and Aparajita Das. 2010. "A Scrutiny of the MP-LADS in India." *Economic and Political Weekly* 45, 2 (9 January), 63.

Paul, Samuel. 2006. "Public Spending, Outcomes and Accountability: Citizen Report Card as a Catalyst for Public Action." *Economic and Political Weekly* 41, 4 (28 January), 333–338.

Polgreen, Lydia. 2011. "India's Voters Send Communists to Defeat in West Bengal." *New York Times*, 13 May.

Prakash, A. Surya. 1995. *What Ails India's Parliament? An Exhaustive Diagnosis* (New Delhi: HarperCollins Publishers).

Sezhiyan, Era. 2005. *Member of Parliament Local Area Development Scheme (MPLADS): Concept, Confusion, Contradictions* (New Delhi: Institute of Social Sciences).

Sezhiyan, Era. 2007. "A Scheme Under Fire." *Frontline* 24, 4 (24 February). Accessed at www.hinuonnet.com/fline/fl2404/stories/20070309002309600.htm 17 January 2011.

Singh, Abhay. 2010. "Govt Decides to Abolish LAD Fund." *Times of India* (11 December).

Sivaramakrishnan, K. C. 2010. "Judicial Setback for Panchayats and Local Bodies." *Economic and Political Weekly* 45, 32 (7 August), 43–46.

Supreme Court of India. 2010. Bhim Singh versus Union of India & Others, Writ Petition (Civil) No. 21 of 1999. (New Delhi, May 6). Accessed at http://judis.nic.in/supremecourt/imgs.aspx 4 February 2011.

Tribune News Service. 2005. "MPLADS Scam Rocks Parliament." *Tribune* (Chandigarh daily newspaper), 21 December.

Unnithan, Sandeep. 2010. "Adarsh Scam: Betrayal of the Martyrs." *India Today*, 6 November.

Chapter 8

Conclusion

Constituency Development Funds and the Role of the Representative

Michael L. Mezey

One of the great challenges that all democratic political systems face is to define an appropriate role in the policy-making process for its citizens. For proponents of pure democracy, this is not a difficult question; they argue that the appropriate role for citizens in a democracy is to actually make the decisions—to have the final say on the public policies under which they will live. From this perspective, representative institutions such as legislatures are inadequate substitutes for the voice of the people and the very concept of representative democracy is a contradiction in terms. In democracies, the people—all the people—decide, not a small group of representatives.

POPULAR CONTROL OVER PUBLIC POLICY

One response to this critique is that because representatives reflect the views and interests of those who elect them, a representative assembly constitutes a reasonable substitute for the public at large. But such an argument ignores the empirical evidence that representative assemblies seldom reflect the economic, social, and demographic composition of their nations and that often there is only the most tenuous connection between the views of constituents and the actions of their representatives. To the extent that the views and actions of representatives are at variance with the wishes and interests of constituents, control over policy is in fact in the hands of elected elites rather than the people.

Furthermore, in modern nation states, even the control that representative assemblies are supposed to exercise over public policy seems to be waning. To an increasing degree, executive power wielded either by elected presidents or prime ministers, or by unelected bureaucrats, has become the dominant force in public policy making. In some instances, these executive centered elites have usurped legislative power, and in other instances legislatures have voluntarily ceded their power. Whatever the case, policymaking power has gravitated toward experts in the executive branch whose views often prevail over the elected legislative and executive leaders to whom they are ostensibly accountable. This phenomenon further erodes citizen control over the policies under which they live.

In opposition to the proponents of pure democracy, others argue that decision-making by the general public is a romanticized notion that might have been fine for ancient Athens or for New England town meetings but is neither practical nor wise in the modern world. First, in a large nation state, it is not possible to assemble all citizens and afford them the opportunity to discuss and select among policy options. Second, even if this was possible (and advances in technology make it at least a "virtual" possibility) it would be quite unlikely that citizens would make informed decisions. Policymaking, after all, is not simply about selecting a particular policy option; it is about selecting wisely. Such wisdom results from familiarity with the issue involved and careful deliberation among competing options that exposes their strengths and weaknesses. It is unrealistic to expect that average citizens, consumed as they are with the challenges and joys of their own lives, would be willing to allocate the necessary time to become informed enough to participate effectively in such a process. And it is obvious that relatively few citizens would be capable of understanding the information necessary to make wise policy choices in an ever more complex world of specialized knowledge. Instead of informed decision-making, citizen decisions likely would be swayed by the simplistic arguments and demagoguery that often characterize political campaigns. On this logic, the choice is between democratically pure decision making that may be less informed and less likely to produce policies that will effectively address the challenges at hand and the more informed and effective decisions that are likely to be made by elected and unelected elites.

In all political systems, the arguments for elite decision-making have for the most part prevailed over those in favor of direct democracy. The disposition is reflected in the relatively few opportunities and institutions that exist for citizens to exercise direct control over public policy decisions, the shifting and usually uninformed nature of public opinion, the persistent disparity between measurements of constituency views and the actions of representatives, and the degree to which polities have come to rely on the expertise resident in their bureaucracies to create solutions for the highly complex challenges that states confront.

But a political system that relegates its citizens to the role of subject or at most periodic voter as opposed to substantive decision-maker runs the risk that its people will become alienated from a regime in which they perceive themselves to have little influence over policy decisions. This risk will increase if citizens perceive a large gap between their preferences and government performance. Signs of such citizen alienation can be found in the low level of public confidence in popularly elected legislative institutions in most countries in the world,[1] in the street protests that took place during 2013 in representative democracies such as Brazil and Turkey, in the various "color revolutions" in Central Europe, in the various events associated with the Arab Spring, and in the "occupy" movements that swept the United States. In different ways and for different reasons, all of these phenomena suggest at least some level of citizen discontent with what they believe to be the non-responsiveness of their political leaders to their needs and opinions.

Such public perceptions and actions should not be written off as simply low level episodic griping with minimal to no systemic implications. Government decisions made by centralized elites—and especially unelected elites—located in the nation's capital, may not reflect the needs and concerns of ordinary citizens. Such elites do not necessarily understand how average people live their lives, and what they do may not be informed by local knowledge about what works and what doesn't work. Technically superior policy decisions may have adverse effects on the ground and thereby exacerbate citizen discontent. Especially in a geographically large nation characterized by political, economic, and/or ethnic diversity, centralized policy decisions may not address the conditions and priorities of those at the periphery. When, over an extended period of time, citizens come to believe that there is little or no relationship between their needs and government actions, systemic legitimacy is imperiled.

INSTRUMENTS OF DIRECT DEMOCRACY

In response to these concerns, various political systems have experimented with forms of direct democracy that seek to return at least some power to individual citizens. One venerable mechanism is the referendum process that allows political leaders to place certain policy questions before the electorate for their approval or disapproval. There is a great deal of variation in the way referendum systems are structured—what sort of items can be referred to referendum, the process by which an item can be placed on the ballot, and whether or not its results are advisory or binding. In some states in the United States, there also is an initiative process that allows citizens who gather a sufficient number of signatures to place policy proposals on the ballot without the approval of government officials. Although such mechanisms of direct democracy exist in a number of countries, the use of these procedures is the exception rather than the rule.

Another way to inject an element of democracy into decision making processes and to respond to center-periphery issues is to empower local citizens to influence or even make small scale policy decisions. One example of this approach is public budgeting—a mechanism that delegates to local groups the power to decide how a specific allocation of public funds should be spent. First used in Brazil, this mechanism has been adopted in other jurisdictions around the world, assuming a variety of forms, depending upon the structures for arriving at group decisions, the relationship between these groups and the local authorities who actually administer the funds and the extent to which the population at large has access to the process.[2]

The various community development fund (CDF) schemes that have been discussed in this volume resemble public budgeting in the sense that they can provide a space for citizens to influence the allocation of public funds. In their ideal form, these schemes disburse a portion of the national budget to members of parliament who, working together with local government officials, individual citizens, and organized interests in their constituencies, identify specific local projects toward which these resources are to be directed. CDFs provide citizens with the opportunity to influence decisions about such things as which highway will be paved, whether funds will be allocated to build a new school or a new health care facility, and where such projects should be located. But unlike public budgeting plans that allocate resources and the discretion about how the funds will be disbursed directly to community groups, CDFs are channeled through the area's representative in the legislature who typically has a key role in designing the decision-making process and influencing the specific allocation decisions.

Public budgeting along with CDF plans constitutes a very limited form of direct democracy. Citizens are not exercising policy control as they would under referenda or initiative procedures. Decisions about how much of the national budget will be devoted to local development projects are still made by central policymakers who in turn delegate to citizens some measure of influence over how a small portion of these funds will be spent.

CDFS AND THE ROLE OF THE LEGISLATOR

By now, it is widely understood that legislators play both lawmaking and representational roles. And while the influence that legislators have over lawmaking varies substantially across nations—from the powerful role of members of the US Congress to the rubber stamp role of representatives in the old Soviet Union—the performance of representational functions is universal.

Representatives throughout the world always have been subjected to requests for assistance from individual constituents as well as from elites and groups within their constituency. Sometimes individual constituents ask for a legislator's help in the often daunting task of navigating the state bureaucracy. In some cases, individuals request help on personal matters that have little to do with the state—for example, money to pay school fees for their children, or assistance in finding a job. A separate class of requests is for government funds for local projects such as highway repairs, irrigation initiatives, or the construction of health or educational facilities. These requests normally come from groups of constituents or from elites within the constituency. The expectation that representatives have an obligation to respond to these requests is reflected in research across a variety of nations, from those with very weak legislatures to those with stronger, more institutionalized legislatures.[3]

These expectations are especially prominent in countries with single member district electoral systems as well as cultures that emphasize clientelism. In multimember district systems, it is more difficult for citizens to focus demands on specific legislators. Also, because such systems usually have strong political parties that influence the outcome of legislative elections, representatives do not rely as much on the personal vote generated by constituent service activities for reelection. In single member district systems, citizens know exactly who their representative is and can direct their requests and concerns to him or her. Even in those single member district systems with reasonably strong political parties, a representative's reelection may well turn on his ability to respond to these constituency concerns.

In the case of political cultures characterized by clientelism, political support is viewed as a transaction between the office holder and the electorate with the latter providing votes to the former in exchange for the representative's delivery of goods and services to the constituency. Rather than demonstrating that his position on national issues fits the views of those whom he represents, or exhibiting a high level of personal integrity, or an acute understanding of public policy, a political leader who wishes to retain the favor of his constituents needs to be able to display above all an ability to bring tangible benefits to the constituency. If a political leader wishes to gain the votes of citizens, he must "pay" for such votes, sometimes in terms of personal services, in other contexts with actual cash, and in still others with local projects for which he can claim credit.

In Africa, single member district systems combine with a culture of clientelism to create a strong local orientation for MPs. But as Barkan and Mattes demonstrate in their chapter in this volume, although there is a general expectation among Africans that their representatives will be locally oriented, such expectations can take the form of either a demand that the representative provide goods and services, or as a wish that the representative listen to their concerns and facilitate an appropriate government response. In either case, however, the representative will spend a great deal of his time advocating to government agencies on behalf of those whom he represents and working diligently to see to it that the constituency receives its share of government resources. Research on legislatures outside Africa has arrived at much the same conclusion.[4]

In the United States, representatives devote a significant amount of their own time and a disproportionate amount of their staff time to dealing with personal requests from individual constituents as well as allocational requests from constituency centered elites. In response to the latter, representatives earmark funds in appropriation bills for particular projects in their constituencies and have championed expenditure and tax provisions that have had a beneficial impact on important economic interests in their constituencies. Representatives also regularly lobby members of the bureaucracy on behalf of constituency groups as well as non-constituency groups, often groups that contribute funds to their election campaigns. As Diane Evans makes clear, although earmarks for specific projects are now restricted in the United States, representatives have found alternative ways to assure that the needs of their constituents are served. Members of the United States Congress often succeed in these efforts because of the influential role that they as individuals and the institution as a whole plays in the public policymaking process, and more specifically in budgetary decisions.

In those countries where the legislature's policymaking role is less robust, it is more difficult for representatives to use the statutory process to generate funds for their constituents, but the demands on these members from their constituents are just as intense if not more so. Even though the policymaking influence of representatives may be limited, their constituents still expect them to be responsive to their service and allocational expectations. Legislators the world over report that such demands are never ending and often overwhelming and most believe that their ability to remain in favor with their constituents and to achieve reelection depends at least in part upon whether or not they can show their constituents that they can respond to these demands. When these expectations are disappointed, representatives fear that their constituents will not be impressed by their claim that both the resources at their disposal and their ability to influence these decisions are limited. CDFs are a response to these pressures.

POLITICAL vs. DEVELOPMENTAL ENDS

Although CDFs contribute to development goals and provide some opportunity for local influence, when they were created their primary purpose was to help legislators cope with constituency demands. In all of the countries where they or their equivalent function, MPs are keenly aware of their potential electoral advantages. In Uganda, members pressed for CDFs because the country's non-party system required them to fund their own campaigns for office and these expenses as well as the expenses they incurred attempting to respond to requests from their constituents far exceeded their own resources as well as their normal parliamentary stipends. In Jamaica, CDF funds allowed MPs to enhance their status so that they could compete more effectively with the power of the local dons who typically controlled the constituencies. Members of the Indian Lok Sabha demanded the creation of these funds after they saw how their counterparts at the state and local levels exploited these schemes for their political benefit. In Kenya, the political needs of MPs apparently were not specifically cited, but the interest of MPs in seeing to it that there were funds available to support the "small things" in their constituencies almost certainly had a political dimension to it.

In the United States, members used earmarks to demonstrate to their constituents that they had the ability to deliver national funds for local projects. During the last part of the twentieth century, congressional party leaders dramatically expanded the use of earmarks, specifically to help their members to get reelected and thus maintain party control of the legislature. Thus, Members from highly competitive districts often had more earmarks approved than their colleagues from electorally safe districts.[5] Even when earmarks are not involved, legislators work diligently to take credit for every form of government spending in their constituency, whether or not they had any direct responsibility for these decisions.

The popularity of CDFs and earmarks speaks to a greater emphasis on the legislator's role as a representative than his role as a lawmaker. Legislators always have played both of these roles, but even in more institutionalized political systems, the influence that individual legislators exert on public policy has waned in the face of waxing bureaucratic and executive power; therefore, greater attention has been accorded to the manner in which legislators deal with their representative responsibilities. Indian MPs, for example, supported MPLADs because they sensed that their constituents were not particularly aware of, or impressed by the votes that they cast, or the speeches that they made on the great issues of the day, but they were impressed by their ability to provide funding for local projects. Especially in countries such as Jamaica and Kenya, citizens expect to be rewarded for their votes, and the projects funded by CDFs constituted the MP's response to this expectation.

Interestingly enough, there is ambiguous empirical evidence that a representative's success in generating CDF funds or earmarks for his or her constituency is a decisive factor in the member's reelection efforts. Barkan and Mattes demonstrate that MPs in Africa *believe* that CDFs help them to get reelected, but research in Kenya, India, and the United States has shown that among those members who have been able to deliver a great deal of resources to their constituencies, many have won reelection but others have lost. In Kenya, the first election after the introduction of CDFs witnessed the highest turnover of MPs in the nation's electoral history. It may be that providing resources to one's constituency is a necessary but not sufficient requirement for reelection; those who bring little or nothing to the constituency are much more vulnerable to defeat while the fate of those who are perceived to have brought funds to the constituency will depend upon a variety of other factors.

An emphasis on the political needs of representatives as the driving force behind CDFs should not obscure the fact that these funds do generate actual projects aimed at serving the needs of citizens. In this connection, it is important to remember that MPs are not motivated solely by their desire for reelection. Members also wish to serve their constituents—to "do good"—and providing needed facilities and services for their constituencies addresses that goal and provides MPs with the intangible rewards of constituent gratitude and enhanced status, quite apart from the more tangible rewards associated with electoral support. The studies in this volume from India, Jamaica, and Kenya demonstrate the wide range of projects supported by CDFs, including road improvements, health clinics, educational facilities, and community centers. In Kenya, public opinion data suggest a high level of approval for both the CDF concept as well as the specific projects funded. Although public opinion in the United States seems to be hostile to the idea of earmarks in the abstract, it is difficult to find instances when citizens or groups condemn or refuse earmarks that benefit them. Cynically put, citizens tend to view other people's earmarks as wasteful spending while viewing those that come to them or to their community as necessary and well deserved.

Presumably, such projects, channeled through the representative, are supposed to better reflect the needs of the constituency than projects that are identified by central authorities. Particularly in large nations such as the United States and India, it is reasonable to believe that representatives and their constituents may have a better sense of local needs than central government agencies. And in these and even smaller nations, the technical criteria typically employed by bureaucrats as they make distributional decisions may not speak to the preferences of those most in need of, or affected by the proposed projects. If properly designed and executed, earmarks and CDFs can provide a degree of democratization to the extent that citizens are empowered by their ability to have a voice in at least a small part of the policy decisions that affect their lives. And to the extent that citizens see concrete examples of government funds addressing local needs, they also can contribute to regime support and stability.

CRITIQUES

Although there are clear benefits for both representatives and citizens in these transactions, there are also concerns. These concerns deal with issues of democratization, efficiency, and corruption. From a democratic point of view, the question is whether funding decisions are made entirely by the representative and his appointees, or whether individual citizens, representatives of civil society, and/or other local leaders are actually involved in these allocation decisions. From a development perspective, it is fair to ask whether in societies where funds are scarce, is it wise to allow politicians, either with or without the assistance of community groups, to decide where these funds should be allocated, or are such decisions best left in the hands of policy experts and bureaucratic officials at the national and local level. Finally, there is a suspicion that representatives use these resources as extensions of their own reelection campaigns, responding primarily to the demands of their supporters, or diverting the funds directly to campaign uses. When representatives decide what constituency projects will be supported, are they directing funds to the projects with the greatest need, or to the ones that will do the most good for the largest number of people, or are they motivated solely by the desire to serve their political supporters and therefore their own political future? Similarly, political corruption also has been a concern with some charging that CDFs have been used to enrich the representative, his family members, or close political allies?

From a democratic perspective, the issue is whether or not CDFs provide a genuine opportunity for citizen input into distributive decisions. In Uganda, it seems clear that local citizens had little role in these decisions. In the United States, while local elites—mayors, leaders of business, labor, and nonprofit groups, local party leaders—influence which earmarks are proposed and approved, it is not at all clear that average citizens have much of a say. Certainly, there seems to be no process by which citizens or groups choose among different possible projects; rather, these decisions seem to be taken entirely by the representative who sponsors the earmark. In India, decisions about allocations seem to be solely in the hands of the MP, but, like earmarks in the United States, there seems to be some level of consultation with local elites as well as coordination among local, state, and national representatives. But in Kenya, there appears to be more extensive citizen involvement on the Constituency CDF committees that identify projects and on the Project Management Committees that supervise the implementation of the selected projects.

From a development standpoint, the issues are a good deal more complicated and implicate the classic tension between bureaucratic and democratic criteria for policy decisions. The former approach privileges careful analysis of competing demands by policy experts employing technical criteria. The latter approach privileges the opinions and perceived interests of citizens, local community groups, and their elected representatives. The bureaucratic approach, its advocates argue, is more effective, less likely to produce wasteful spending, less vulnerable to corruption, and constitutes a more efficient use of scarce resources. Because legislators as a rule will not have very much in the way of policy expertise, to the extent that they have a significant role in identifying specific projects, their decisions are likely to be informed by political rather than policy criteria.

It is also possible that the hostility of central bureaucrats toward CDFs and earmarks can be attributed at least in part to their desire to protect their own prerogatives. This turf perspective is suggested by the persistent critique that CDFs violate the principles of separation of powers—that is, legislators, by selecting projects, are performing executive rather than legislative functions. In response, legislators argue that the power of the purse is the fundamental prerogative of legislatures and that entitles them to determine the projects that will be supported by public funds. In addition, the meaning of separation of powers is hardly unambiguous and certainly not a necessary requirement for democratic government. In the United States, the ostensible model for separation of powers, presidents, through executive orders, signing statements, and the exercise of unilateral powers in regard to foreign and defense policy have been to an increasing degree engaged in de facto lawmaking. Supreme Court decisions declaring acts of state legislatures, the Congress, and the President unconstitutional have been characterized by both the right and the left as "law making by judges." And, of course, in parliamentary systems, the concept of separation of legislative and executive powers is nearly irrelevant.

No doubt, CDFs can lead to confusion and inefficiencies; the multiple CDF programs in India at the national, state, and local levels, combined with the funds that are under the direct control of administrators at the various levels of government certainly creates problems of coordination and increases the likelihood that scarce funds will be wasted. Nonetheless, this hardly seems a sufficient reason to condemn such schemes. First, bureaucratic structures themselves are not necessarily models of clarity and efficiency. After all, the term "red tape" traditionally refers to the operation of bureaucracies, not legislatures. Second, in most instances, something is produced by the CDF—a health facility, a paved road, a community center. Even if the specific project does not score high on the priority list of a bureaucrat, it would be difficult to argue that it doesn't serve at least some members of the local community. Third, CDFs and earmarks typically constitute a very small portion of the national development budget. Even if some of this money is not spent in the most efficient manner, it can be argued that this is a small price to pay for creating the sense among citizens that they have some say in the allocation of resources. Finally, one cannot help but detect a whiff of elitism in the bureaucratic critique, a disposition to argue that only the experts can correctly discern what citizens truly need from what they claim to want. In democratic systems, it can be argued that citizens, or at least their elected representatives, should decide what they want and need, and such systems do not and should not offer a guarantee that citizens will always do what is wisest, most efficient, or in their best interests.

Advocates of the bureaucratic approach make the point that CDF funds are more likely to be misappropriated, either for corrupt purposes, or because the decentralization of the process makes the "leakage" of funds inevitable. Certainly, it would be surprising if no funds or projects were directed toward the political allies of MPs, or if there was no corruption in the disbursement of these funds. In Kenya, MPs are regularly accused of stacking CDF committees with political allies and cronies, a process that results in projects that reflect the political needs of MPs rather than the objective development needs of constituents. As a result of these complaints, the 2013 reforms diminished the role of the MP in selecting committee members. In the United States, one of the reasons that earmarks have been criticized and restricted is the assumption that members use these funds to advance their interests and those of their supporters, and that money is too often wasted on frivolous or low priority projects.

But it is also the case that in most countries, the media seem to relish reports of corruption among legislators. Because the legislature is a more open institution than the executive and because it has no control over the coercive elements of the state, stories of corrupt activities by individual MPs are easy to write and those who write them are unlikely to face sanctions. Because politicians in most countries are viewed with suspicion, such stories tend to resonate with the public. Finally, because CDF funds are limited and all proposed and worthwhile projects cannot be funded, it is easy for those who do not receive funding to conclude that those who succeeded did so because of corruption, or political favoritism.

But we also know that bureaucracies and executive leaders are not immune from political pressures and that at least some level of corruption exists in those precincts as well. In many countries, the bureaucracy has been colonized by governing political parties and their decisions made there are heavily influenced by political factors. As David Ndii's chapter on Kenya indicates, CDFs in that country were in part a legislative response to a corrupt national bureaucracy. A more general discussion of African bureaucracies concludes that "corrupt practices have permeated the civil service" and "structures intended as institutional vehicles of development, by their inefficiency, became obstacles to effective growth."[6] In Latin America, one scholar concludes that many programs designed as part of economic development plans "end up transformed into particularistic benefits as they are implemented by a partisan bureaucracy" with supporters of the president and the governing party benefiting to the detriment of those for whose benefit the program was originally designed.[7]

But because bureaucrats are viewed as policy experts and because most of their work is done behind closed doors, they are not as easy targets for charges of corruption as are legislators who are not viewed as experts and who do their work in public. As for presidents and prime ministers, because they control the coercive power of the state, the risks associated with charges of corruption directed against them are in many countries greater than is the case with MPs.

CONCLUSION

It would be difficult to argue that CDFs wherever they are found are consistent, corruption free instruments for democratic participation in development decisions. Clearly, there are situations such as Uganda where they were little more than grants to MPs to be used for their own political purposes. On the other hand, in India and Kenya it seems clear that local groups had a significant voice in deciding the purposes to which CDFs would be deployed and real projects materialized from these funds. In the case of the United States, local elites are involved in earmark decisions and although they never accounted for more than one half of 1% of the national budget, real projects—some, of course, of dubious value—were produced by these funds.

As for corruption, it would be difficult to find any political system without some level of corruption, whether it is the petty corruption of bribe taking that one sees in so many "less developed" countries, or the corrosive influence of wealth that one finds in countries such as the United States. Decisions about the distribution of public funds always have a political dimension to them, and that means that those in favor with the politicians who are in power are at an advantage. Certainly, as several of the papers in this volume make clear, oversight and accountability procedures are not as effective as they should be and need to be strengthened, along with transparency. Nonetheless, it would be a stretch to say that CDFs and earmarks raise the level of public corruption beyond what one would normally find in a given political system. This is not to say that one should be sanguine about corruption; it is simply to say that if one wishes to stamp out corruption, CDFs and earmarks would not be the most obvious place to start.

NOTES

1. See Mattei 2005.
2. Wampler 2007.
3. See Mezey 1978.
4. Mezey 2008, chapter 4.
5. Mezey, Representatives and their Constituents, pp. 99–100.
6. Chazan, Mortimer, Ravenhill, and Rothchild, 1992, 57.
7. Geddes 1994, 136

REFERENCES

Chazan, Naomi, Robert Mortimer, John Ravenhill and Donald Rothchild. *Politics and Society in Contemporary Africa.* 2nd ed. Boulder, Colorado: Lynne Rienner, 1992.

Dogan, Mattei, ed. "Erosion of Confidence in Thirty European Democracies." In *Political Mistrust and the Discrediting of Politicians*. Leiden: Brill, 2005.

Geddes, Barbara. *Politician's Dilemma: Building State Capacity in Latin America.* Berkeley: University of California Press, 1994.

Mezey, Michael L. *Comparative Legislature*. Durham: Duke University Press, 1979.

———. *Representatives and their Constituents.*

———. *Representative Democracy: Legislators and their Constituents.* Lanham, MD: Rowman and Littlefield, 2008.

Wampler, Brian. *Participatory Budgeting in Brazil: Contestation, Cooperation, and Accountability*. University Park, PA: The Pennsylvania State University Press, 2007.

Appendix 1

Table A1.1 Characteristics of Selected Decentralized Funds[1]

	X-Axis: Country and name of fund *Y-Axis: Descriptive Characteristics*	*Bhutan*	*Ghana*	*India*	*Jamaica*
	Official name, year created	Constituency Development Grant (CDG), created in April 2009	District Assemblies Common Fund (DACF)	Member of Parliament Local Area Development Scheme (MPLADS), launched in December 1993	CDF, created in 2007, began in 2008
	CDF?	Yes	No	Yes	Yes
	Type of electoral parliamentary system (according to IDEA)	No provisions for direct elections	Plurality/Majority: First Past the Post	Plurality/Majority: First Past the Post	Plurality/Majority: First Past the Post
Legal Basis	*Legal method of creation*	Executive order by the Finance Minister; confirmed at 35th session of Council of Ministers	Established in 1992 constitution and institutionalized by the DACF Act 1993. President Promised CDF in 2009 State of Nation	Parliament created the scheme and persuaded the then Prime Minister to support and announce it in 1993	Established out of Office of the Prime Minister (OPM)
	If applicable, name of legislation or directive creating fund	Constituency Development Grant Rules 2009	Article 252 (2) of 1992 Constitution of Ghana and the DACF Act 1993	1994 MPLADS Guidelines (amends. 1997, 1999, 2002, 2005)	n/a
Funding	*% or amount of annual budget allocated to Fund*	0.53% of national budget for 2010–2011. Nu. 168 million (US$2,622,480[2]) for 47 constituencies.	5% annual budget for DACF, of which 5% shared by 230 MPs (US$92,115 per MP for 2011)	0.14% of 2010–2011 national budget. 20 million rupees (US$441,697) per MP/ Constituency per year. For FY 2011/2012, the fund is increased to 50 million rupees per MP/constituency	0.5% of annual budget, JA$40 million (US$ 394,205) per MP for 2008; 0.23% and 0.24% of annual budget, JA$20 million (US$ 197,102) per MP for 2009 and 2010, respectively

Funding	*Direct or indirect disbursement of funds to MPs*	*Indirect:* CDG is managed by the Ministry of Finance, who transfers fund allocation to respective Gewog (constituency) through Letter of Credit (LC), the latter then transfers the fund to implementing agencies	*Indirect*: District Assemblies (constituency local governments) receive funds from Ministry of Local Government and Rural Development (MLGRD)	*Indirect:* MPLADS is implemented by the District Authority. The Government of India releases the fund to the District Authority, who then releases the fund to the Implementing Agencies.	*Indirect:* CDF is administered by the CDF Unit under the OPM. Funds are allocated by the Financial Officer in the OPM to the implementing agency
PBP	*Parliaments' constitutional budgetary power*	Finance Minister presents the annual budget to the National Assembly for approval	The president prepares and includes the budget into the Appropriation Act for Parliament to approve	Parliament has the power to make grants and appropriations	Financial Minister introduces the Appropriation Bill for the House of Representatives to pass
Process (implementation and oversight)	*Types of funded projects permitted/ prohibited*	*Permitted:* infrastructure (roads), education *Prohibited:* supplementing gov't activities/programs, resources for local gov't, contributions or donations	*Permitted:* education and health care	*Permitted:* water treatment, healthcare, infrastructure, sanitation, emergency assistance	*Permitted:* infrastructure, water treatment, electricity, education, social safety nets
	Who controls administration of the Fund?	Provincial gov't (Dzongkhag) requests funds released to individual Gewog by Finance Ministry when National Assembly approves grant	DACF Administrator, who is appointed by the President with prior approval from Parliament, and the Ministry of Finance	MPLADS housed within the Ministry of Statistics and Programme Implementation; District Authority prioritizes, selects, and oversees projects	OPM; CDF Programme Management Unit; various Parliamentary committees
	Which entities are tasked with oversight?	Ministry of Finance, National Assembly Budget Committee, provincial gov't, constituency gov't, Royal Audit Authority (audit Ministry of Finance)	DACF Administrator tasked with monitoring and issuing reports to MLGRD	District Authority of MPLADS; implementing agencies	CDF Unit; Constituency Project Oversight Committee per region; OPM consulted on arising issues; implementing agencies

Table A1.1 (Continued)

	X-Axis: Country and name of fund *Y-Axis: descriptive Characteristics*	*Kenya*	*Malawi*	*Malaysia*	*Nigeria*
	Official name, year created	CDF, created in 2003, amended in 2007, amended in 2013	CDF, created in FY2006/2007	CDF (Special Constituency Allocation fund created in 1975)	CDF
	CDF?	Yes	Yes	Yes	No
	Type of electoral parliamentary system (according to IDEA)	Plurality/Majority: First Past the Post	Plurality/Majority: First Past the Post	Plurality/Majority: First Past the Post	Plurality/Majority: First Past the Post
Legal Basis	*Legal method of creation*	Legislation passed in parliament	Introduced by parliamentary administrative decision	The Prime Minister's Office (PMO) created the Special Constituency Allocation fund in 1975	Proposed by the President at the budget meeting with MPs in 2008
	If applicable, name of legislation or directive creating fund	CDF Act of 2003 (Amend. 2007; 2013)	"Guidelines for the Constituency Development Fund" by the Ministry of Local Government and Rural Development, 2006		None
Funding	*% or amount of annual budget allocated to Fund*	2.5% of annual budget; 75% of annual allocation equally distributed per constituency, 25% dispensed on basis of poverty need and population size. Each constituency receives on average KShs.60 million (US$ 684,540). In FY 2011/2012, the CDF amount went up by 19% from Ksh.14.5 billion to Ksh.17.2 billion	MK 2 million (around US$ 5,970) since FY 2006/2007, MK 3 million in FY 2010/2011, and MK 4 million in FY 2011/2012	RM2 million (US$605,878) per MP in FY2006, RM 1 million in FY2007 and FY2008, RM 1.5 million in FY2010	N60 Billion (US$ 371,862,600) (divided into N10 Billion per 6 geo-political areas), approximately 1.93% in FY 2009

Funding	*Direct or indirect disbursement of funds to MPs*	*Indirect:* CDF is administered by the CDF Board nationally. CDF Board disburses money to constituency accounts. Money is then transferred from the constituency bank account to specific projects.	*Indirect:* CDF is administered through local assemblies (local government units). But MPs have exclusive power to decide on how CDF resources can be utilized.	*Direct: only given to Barison National (BN) MPs, and not to Opposition MPs*	*Direct:* funds are given to Senators and Representatives directly.
PBP	*Parliaments' constitutional budgetary power*	National Assembly passes the Appropriation Bill which include the estimates expenditures of national government, the Judiciary and the Parliament (Parliamentary Service Commission is responsible for preparing annual estimates of expenditure of the parliamentary service)	Financial Minister introduces estimates of expenditures into the National Assembly which then approves and passes the Appropriation Bill	Parliament has the power to pass the Supply Bill and authorizes expenditure	The National Assembly approves and passes the Appropriation Act (which contains estimates of revenues and expenditures prepared by the President)
Process (implementation and oversight)	*Types of funded projects permitted/ prohibited*	*Permitted:* healthcare, education, security, electricity, sanitation, water treatment	*Permitted:* communal fisheries, police posts, health clinics, dam construction, etc. *Prohibited*: personal benefit, funerals, personal transport, disaster management or relief, for labor done by communities, for bursaries or competitions	Small projects	*Permitted:* Water supply, rural electrification, roads, or rehabilitation of school facilities
	Who controls administration of the Fund?	CDF Board	MP's with little oversight	Implementation Coordination Unit (ICU) of the Prime Minister's Department	MPs
	Which entities are tasked with oversight?	CDF Board; Constituencies Fund Committee; National Management Committee; all stakeholders in implementing	District DCs and town CEOs	ICU of the Prime Minister's Department	Independent Corrupt Practices and Other Related Offences Commission

Table A1.1 (Continued)

	X-Axis: Country and name of fund *Y-Axis: Descriptive Characteristics*	*Pakistan*	*Papua New Guinea*	*Philippines*	*Sierra Leone*
	Official name, year created	Khushal Pakistan Programme-I (KPP-1), created in 2003 (it was initially called Tameer-e-Pakistan Programme and renamed later)	Electoral Development Funds (a.k.a. Rural Development Program), created in 1970s and amended in 1995 and 2007	Priority Development Assistance Fund (PDAF) transformed in 2000 from the former Countrywide Development Fund created in 1990	CDF, created in 2009
	CDF?	Yes	Yes	No	No
	Type of electoral parliamentary system (according to IDEA)	Mixed: Parallel	Plurality/Majority: Alternative Vote	Mixed: Parallel	Proportional Rep.: First Past the Post
Legal Basis	*Legal method of creation*	Program launched by the government in 2003 in order to enhance its social interventions.	Executive order	Created by the Congress as a congressional initiative; included in the annual General Appropriations Act (GAA) since 1990	Legislation passed in parliament
	If applicable, name of legislation or directive creating fund	Update given under: Five Points Program (not CDF name). CDF funding comes from the regular budget processes of the Public Sector Development Programme	n/a	GAA	Article 34.A of the Mines and Minerals Act of the Republic of Sierra Leone 2009
Funding	*% or amount of annual budget allocated to Fund*	Rs. 5 million (US$48,265) per Member of the National Assembly (MNA, 342 in total) and each member of the Senate (100 in total) per year in 2003–2004. In 2009–2010, total KPP-1 budget amounted to Rs. 4.4 billion which was 0.18% of national budget, with Rs. 9.95 million per MP (US$96,047)	Kina 500,000 (US$201,050) per MP district; additional Kina 2 million for open and provincial electorates	House members P70 million (US$1,584,450; P200 million (US$4,527,000) per Senator	10% of the surface rent paid by the mining companies goes to the CDF. Amounts vary and are uncertain.

Funding	*Direct or indirect disbursement of funds to MPs*	*Indirect:* CDF funds are disbursed to Executing Agencies in the Federal/ Provincial/District Governments legislator	*Direct:* 50% of fund allocation is used at MPs discretion on any project. The fund is often deposited into MPs' private accounts. Joint Budget and Planning Committees of each electorate allocate other 50%	*Indirect:* Department of Budget and Management (DBM) releases money to implementing agency's bank account	*Indirect:* checks were handed over to the Minister of Local Government and Rural Development for onward handing over to the respective Paramount Chiefs. Members of parliament provide consultation and identify the beneficiaries.
PBP	*Parliaments' constitutional budgetary power*	The Federal government presents annual budget to the National Assembly, which authorizes the spending. The National Assembly has the power to make grants in advance	The National Gov't prepares the national budget which includes separate appropriations for the service of that year in respect of the services of the Parliament, general public services, the services of the Judiciary. The Speaker of the Parliament has the power to submit to the Prime Minister estimates of expenditure for the services of the Parliament	Legislature holds firmly the power of purse. In the Philippine Constitution, Article VI, Section 24 states that "All appropriation, revenue or tariff bills, bills authorizing increase of the public debt, bills of local application, and private bills shall originate exclusively in the House of Rep., but the Senate may propose or concur with the amendments."	
Process (implementation and oversight)	*Types of funded projects permitted/ prohibited*	*Permitted:* Health, education, sanitation, roads, electrification of villages, gas, and telephones, improvements to small roads and drains.	*Permitted:* infrastructure (roads), healthcare, education, water treatment, rule of law	*Permitted:* education, health, livelihood/social service, rural electrification, water supply, financial assistance, public works, irrigation, peace and order, housing, forest management, and projects in historical/art/ culture and music	
	Who controls administration of the Fund?	KPP-I is managed by the federal department of Local Government and Rural Development (LGRD). MPs submit 2–3 schemes to LGRD and identify executing agencies. Funds are allocated to the executing agencies MPs identified.	The Office of Rural Development requires MPs or committees (depending on type of fund) to seek approval from Joint Budget and Planning Committees or Joint Planning and Budget Priority Committees in projects accordance with Public Finance (Management) Act	Department of Budget and Management processes, approves and releases the fund	Ministry of Local Government and Rural Development
	Which entities are tasked with oversight?		Joint Budget and Planning Committees; Joint Planning and Budget Priority Committees; Ombudsman Commission	The Commission on Audit (COA)	Parliamentary Oversight Committee on Mines and Mineral Resources

Table A1.1 (Continued)

	X-Axis: Country and name of fund *Y-Axis: Descriptive Characteristics*	*Solomon Islands*	*Southern Sudan*	*Swaziland*	*Tanzania*
	Official name, year created	Rural Constituency Development Fund (RCDF), created in 1989	CDF, created in 2007	Regional Development Fund (RDF)	Constituencies Development Catalyst Fund (CDCF), created in 2009
	CDF?	Yes	Yes	Yes	Yes
	Type of electoral parliamentary system (according to IDEA)	Plurality/Majority: Alternative Vote		Plurality/Majority: First Past the Post	Plurality/Majority: First Past the Post
Legal Basis	*Legal method of creation*	Program proposed and devised by the government	Legislation passed in parliament	Government initiative	Legislation passed in parliament
	If applicable, name of legislation or directive creating fund	Constituency Development Plan created to guide RCDF 1998–2001 and was updated in 2002, 2005, 2006; legislation was passed in 2013	The Constituencies Development Fund Act, 2007	RDF Regulation established by the Ministry of Tinkhundla Administration and Development (MTAD)	The Constituencies Development Catalyst Fund Act 2009
Funding	*% or amount of annual budget allocated to Fund*	SI$400,000 (US$56,243) per constituency (funded by Taiwan)	Sudanese pounds (SDG) 140,000 (US$31,800) per MP (171 MPs in total) for 2007, SDG733,333 (US$166,572) for 2009	E80 million (US$**7,819,372**) FY 2009/2010	TZS 9,560,000,000 (US$5,912,181) FY 2010, 0.1% of national budget
	Direct or indirect disbursement of funds to MPs	*Direct:* MPs receive and have control over the use of RCDF disbursements.	*Indirect:* funds are allocated to CDF bank account maintained by local CDF committees where MPs serve as one of the members	*Indirect:* Ministry of Finance budgets and releases the fund to the MTAD. Inkhundla committee (where MP is a member) approves the application submitted by local association, MP submit applications to the regional secretary for onward handing over to the project committee. Once approved, funds are distributed from MTAD to the local association	*Indirect:* the Treasury disburses the fund to each constituency bank account opened and maintained by the corresponding Constituency Development Catalyst Committee (CDCC)

PBP	*Parliaments' constitutional budgetary power*	The Minister of Finance presents the annual budget to the parliament, which approves and passes the Appropriation Act			The National Assembly approves the government budget and enacts the Appropriation Act
Process (implementation and oversight)	*Types of funded projects permitted/ prohibited*	*Permitted:* infrastructure, healthcare, water treatment, electricity, sanitation, telecomm.		*Permitted:* community infrastructure (local roads; electricity extensions; school buildings), but may also be for investments that solely benefit the association (e.g., funds to establish a chicken hatchery for a cooperative, or to purchase a mill)	
	Who controls administration of the Fund?	RCDF housed under Ministry of Rural Development in Office of Prime Minister but MPs have primary responsibility for fund administration	Chairman of Southern Sudan Legislative Assembly (SSLA) specialized committee on Economic, Development and Finance; Local CDF committees	MTAD	CDCC chaired by MPs in individual constituency. The Minister responsible for local governments coordinates the administration and management of the funds
	Which entities are tasked with oversight?	Ministry of Rural Development; MPs	Local CDF committees, CDF parliamentary committee, Clerk of the Assembly	MTAD	Council Planning Officer

Table A1.1 (Continued)

	X-Axis: Country and name of fund *Y-Axis: Descriptive Characteristics*	*Uganda*	*Zambia*	*Zimbabwe*
	Official name, year created	CDF created in 2005–2006 fiscal year; abrogated 2011.	CDF, created in 1995	CDF, created in 2009, implemented in 2010
	CDF?	Yes		
Legal Basis	*Type of electoral parliamentary system (according to IDEA)*	Plurality/Majority: First Past the Post	Plurality/Majority: First Past the Post	Plurality/Majority: First Past the Post
	Legal method of creation	Established from talks between Presidency and MPs from 7th Parliament	Created by Cabinet Circular No. 10 and approved by Parliament	Proposed and established by Financial Minister Tendai Biti
	If applicable, name of legislation or directive creating fund	n/a	The guidelines on the management and utilization of CDF by the Ministry of Local Government and Housing, revised in 2006 and 2010	n/a
Funding	*% or amount of annual budget allocated to Fund*	2.95 Billion Shillings was initial total CDF portion of budget (US$3,942.35 per MP)[3]	0.53% of 2011 budget, ZMK720 million (around US$150,000) per constituency	US$50,000 per constituency (0.38% FY 2011) (to lower House members only)
	Direct or indirect disbursement of funds to MPs	*Direct*: CDF disbursements allocated to MPs' bank accounts, who in turn identify projects funded by this allocation	*Indirect:* The Council (Local Authority) shall administer the channeling and utilization of the CDF. The Ministry of Local Government and Housing (MLGH) placed allocated funds in the bank account opened by the Council per constituency	*Indirect:* The money is administered by the Ministry of Parliamentary and Constitutional Affairs. Respective Member of the House of Assembly is to chair the fund.
PBP	*Parliaments' constitutional budgetary power*	The President presents the financial budget to the Parliament. An appropriate committee of Parliament may discuss and review the estimates. Parliament passes the Appropriation Bill	Financial Minister presents the budget to the National Assembly, which approves it and passes the Appropriation Act	Financial Minister presents the budget to the House of Assembly, which approves the budget and passes the Appropriation Bill

Process (implementation and oversight)	*Types of funded projects permitted/prohibited*	*Permitted:* infrastructure, water treatment, electricity, local economic enablement *Prohibited:* infrastructure projects already under local or national gov't programs, religions/political activities	*Permitted:* rehabbed schools, infrastructure (bridges), chief's palaces	*Permitted:* construction of boreholes, repair of schools and clinics, purchase of generators, creation of market stalls
	Who controls administration of the Fund?	MPs must devise 5-person committees (Chairperson, a Secretary, Treasurer, 2 accountants) to administer individual CDF allocations	The Council (Local Authority) shall administer the channeling and utilization of the CDF	Constitution and Parliamentary Affairs Ministry; local CDF fund committee chaired and administered by MPs
	Which entities are tasked with oversight?	Each MP is accountable to the Accounting Officer (Clerk of Parliament) in using CDF allocation	District Development Coordinating Committee (DDCC), Constituency Development Committees (CDC); MLGH	Ministry of Constitution and Parliamentary Affairs, CDF Board; The Comptroller and Auditor General and the office of the Accountant General

[1] This information comes from a variety of official sources, academic articles and mass media. The information in this table has been added over time, with the last, update in Kenya following the legislation in 2013.

[2] Exchange rate as of August 2013.

[3] Rate taken from Kasfir and Twebaze Chapter.

Appendix 2

CDF Variables

INSTITUTIONALIZATION

To calculate the degree of CDF institutionalization, we counted the number of steps involved in the distribution of CDF funds. First, we identified each actor in the distribution process. Second, we counted all relationships between actors as a distribution step. Last, each distribution process ends with a project funding step.

ACCOUNTABILITY

To calculate the degree of accountability, we counted every governmental location (central, regional, local) that exercises either administrative and oversight control over the CDF process. This creates a range of accountability score based on administration and oversight from 0–6. In addition, we added a single point to a country's accountability score if it had a Freedom of Information Law, which enables citizens to track how government funds (and CDFs) are spent.

MP INVOLVEMENT

To calculate this variable, we created two indices. The first index measures the degree of direct MP control of CDF funds, ranging from 0 (no MP control) to 1 (complete MP control). The second measures the degree of MP discretion over how CDF funds were spent, ranging from 0 (no MP discretion) to 1 (MPs have exclusive discretion). The scores of these two indices were then added together yielding a composite MP Involvement score.

Appendix 3

Code Sheet for CDF Institutionalization and Accountability Steps, by Country

INSTITUTIONALIZATION STEPS

Method for Counting Steps

1. Identify every actor in the process
2. Count all relationships between actors as a step
3. Each process ends with the funding of the project (this could be eliminated after)

Kenya[1] – 5 Steps

Step 1: MP and Constituency Development Committee (CDC, MP chairs committee) submit proposals to the Constituency Development Fund Board (CDFB).

Step 2: The CDFB approves or denies funding. If approved, funds go to the constituency bank account

Step 3: The constituency executes the projects

Step 4: If the CDFB denies the project, it is reviewed by the Constituency Fund Committee (CFC), in Parliament.

Step 5: If approved, the CFC releases funds to the constituency bank account for project implementation

Uganda[2] – 3 Steps

Step 1: Ministry of Finance, Planning and Economic Development (MFPED) transfers the fund to the Parliamentary Commission (PC).

Step 2: The Clerk to Parliament disburses the fund to each MP's personal account.
Step 3: MPs fund projects.

Jamaica[3] – 5 Steps

Step 1: MPs consult with constituency development committees (CDC) to determine priority projects.
Step 2: Based on the priorities determined by the communities, MPs develop the project documents with the CDF Unit staff assigned to their area, and then submit the documents to the CDF Unit located in the Office of the Prime Minister (OPM) for consideration.
Step 3: The CDF Unit analyzes the proposals, initially approves them and then passes them to the bipartisan Parliamentary Committee for final approval.
Step 4: The Parliamentary Committee (PC) approves the projects.
Step 5: The Finance Officer at the OPM then allocates the funds to the implementing agency identified in the proposal.
Step 6: Implementing agency implements project

India[4] – 4 Steps

1. Government of India releases funds to District Authority
2. MP submits proposals for projects to District Authority
3. District Authority approves or denies project based on feasibility and selects implementing agency
4. Implementing agency executes project

Bhutan[5] – 6 Steps

1. Member of National Assembly (MNA) consults with Dzongdag, GTs and NGOs
2. Project proposals are endorsed by the Gewog Tshogde (GT)
3. Proposals are recommended by the Dzongdag to the MNA (MNA should approve what the Dzongdags recommendation (hence double arrow)
4. Dzongdag requests fund release from Finance Ministry
5. Finance Ministry transfers funds to Gewog
6. Gewog implements project

Ghana[6] – 3 Steps

Step 1: Ministry of Local Government and Rural Development (MLGRD) releases funds to MPs

Step 2: District Assembly (DA, the local government unit) oversees MP project selection
Step 3: MPs fund projects

Malawi[7] – 3 Steps

Step 1: CDF funds are released to the District Assembly (DA)
Step 2: DA and MP consult and make determinations about projects
Step 3: DA funds projects based on MP choices

Malaysia[8] – 2 Steps

Step 1: The Implementation Coordination Unit (ICU) of the Prime Minister's Department allocates the funds to BN (Barison Nasional) MPs (not to opposition MPs)
Step 2: MPs fund the projects in their respective constituencies.

Nigeria[9] – 2 Steps

Step 1: Office of the Senior Special Assistant to the President – Millennium Development Goals (OSSAP-MDGs) pay money directly to MPs
Step 2: MPs would decide which project to put the fund into.

Pakistan[10] – 3 Steps

Step 1: MPs identify local projects for development
Step 2: Local Government and Rural Development (LGRD) distributes funds to implementing agencies
Step 3: Implementing agencies implement projects

Papua New Guinea[11] – 2 Steps

Step 1: Electoral Development Fund (EDF) releases 50% of funds to MPs
Step 2: MPs choose and fund projects

Philippines[12] – 3 Steps

Step 1: MP chooses PDAF projects
Step 2: Priority Development Assistance Fund (PDAF) releases funds to implementing agency
Step 3: Implementing agency funds projects

Solomon Islands[13] – 2 Steps

Step 1: Solomon Island government pays out the fund directly and evenly to 50 Solomon Islands' MPs.
Step 2: MPs administer projects in their constituencies.

Southern Sudan[14] – 3 Steps

Step 1: MPs propose projects to CDF committee
Step 2: Local CDF committees disburse funds to government departments who implement the projects.
Step 3: Implementing agencies execute projects.

Tanzania[15] – 3 Steps

Step 1: The Treasury posts the funds directly to the respective Constituency Development Catalyst Fund account maintained by corresponding Constituency Development Catalyst Committee (CDCC).
Step 2: MP collects project proposals and submit to the CDCC for consideration. Then CDCC approves the record of projects by the end of December.
Step 3: The CDCC in each constituency (composed and convened by MP) shall approve allocation and disbursement of the funds to specific projects.

Zambia[16] – 3 Steps

Step 1: the Constituency Development Committee (CDC) submits project proposals to the Local Council (via the District Development Coordinating Committee (DDCC)).
Step 2: The Town Clerk/Council Secretary notifies the Constituency Development Committee (CDC) on which projects have been approved by the Council for funding and implementation.
Step 3: The Ministry of Local Government and Housing (MLGH) disburses the funds either by Bank Transfer or by checks to Constituency Development Fund Accounts maintained by the Councils.
Step 4: Funds are paid to the authorized Contractor or Supplier directly for implementation of approved projects.

Zimbabwe[17] – 4 Steps

Step 1: Local Committees (chaired by MPs) choose projects
Step 2: MPs make official requests to the Ministry of Constitutional and Parliamentary Affairs for releasing the funds.
Step 3: Funds are released to the Local Committees.
Step 4: Local Committees administer funds and projects.

ACCOUNTABILITY STEPS

Method for Counting Steps

1. Identify all the agencies or organizations (including MPs) which receive information about CDFs from other agencies that execute and implement projects.
2. Each one of these relationships should be counted as an accountability step.
3. Do not double-count relationships even if different data is provided at different times or on a different basis.
4. Any specification of regular auditing by any one agency or organization over another should be counted as one additional step. Do not count auditing relationships that refer to the potential for an audit, which is based on existing standard procedures (instead, this is reserved for regular auditing on a recurrent basis).
5. Add one extra step to the total number of steps if the country has a Freedom of Information Law.

Kenya – 3 Steps[18]

Relationships of Accountability

1. CDFB (Constituency Development Fund Board) to CFC (Constituency Fund Committee, Parliament)
2. MP/CDC (Constituency Development Committee) to CDFB

Actual Regular Auditing Authority

1. Controller and Auditor General

Presence/Absence of FOIL

0. Absent

Uganda – 3 Steps[19]

Relationships of Accountability

1. MP to Accounting Officer (Clerk of Parliament)
2. MP to District CDF Committee

Actual Regular Auditing Authority

0. None

Presence/Absence of FOIL

1. Present- Access to Information Act

Jamaica – 6 Steps[20]

Relationships of Accountability

1. CDF-POC (Project Oversight Committee) to OPM (Office of the Prime Minister)
2. OPM to Auditor General
3. OPM to Financial Secretary
4. Implementing Agency to OPM
5. Implementing Agency to CDF-POC

Actual Regular Auditing Authority

0. None

Presence/Absence of FOIL

1. Present

India – 4 Steps[21]

Relationships of Accountability

1. Implementing Agency to District Authority
2. District Authority to State Government
3. District Authority to Ministry of Statistics and Programme Implementation

Actual Regular Auditing Authority

0. None

Presence/Absence of FOIL

1. Present

Bhutan – 4 Steps[22]

Relationships of Accountability

1. Gewog/Gup to Dzongdag
2. Gewog/Gup to Member of the National Assembly (MNA)
3. MNA to National Assembly

Actual Regular Auditing Authority

1. Dzongdag internal auditor

Presence/Absence of FOIL Law

0. Absent

Ghana – 4 Steps[23]

Relationships of Accountability

1. District Assemblies to District Assemblies Common Fund (DACF) Administrator
2. DACF Administrator to Parliament
3. DACF Administrator to Ministry of Finance; Ministry of Local Government and Rural Development

Actual Regular Auditing Authority

1. Auditor General (required by Law)

Presence/Absence of FOIL

0. Absent

Malawi – 2 Steps[24]

Relationships of Accountability

1. MP to Ministry of Local Government and Rural Development
2. Local Councilors to National Assembly

Actual Regular Auditing Authority

0. None

Presence/Absence of FOIL

0. Absent

Nigeria – 2 Steps[25]

Relationships of Accountability

1. MP to Office of Special Assistant to the President on Millennium Development Goals

Actual Regular Auditing Authority

0. None

Presence/Absence of FOIL

1. Present – Freedom of Information Bill

Pakistan – 2 Steps[26]

Relationships of Accountability

1. MP to Ministry of Local Government and Rural Development

Actual Regular Auditing Authority

0. None

Presence/Absence of FOIL

1. Present – Freedom of Information Ordinance

Solomon Islands – 2 Steps[27]

Relationships of Accountability

1. Member of National Parliament to Ministry of Rural Development
2. Member of National Parliament to Constituency Development Committee

Actual Regular Auditing Authority

0. None

Presence/Absence of FOIL

0. Absent

Southern Sudan – 2 Steps[28]

Relationships of Accountability

1. Local CDF Committee to Parliament (Southern Sudan Legislation Assembly [SSLA] Constituencies Fund Committee; Clerk of Parliament)
2. District Authority to Ministry of Local Government

Actual Regular Auditing Authority

0. None

Presence/Absence of FOIL

0. Absent

Tanzania – 4 Steps[29]

Relationships of Accountability

1. Member of National Assembly to District Constituency Development Catalyst Committee
2. District Constituency Development Catalyst Committee to District Council/ Planning Officer
3. Council Planning Officer to Local Government Minister/Union Minister (Zanzibar)

Actual Regular Auditing Authority

0. National Audit Office

Presence/Absence of FOIL

0. Absent

Zambia – 4 Steps[30]

Relationships of Accountability

1. Constituency Development Committee to Ministry of Local Government and Housing
2. Constituency Development Committee to District Development Coordinating Committee
3. District Development Coordinating Committee to District Council

Actual Regular Auditing Authority

1. Local Government Auditors of Ministry of Local Government and Housing

Presence/Absence of FOIL

0. Absent

Zimbabwe – 2 Steps[31]

Relationships of Accountability

1. CDF Committee (Chaired by Constituent's MP) to Ministry of Constitutional and Parliamentary
Affairs

Actual Regular Auditing Authority

0. None

Presence/Absence of FOIL

1. Present – Access to Information and Privacy Act

NOTES

1. The Parliament of Kenya, 2003/2007. The Constituencies Development Fund Act.

2. Uganda Debt Network, 2007. "Briefing Paper on the Constituency Development Fund (CDF) in Uganda."
http://www.udn.or.ug/pub/CDFbriefingpaper.pdf

3. Office of the Prime Minister, Jamaica. Ministry Paper No: – Constituency Development Fund.

4. Government of India, 2005. Guidelines on Member of Parliament Local Area Development Scheme.

5. Royal Government of Bhutan, 2009. Constituency Development Grant Rules. A Dzongdag is governor of a Dzonkhag, one of 20 administrative-judicial units in Bhutan. A Gewog is one of 205 administrative units below that of the Dzonkhag. The Gewog Tshodey is the district council.

6. Ayee JRA. 1995. "Financing sub-national governments in Ghana: the District Assemblies' Common Fund." Regional and Federal Studies 5(3):292–306. The Ghanaian Government. "How the Fund is Distributed." See http://www.commonfund.gov.gh/how_fund_is_distributed.html

7. Blessings Chinsinga, 2010. "The Interface between Local Level Politics, Constitutionalism and State Formation in Malawi through the Lens of the Constituency Development Fund (CDF)." http://www.nimd.org/documents/T/the_interface_between_local_level_politics_-_constitutionalism_and_state_formation_in_malawi_through_the_lens_of_the_constituency_development_fund.pdf

8. The Malaysian Insider, 1 May 2011. "Opposition MP's bid for funds to be decided Feb 8." http://www.themalaysianinsider.com/malaysia/article/opposition-mps-bid-for-funds-to-be-decided-feb-8/

9. See *Ripples in the Senate Over Constituency Fund.* Available from: http://allafrica.com/stories/200904020051.html. *Nigeria news: Senators get N45m each for constituency projects.* Available from: http://assemblyonline.info/?p=962

10. Mohammed Rizwan, 30 December 2011. "The Politics of Development Spending." *The Express Tribune.* http://tribune.com.pk/story/313996/the-politics-of-development-spending/

11. Joseph Ketan, 2007. "The Use and Abuse of Electoral Development Funds and their Impact on Electoral Politics and Governance in Papua New Guinea." *CDI Policy Papers on Political Governance.* http://www.cdi.anu.edu.au/_research/2007-08/D_P/2007_08_PPS4_PNG_Ketan/2007_08_PPS4_KETAN.pdf

12. Hon. Prospero C. Nograles and Hon. Edcel C. Lagman, 2007. "Understanding the 'Pork Barrel'." http://www.google.com/url?sa=t&source=web&cd=1&sqi=2&ved=0CBYQFjAA&url=http%3A%2F%2Fwww.congress.gov.ph%2Fpdaf%2Fnews%2Fpork_barrel.pdf&ei=cePnTYbcJorqgQeHjZX4Cg&usg=AFQjCNFsYuJcMfgbuA7OPZWvz863i5Hbyw&sig2=p2RpW8pJlEMPgF1g1-Lvbg

13. Fred Fono, 2007. "A perspective on constituency development in Solomon Islands." *Pacific Economic Bulletin*, 22(2) 127–130.

14. Sudan Tribune. (2009, Feb 17). "South Sudan MPs pass corruption bill to final reading." Available from: http://www.sudantribune.com/South-Sudan-MPs-pass-corruption,30203. Wanichan, Jennifer. (2009, Sep 24). "Focus On South: Constituency Development Fund: Crooked theft by MPs." Available from: http://www.sudanvisiondaily.com/modules.php?name=News&file=article&sid=49589

15. United Republic of Tanzania, 2009. "The Constituencies Development Catalyst Fund Act."

16. Ministry of Local Government and Housing, Zambia, 2010. "Constituency Development Fund (CDF) Guidelines." http://www.mlgh.gov.zm/index.php?option=com_docman&task=doc_download&gid=65&Itemid=58

17. Zimvest. (2010, Sep 8). "Constituency funds delay: MPs blame outreach programme." Available from: http://zimvest.com/constituency-funds-delay-mps-blame-outreach-programme. Newsday. (2011, Jan 3). "Development fund brings positive change." Available from: http://www.newsday.co.zw/article/2011-01-03-development-fund-brings-positive-change. Allafrica. (2011, Apr 8). "Zimbabwe: Development Fund 'Prone to Political Hijack'." Available from: http://allafrica.com/stories/printable/201104110041.html

18. The Parliament of Kenya, 2003/2007. The Constituencies Development Fund Act.

19. Uganda Debt Network, 2007. Briefing Paper on the Constituency Development Fund (CDF) in Uganda. Available from: www.udn.or.ug/pub/CDFbriefingpaper.pdf

20. Government of Jamaica; Ministry of Finance and the Public Service, 2011. Revised Constituency Development Fund (CDF) Operational Procedures.

21. Government of India, 2005. Guidelines on Member of Parliament Local Area Development Scheme.

22. Royal Government of Bhutan, 2009. Constituency Development Grant Rules.

23. Government of Ghana, 1992. Constitution of the Republic of Ghana; Parliament of Ghana, 1993. District Assemblies Common Fund Act; District Assemblies Common Fund website. Available from: http://www.commonfund.gov.gh/index.html

24. Chinsinga, B. "The Interface between Local Level Politics, Constitutionalism and State Formation in Malawi through the Lens of the Constituency Development Fund (CDF)." Available from: http://www.eldis.org/vfile/upload/1/document/1106/The%20interface%20btn%20local%20level%20politics,%20constitutionalism%20and%20state%20formation.pdf

25. Website of the Office of the Speaker of the House of Representatives of the Federal Republic of Nigeria (2010, October 21). "House Orders Probe of MDG Constituency Projects." Available from: http://www.speakersoffice.gov.ng/news_oct_21_10_1.htm.

26. Asian Development Bank, 2007. Sindh Secondary Cities Urban Sector Assessment. Available from: http://scip.gos.pk/Reports%20and%20Publication/Sindh%20

Urban%20Sector%20Assessment.pdf. Funding for the Pakistan CDF comes from the regular budget process of the Public Sector Development Programme. We could find no guidelines as to the regulation and auditing of activities as part of the Khushal Pakistan Programme-I.

27. Solomon Star. (2010, May 1). "Is the RCDF Moving Away from Parliament?" Available from: http://www.solomonstarnews.com/viewpoint/editorial/5374--is-the-rcdf-moving-away-from-mps; National Parliament of the Solomon Islands, Parliamentary Entitlement Regulations, 2009.

28. Government of Southern Sudan, 2011. Participatory Planning and Budgeting Guide for Local Governments in Southern Sudan; Sudan Vision Daily Newspaper. (2010, September 24). "Constituency Development Fund: Crooked Theft by MPs." Available from: http://www.sudanvisiondaily.com/modules.php?name=News&file=print&sid=49589

29. Government of Tanzania, 2009. The Constituencies Development Catalyst Fund Act.

30. Government of the Republic of Zambia, Ministry of Local Government and Housing, 2010. Revised Guidelines on the Management and Utilization of the Constituency Development Fund.

31. ZimEye. (2009, December 3). "Constituency Development Fund Established." Available from: http://www.zimeye.org/?p=10848

Appendix 4

Principles and Guidelines for Constituency Development Funds

CONSTITUENCY DEVELOPMENT FUND WORKSHOP 2011

The Commonwealth Parliamentary Association (CPA) in collaboration with the State University of New York organized this workshop to investigate the operations of Constituency Development Funds (CDFs) in Commonwealth jurisdictions. The Workshop explored the operations of these funds by asking about: the efficiency of service delivery in constituencies, the extent to which such policymaking contributes to effective administration, and the best ways to enhance the accountability and transparency of policy making on such funds.

The Workshop, hosted by the Jamaica Branch of the CPA in June 2011, brought together 11 Parliamentarians from the CPA's Asian, Indian and Caribbean Regions. It followed on a larger workshop held during the CPA's 56th Commonwealth Parliamentary Conference in Nairobi, Kenya, in September 2010 which identified the growth of CDFs and highlighted the need for a common set of guidelines for these funds.

The Parliamentarians attending the Jamaica workshop, together with civil servants and academics, compared the delivery of CDFs in their own jurisdictions as well as case studies from other regions. The discussion revealed that, though there was great diversity in how the funds were administered and allocated, there was an overall consensus on the need for effective governance. The workshop therefore identified the following key principles and guidelines for CDFs.

INTRODUCTION

Parliamentary involvement in grassroots community development has grown considerably across Commonwealth countries. One important tool in this effort has been the Constituency Development Fund (CDF), which appropriates national funding for MP-influenced, locally determined constituency-level development. CDFs become legitimate mechanisms of development through their creation in parliamentary legislation. They also facilitate the legitimate connection between members of parliament and their constituencies. A central hope behind CDFs is that local input promotes better targeting of projects to the needs of constituents, more attention to implementation, and a way of holding government officials responsible for results by giving MPs the capacity for development whose electoral fate will be locally determined.

The Commonwealth Parliamentary Association recognizes that CDFs should take steps to eliminate opportunities for corruption and be part of comprehensive development efforts. Below are principles and guidelines for the operation of CDFs that are consistent with international norms and values about legislative performance and socioeconomic development. These principles highlight the importance of transparent project selection and implementation in a manner that enables citizens to work together for the development of their constituency, demand accountability, and maintain regular oversight. Further, the administration and management of CDFs can empower provincial and district governments and professional experts to apply their own contextual knowledge to solve local development problems. CDFs also should foster public learning through monitoring and evaluation about what types of development projects are most successful in meeting the needs of citizens and promoting community development.

It is clear that the successful operation of any CDF is contingent upon strong MP involvement and leadership. As representatives of a constituency's citizens, MPs play an essential role in facilitating citizen participation to make claims upon government services. In this role, MPs can ensure that CDF resources are used efficiently and honestly, with the intent to meet the public interests of their constituencies. Thus, the potential offered by CDFs hinges on the initiative of MPs and their dedication to empowering citizens to participate in their own development.

PRINCIPLES AND GUIDELINES FOR CDFs

The following are general principles of good governance that should apply to all CDFs across cases.

Responsiveness

CDFs are a distributive policy tool designed to meet the development needs of citizens. Their success is contingent upon an inclusive process of consultation which fosters cooperation among constituents, MPs, and technocratic experts. CDF initiatives should respond to local developmental needs. On this basis, CDFs require channels of input for local citizens and civil society at all steps in decision making on CDFs.

- CDFs shall improve the well-being and livelihoods of constituents. The primary purpose of a CDF is to redirect additional resources to constituencies to solve socioeconomic and humanitarian problems identified by citizens and elected representatives.
- Civic participation in government and MP-constituent relations shall be improved through the operation of CDFs.
- CDFs shall respond to constituents' needs regardless of political party affiliation or their relationships to MPs and CDF committees and/or implementers. CDFs shall not be used vindictively to retaliate against any public official's electoral opponents.
- Project selection and implementation shall be based on the needs of the people, who will be provided opportunities to communicate their diverse development needs to MPs and CDF committees and/or implementers for the duration of the project.
- Responsiveness can be achieved through a variety of means, including public forums and discussions about a community's development needs. A responsive CDF process shall also solicit input from all legitimate stakeholders by regularly including them in project selection and implementation.

Transparency

Transparency, as in the case of CDFs, is the fundamental cornerstone of an open government that promotes citizen engagement. Transparency refers to the administration of government services in an open and publicly observable manner that creates opportunities for public participation. MPs, CDF committees and/or implementers shall open decision-making processes to the public.

- The process of CDF project selection and implementation shall be transparent. MPs and CDF committees and/or implementers shall consult constituents about local development problems and all possible solutions.
- All deliberative decisions made by MPs, CDF committees and/or implementers and other bodies shall be open to the public. The flows of all CDF funds shall be transparent and traceable to specific decision-making processes.
- All financial information regarding the use of CDF funds on projects shall be publicly available and documented according to standard and auditable

accounting principles. Documentation of CDF funding shall be made publicly available in a timely manner.

- CDF programs shall ensure ease of access for all citizens, who shall be allowed to make claims of redress and appeal regarding the CDF process according to government regulations.

Administration and Management

CDFs shall be administered and managed in an efficient, effective and transparent manner. In this regard, MPs and committees and/or implementers shall facilitate the process by mobilizing citizen participation, streamlining implementing mechanisms, and proactively complying with them. Such actions ensure that CDF administration and management will be performed in a timely fashion and remain faithful to the intent of CDFs.

- CDF funds shall be allocated to individual constituencies in a fair and equitable manner, regardless of MPs' partisanship, gender, religion, race, or ethnicity.
- CDF funds shall be released in a timely manner and CDF projects shall be completed in a timely manner. The release of funds shall not be employed as part of a legislative election campaign.
- CDF funds shall be channeled to a separate account of a public agency. Access to the funds shall be limited to officially authorized administrators. Funds shall be managed according to the best practices of public financial management.
- The structure of CDF administration shall be clearly defined. Each administering body at corresponding levels shall function with unambiguous legitimate authority, explicit responsibility and substantive commitments. The structure of authority will be clearly stated to the public to ensure that citizens are knowledgeable about the decision-making process of CDF management.
- A set of policies and procedures shall be made public to guide the implementation of the fund and the projects.
- Funding shall be devoted to development in constituencies. Funded areas may include poverty reduction, infrastructure, water, education, health care, sanitation and disaster mitigation, and shall address specific needs of individual constituencies.
- CDFs shall utilize all available technical expertise relevant to a particular project. Governments should make available to CDF implementing agencies relevant technical expertise. For example, public health professionals should be consulted about any CDF project that seeks to improve the health care of constituents. Such expertise is essential to ensure that development

projects are carried out in effective and efficient ways that improve livelihoods.

- CDF committees and/or implementers shall coordinate their projects with similar initiatives of local governments and agencies of the central government in order to avoid waste, utilize resources efficiently, and strive for sustainability of local development.

Accountability and Oversight

Accountability and oversight play essential roles in promoting project quality, improving decision-making, and preventing corruption and abuse of CDF funds. Proper oversight of CDF financing ensures fiscal probity and promotes accountability to the public among MPs and CDF committees and/or implementers.

- Within government regulations, MPs, CDF committees, and implementers shall be held accountable for their respective roles, conduct, and decisions in the process of CDF implementation.
- Procedures and/or legal regulations shall be put in place to hold CDF actors accountable.
- Appropriate entities with adequate monitoring and oversight capability shall be assigned responsibility for overseeing CDF implementation.
- Any findings and/or results of investigations shall be released to the public in a timely manner.

Monitoring and Evaluation

Monitoring and evaluation of CDF projects are essential tasks to help ensure learning about what actions are most effective in fostering constituency development. Monitoring ensures that CDF projects are progressing toward their goal, while evaluation assesses the efficiency, effectiveness, impact, and results of a CDF project. MPs, among other stakeholders, shall engage proactively in facilitating this process.

- Monitoring shall be performed throughout a CDF project to ensure that it is progressing towards its publicly stated goal. Constituents and legitimate stakeholders shall be afforded opportunities to participate in the monitoring process.
- If a monitoring entity determines that a project is deviating from its stated goal; under government regulations, it shall make recommendations about adjusting implementation.

- Evaluation shall be conducted upon completion of projects by appropriate government agencies. Evaluations shall be made publicly available to ensure that CDF committees and/or implementers are aware of the effectiveness of previous CDF projects.
- In addition to monitoring and evaluation, CDF projects will be subject to regular audits by appropriately designated entities for the duration of the project.

Appendix 5

CDF Toolbox

COMPREHENSIVE DESIGN FOR THE CDF TOOLBOX

A "toolbox" provides a set of descriptions, examples, and templates of existing practices in a policy area that can assist policy makers approach specific issues and policies. Toolboxes make available good practices and improve the effectiveness of a particular governance sector or set of institutions. This CDF toolbox will assist Commonwealth Parliaments, MPs, and CDF administrators apply the Principles and Guidelines for Constituency Development Funds that were developed by the CPA with the assistance of the State University of New York Center for International Development (SUNY/CID). These tools will create a practical framework to translate these principles and guidelines into practice.

1. **Sourcing and Financing.** A tool for sourcing and financing will outline alternative models of CDF financing. It will present comparative good practice for financing mechanisms and for the distribution of operating expenses for the funds.
2. **Rules and Procedures.** A tool for rules and procedures will highlight the administration and management of CDFs on responsiveness, transparency, and accountability. The Rules and Procedure tool will present comparative good practices in rules and procedures for CDF operations and includes a template for the necessary issues to be addressed.
3. **Public Participation.** Constituency Development Funds serve to bring MPs together with citizens, CSOs, and other officials from national and local government agencies to address locally developed priorities in constituencies. Their success rests in good measure upon inclusive consultation. The Public Participation tool will present a variety of practical methods

including: constituency needs assessments, public awareness campaigns, Constituency CDF offices, focus groups, community meetings, and participatory budgeting techniques, and coordination of the constituent CDF office with other agencies.

4. **Procurement, Tendering, and Contracting.** A transparent process of procurement, tendering, and contracting will promote more effective implementation of CDF projects and increase public confidence in the integrity of the process. The Procurement, Tendering, and Contracting Tool will present templates for the entire procurement process: issuing tenders, evaluating bids, ensuring timeliness in the contracting, awarding contracts for CDF projects, and enhancing the value for money of CDF projects.
5. **Implementation and operations.** To ensure efficient, effective, and accountable project implementation, this tool will provide guidance on operational procedures such as identification of CDF implementers and CDF Constituent Committees, financial distributions to CDF projects, implementers, invoicing processes, reporting templates, and dispute resolution mechanisms.
6. **Impact Assessment, Monitoring and Evaluating CDFs.** Monitoring and evaluation is essential to ensure the accountability of CDFs to constituencies and stakeholders, such as government bodies and national CDF Boards that may be enshrined in legislation. The Impact Assessment, Monitoring and Evaluation Tool will provide guides for: internal M&E for CDF committees; social audit methodology, and other models of public participation in monitoring and evaluation by constituents and CSOs; Governmental audit procedures; and evaluation of the CDFs' impact on service delivery and local development. This tool will also provide a feedback mechanism to evaluate the implementation of CDFs against broader national priorities in development. It will assist in mapping out the process for understanding the practical matters: identifying needs and links to be made for CDF performance reviews and to annual budgetary perspectives. It will identify challenges of integrating CDFs with contributions of the community and of other agencies to CDF projects.

Appendix 6

Tool #3

Public Participation

INTRODUCTION

A public participation tool will assist MPs to facilitate the participation of citizens to make claims upon government services that are in accordance with the mandates contained in national legislation on CDFs. It includes mechanisms for participation and cooperation with local, regional and national agencies, and for conducting community-based needs assessments and public awareness campaigns, establishing CDF offices, holding community meetings, and initiating community-based budget proposals. This tool may emerge from a strategic plan for the development of the constituency.

This tool serves as a guide for MPs to a range of participatory practices for CDFs: from those addressing problems of inter-governmental coordination to those including constituents in the selection of priorities and projects to be developed with CDF funds. By facilitating inter-governmental coordination, CDFs can help to enhance service delivery through the achievement of positive synergies in development administration. By connecting constituents to MPs and CDF decision-makers, participatory mechanisms can increase the likelihood that CDFs will be responsive to local needs and those of constituents. This tool provides a menu of options for including individuals and organizational actors in identifying development priorities and selecting CDF projects.

In the following section, we propose participatory practices that emerge from the Principles and Guidelines for Constituency Development Funds that the CPA developed and adopted in 2011.

A SPECTRUM OF PARTICIPATION

We now turn to the spectrum of different types of participation that can increase the responsiveness, transparency, and accountability of CDFs to the public.

Figure A6.1 illustrates how CDFs permit a broad range of participation. On one side of the spectrum, participation in CDFs lack clearly defined institutional rules or procedures for participation and place decision-making at the discretion of individuals. In the middle of the spectrum, participation in CDFs is governed by clear rules and procedures, which include local committees of constituent representatives, parastatal committees and other government agencies. At the other end, CDFs can encourage much broader participation by constituents, including in mechanisms that resemble participatory budgeting.

INFORMAL PARTICIPATION

At the left side of the spectrum, there is very narrow participation in decisions about the use of CDFs. Elected officials have great discretion to make decisions over the employment of funds on the basis of personal links with particular constituents' perception of local development needs.

In the absence of broader participation of constituents, CDF projects may neglect important issues in constituencies and, more generally, have difficulty in establishing development priorities that reflect broader needs in constituencies. Overall, this type of CDF relies on the capacity of the MP, alone, to aggregate constituent interests, and provides limited opportunities for other government agencies or constituents to participate in project selection.

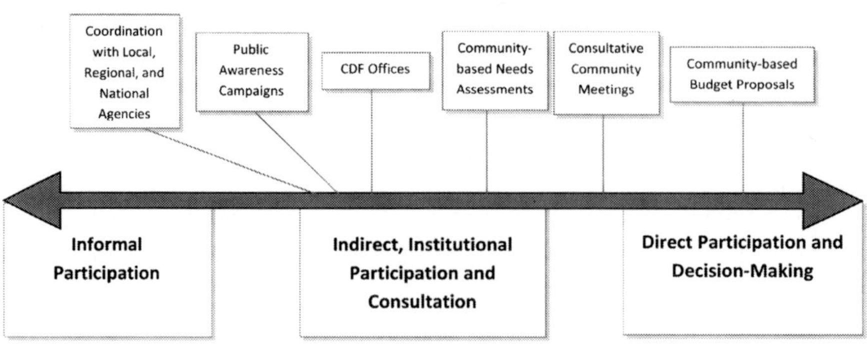

Figure A6.1

INDIRECT, INSTITUTIONAL PARTICIPATION AND CONSULTATION

In the middle of the spectrum, CDFs can feature indirect popular participation and participation of cooperating agencies though clearly defined rules and regulations governing the methods of project selection, implementation, and oversight. Constituent participation in project selection takes place in community needs assessments, such as focus groups, surveys of constituents, and contact with individual participants. Constituents can also participate in consultative local decision-making bodies, such as "CDF Boards," which can be chaired by MPs and staffed by representatives of constituents, CSOs, and local elected officials. These consultative bodies can hold community meetings where citizens can express views on needs of the constituency. CDF programs can also open Constituency/CDF Offices in constituencies to receive constituent input and disseminate relevant information about the CDF activity in that constituency. Project implementation and oversight is often performed by national-level agencies in either the executive or legislative branches. These administrative bodies promote formal compliance with existing rules and provide expectations for appropriate contracting and tendering procedures. In addition, CSOs and parastatal agencies can perform their own oversight activities to inform the public about the progress of project completion and hold project implementers accountable.

Table A6.1

CDF Participation Tools

- **Constituency Needs Assessments:** methods in which constituents can express their preferences in focus groups, surveys, individual meetings and interviews.
- **Public Awareness Campaigns:** increasing awareness among CDF stakeholders about CDF purposes and procedures
- **CDF Offices:** providing constituents with a one-stop clearinghouse for all CDF information relevant to their constituency
- **Consultative Community Meetings:** enabling constituents to pose questions to a panel of CDF decision-makers and CSO representatives about local development
- **Constituency-based Budget Proposals:** empowering constituents to define their own development agenda, make project proposals, and select projects
- **Coordination with Local, Regional, and National Agencies:** forging relationships with government agencies across communities of practice

Table A6.2

	Informal Participation	*Indirect Participation and Consultation*	*Direct Participation*
Who is Mobilized	MP supporters, friends, clients	CSOs, constituencies, ordinary citizens	Ordinary constituents
Method of Project Selection	MP discretion	Local CDF boards including MPs, constituents, CSO representatives	Direct selection by constituents
Method of Information Sharing	Informal communication among MP's network of constituents	Town hall meetings with constituents and CDF offices	Deliberative discussion within community assemblies
Amount of Participation	Limited: dependent on outreach activities of individual MPs	Representative: constituent input via representatives on CDF boards	Direct: constituents specify development priorities in assemblies, community meetings
Role of CSOs	Oppositional: perform oversight independent of MPs	Supportive: CSOs sit on local CDF boards, but conduct independent oversight	Facilitative-supportive: CSOs promote and organize community assemblies
Role of Central Government	Agencies audit or implement projects	Agencies approve project selections, disburse funding, and perform oversight	Informative:agencies provide budget information to citizen assemblies and work with constituents, CSO on oversight

Indirect participation provides constituents with channels to communicate their priorities and preferences about which projects deserve support. MPs may supervise these consultative bodies, play a central leadership role in them, or select the personnel for the local CDF board. Consultative community meetings with constituents can strengthen responsiveness and accountability of a CDF board. Establishing local Constituency/CDF offices in each constituency can strengthen transparency and oversight of CDF operations by public information campaigns. Clearly defined rules and procedures allow constituents and CSOs to perform oversight and improve the efficiency of administration and management.

PARTICIPATORY BUDGETING MECHANISMS

On the right side of the spectrum are participatory mechanisms that enable direct constituent participation in selecting projects for CDFs. Among these mechanisms are: community assemblies to enable constituents to identify local development priorities and articulate individual project proposals. Deliberative forums led by facilitators who provide information to constituents on the legal and actual possibilities for funds. Constituents participating in deliberative assemblies may also elect constituent delegates who become experts in local and national budgeting. Constituent delegates then work with MP staff and facilitators to refine project proposals and present them at community assemblies where participants select projects for funding.

Since constituents are empowered to identify priorities and select projects, these CDF programs guarantee a high degree of responsiveness and ensure that project selection is accountable and transparent. Further, greater participation by constituents in selection of projects for CDFs can lead to increased constituent participation in the implementation and oversight of CDF projects.

CDF Public Participation Tools

Below are six tools designed to ensure broad participation in the implementation of CDFs together with MPs. Each section defines the purpose of the tool and makes suggestions for employment of the tool. Appendix A includes templates for using the tools.

1. Constituency Needs Assessment

A Constituency Needs Assessment (CNA) can be part of a constituency strategic plan. It gathers information from constituencies to identify needs for local development and service delivery, and to assist in developing projects that address those concerns. A CNA can be performed using multiple methods of assessment, including:

- **Surveys:** posing specific questions to a large number of constituents about local development
- **Focus groups:** meetings with groups of selected constituents about local development
- **Constituent interviews:** enabling constituents to directly inform MP or CDF staff about local development
- **Informal constituent contacts:** reaching out to constituents active in local communities for information about local development

Suggested Components of a Community Needs Assessment Survey:

- **Constituent Contacts:** An effective way of learning about development in a constituency is from informal contact with constituents, who express their preferences and priorities for local development. These contacts can also be used to build a list of respondents who may be interested in participating in surveys, focus groups, or interviews.
- **Preliminary Consultation with Local Stakeholders:** Local stakeholders such as CSOs, local elected officials, and community leaders, can provide input into the development of CDF proposals and enhance the legitimacy of the assessment as a basis for decision-making on CDFs.
- **User Friendly Assessment Questions**: Needs assessment questions should be written in simple, easy to understand language. Questions asked in either a survey or a focus group should be composed in the primary language spoken by constituents.
- **Selection of Assessment Methodology:** CDF decision-makers should choose an assessment methodology tailored to the type of constituent information they wish to collect. Surveys provide decision-makers with a large number of constituent responses and can provide a more comprehensive description of constituents' priorities. On the other hand, focus groups provide more in-depth understanding of how local constituents perceive their community's development needs.
- **Designated Staff to Perform Needs Assessment:** A small number of CDF staff (2–3 persons) should be designated to develop procedures for executing the needs assessment. Staff members with experience in constituency relations and who are familiar with the demographic composition of the constituency can identify a sample of respondents that is representative of the entire population within the constituency. The size of the sample should reflect good practice in statistical sampling. Staff should also possess a basic understanding of quantitative or qualitative research methods in order to analyze survey, focus group, or interview data.

2. Public Awareness Campaigns

Public Awareness Campaigns, which are under the overall direction of the MP and/or a parliamentary committee, disseminate knowledge about CDFs in trainings, workshops, and produce outreach materials that build stakeholder understanding of a country's CDF program. Such campaigns inform constituents and stakeholders about the rules and procedures governing CDF operations including project selection, approval, and implementation. Public awareness campaigns can strengthen relationships among stakeholders and increase cooperation between CDF officials and other stakeholders, and give to constituents a greater sense of ownership of CDFs.

Suggested Components of a Public Awareness Campaign:

- **Informational Literature and Public Service Announcements:** CDF Campaign organizers should distribute information on the rules and procedures of the country's CDF to the general public. These pamphlets or brochures should describe CDF rules to ensure comprehension by all sectors of the public. It should also include contact information for meetings of local CDF boards or committees to facilitate public participation. CSOs and other officials can also distribute these pamphlets and brochures on CDFs.
  Public service announcements can inform the public about CDFs. These are short commercials or advertisements produced and purchased for broadcast in local media and uploaded to institutional web sites to inform the general public about the purpose of a CDF program.
- **Workshop Planning and Agenda:** Workshops can build relationships between MPs, CSO leaders, and other elected officials with information to participants on project selection, approval, and implementation to facilitate broadly legitimate participation in CDF programs. Workshop facilitators should also pose questions to participants that enable them to deliberate on their communities' development needs and priorities.
- **Media Contacts:** Public awareness campaigns are strengthened by publicity from local, regional and national media, and web sites that provides constituents with information about CDF programs. MPs and CDF staff should actively reach out to reporters and journalists to keep them informed about the venue and dates of awareness campaign events. Media advisories and press releases should be regularly provided to reporters and journalists at least one week prior to campaign events.
- **Outreach to CSOs and Local Elected Leaders:** Public awareness campaigns can also help to strengthen relationships among stakeholders, CSO leaders, and local government officials. Campaign organizers should invite the relevant local CSO and government officials to campaign events, and publicize this cooperation to demonstrate broad approval of the CDF program.

3. Constituency/CDF Offices

A Constituency/CDF Office provides a one-stop clearinghouse for all CDF-related activities and information in a single constituency. It may be necessary to set aside funding for these offices that provide citizens with a space to review potential CDF projects and submit feedback regarding their priorities and preferences.

Suggested Components of a Constituency/CDF Office:

- **Constituent Contacts:** Constituency/CDF Offices permit regular contact with constituents that provide MP's with information on the preferences and priorities for development of constituents. Office staff should maintain a database of all constituent requests to the CDF Office, which can serve as a quick and reliable information resource for CDF decision-makers.
- **Office Staff Trained in Constituency Relations:** CDF office staff should have experience in constituency relations, be familiar with the constituency's communities, and understand CDF operations. They should also be trained to develop and maintain a database of constituent preferences and to communicate this information to the MP and CDF board.
- **Official Records of CDF Operations:** CDF offices should maintain multiple copies of official records of CDF operations, which include a list of all selected projects, their locations and implementers, tendering and contracting documents, and comments of constituents on the project or its implementers. Such offices will provide minutes of meetings of local CDF boards or other bodies about decisions concerning CDFs to constituents.
- **Easily Accessible Location and Hours**: CDF offices should be accessible to all constituents and office hours should be scheduled to maintain accessibility during normal business hours.

4. Consultative Community Meetings

Community meetings are gatherings that enable MPs, constituents and government officials to identify community needs and develop priorities for local development. They provide opportunities for constituents to consult with MPs and other officials on the use of CDF funds. These meetings also allow MPs to demonstrate their responsiveness to constituents by publicizing recent activities.

Suggested Components of a Community Meeting:

- **Meeting Planning:** The location and format of the community meeting should be publicized well in advance, and invitations containing the agenda should be sent out. Members of a CDF board and other stakeholders should participate in the community meeting. Planners should publicize the meeting in local media and post notices of the meeting throughout the constituency.
- **Outreach to CSOs, local elected leaders, CDF decision-makers:** Meeting planners should reach out to CSOs and government officials to encourage their participation. Advanced coordination will improve prospects for a successful public, community meeting.

- **Agenda and Format:** The meeting agenda should be publicized in advance and distributed at the meeting. The MP or her/his representative can make a brief opening statement about recent development initiatives in the constituency. Constituents may then address comments and/or questions to the panel for brief responses. At the end of this dialogue, the MP and panelists can conclude by summarizing what was discussed at the meeting.
- **Meeting Organization and Follow-up:** The meeting should take place in an orderly fashion: *moderators* from local CSOs or interested constituents can help to manage the meeting to ensure that it maintains a tone of civil dialogue. Organizers can reach out to local police for security. Other *staffers* should maintain a record of the community meeting (either audio, video, or a written record) for the MP and the CDF local board as well as making a copy publically available.

5. Constituency-based Budget Proposals

Participatory budgeting mechanisms confer some direct decision-making authority to constituents in the use of CDFs. They are based around citizen assemblies that enable constituents to identify development priorities and select projects to be funded by a CDF. MPs, CDF Board staffers, and CSOs can facilitate participation and assist constituents to make decisions that address needs in constituencies. These constituency-based budget proposals can demonstrate the manner in which CDFs can contribute to developmental synergies between local and national initiatives in service delivery in constituencies.

Suggested Components of Participatory Community Assemblies:

- **Formation of Steering Board:** A Steering Board helps to establish and organize community assemblies. They are composed of the MP, CSO representatives, and other constituency stakeholders. The Steering Board determines when and where to hold citizen assemblies to guarantee to all constituents the opportunity to participate in assemblies. The board typically addresses questions or comments about community assemblies and informs the public about the purpose, time, and place of the assemblies.
- **Trained Assembly Facilitators:** Trained facilitators enhance prospects for successful participatory assemblies. Facilitators guide discussion among constituents to identify problems and propose practical solutions. Facilitators must also ensure that all participants have an opportunity to speak during the assembly, especially those participants from marginalized and dispossessed groups, and members of the opposition who may otherwise lack opportunities for participation.

- **Trained Budget Delegates:** Budget delegates are constituents who volunteer at the initial community assembly to develop expertise on a development sector that identified as a priority, refine initial project proposals to ensure compatibility with existing capacities and budgetary rules, and inform other constituents about existing CDF proposals.
- **Publicly Accessible Information:** The Steering Board will provide constituents with up-to-date data about local economic growth, poverty, health, and education, as well as on service delivery in these areas. This information should be made available by facilitators and CDF staff in formats that are accessible to all citizens, regardless of language, and in both hard and soft copies.

Proposed Timeline for Community-based Budgeting Proposal Process

Community-based Budget Proposals are developed in a series of events and meetings. It begins with initial deliberative community assemblies and results in project proposals selected by direct constituency voting. The community-based budgeting timeline should provide sufficient time to develop alternative proposals: below is a five-month process of decision making on project selection. This time line can vary according to national legislation and in a manner that is in harmony with national budget cycles.

Month 1: Steering Board Formation

Local stakeholders (MPs, CSOs, government officials) meet and plan the logistics of the community-based budget process. The Steering Board should select accessible locations for community assemblies, designate facilitators and budget delegate trainers among CDF staff, and determine what technical information will enable constituents to develop initial project proposals.

Month 2: Community Assemblies

Constituents meet to discuss development priorities in their constituencies. These discussions specify current shortcomings in service delivery and development, and identify potential project proposals.

Month 3: Delegate Meetings

Individuals who have been selected as delegates at community assemblies will meet with facilitators and CDF staff to refine proposals according to pending legal regulations and existing infrastructure capacity.

Month 4: Second Community Assemblies

Budget delegates present refined project proposals to community assemblies to solicit feedback. Constituents deliberate about which proposals are most needed.

Month 5: Project Selection and Voting

Constituents vote on projects to receive funding, which will then be implemented through the CDF.

6. Coordination with Local, Regional, and National Agencies

Communication across government agencies is an important guarantee that CDF projects improve local development and service delivery, and that CDF projects are coordinated with parallel development initiatives of other government agencies. Officials from other agencies can provide technical expertise on development issues, and assist CDF decision-makers to anticipate likely costs and implementation problems of potential CDF projects.

- **Identifying Policy Communities:** A Policy Community is a network of officials involved in a specific area of service delivery or governmental operations who share a common definition of the issues at hand. CDF decision-makers should consult with officials across the policy community to ensure that the selection and implementation of projects are consistent with existing regulations and operational standards. Coordination with local and national ministerial officials throughout project selection and implementation will increase the likelihood of smooth CDF operations.
- **Coordination Mechanisms:** Communication across the diverse policy community of government, parastatal agencies and CSOs will enhance prospects for effective decisions on CDFs that are consistent with national and local development priorities. These individuals should also participate in community meetings, public awareness campaigns, and other activities.
- **Periodic Meetings:** MPs, CDF staff, local government staff and agency staff should meet regularly to coordinate CDF operations with those of line ministries. Meetings should have an agreed-upon agenda that evaluates past developments and upcoming planning associated with CDFs. A record of the meetings should be maintained and distributed among the participants in the meetings.
- **Opportunities for Learning, Innovation, and Adaptation:** Coordination within policy communities on specific issues addressed by CDFs will enable MPs, local officials and ministerial officials to develop new and more effective approaches to development challenges in constituencies. Routine coordination with other agencies thereby enables CDF decision-makers to transform country-wide development practices and accelerate the development of each individual constituency.

Index

About the Contributors

Joel D. Barkan was professor emeritus of political science at the University of Iowa in Iowa City and most recently a Senior Associate, Africa Program for the Center for Strategic and International Studies. A distinguished academic specialist on politics and development policy in sub-Saharan Africa, he served as the Regional Democracy and Governance Advisor for East and Southern Africa to the United States Agency for International Development from 1992 to 1994. He served as a principal investigator of the Africa Legislatures Project and edited the influential *Legislative Power in Emerging African Democracies*. Further, he was published in *Foreign Affairs*, the *American Political Science Review*, *Current History*, *Journal of Democracy*, *Journal of Modern African Studies*, and other journals.

Horace A. Bartilow is associate professor of political science at the University of Kentucky. His teaching and research interests are in the areas of International Political Economy (both licit and illicit IPE), International Relations, and American Foreign Policy. His current research is a systematic study of the human rights effects of the US-funded drug war in Latin America. His recent articles have appeared in Latin American Research Review, the National Political Science Review, International Studies Quarterly, Foreign Policy Analysis, Latin American Politics and Society and International Politics. His research has addressed issues that relate to the human rights effect of the drug war, the politics of international counter-narcotic cooperation, the politics of international trade and the politics of the IMF's structural adjustment lending. He is the author of *Debt Dilemma: IMF Negotiations in Jamaica, Grenada, and Guyana* (University of Warwick, London: Macmillan Press)

Mark Baskin is research professor of Political Science at Rockefeller College of Public Affairs and Policy at the University at Albany and a senior fellow at the State University of New York Center for International Development at the State University of New York (SUNY/CID). Earlier, he was director of Research at the Pearson Peacekeeping Centre in Canada, a policy fellow at the Woodrow Wilson International Center for Scholars, a UN official in several Balkan peace operations. He has directed SUNY/CID's project on CDFs, and has contributed to legislative strengthening and capacity building in Europe, the Middle East, Africa and Asia. He has written extensively on development, legislative development, and comparative policy making.

Harry Blair is a visiting fellow in the Yale Department of Political Science. Previously he served as the associate chair of the Department of Political Science, senior research scholar and lecturer in Political Science at Yale. His research interests currently focus on democratization in developing countries, particularly on civil society and decentralization. His numerous articles have appeared in American Political Science Review, Comparative Politics, Journal of Development Studies, and World Development, among others.

Diana Evans is professor of political science at Trinity College. Her current research focuses on the effect of legislative distributive policies in the United States through an examination of how pork barrel politics affects Congress and congressional elections. Her most recent book is *Greasing the Wheels: Using Pork Barrel Projects to Build Majority Coalitions in Congress*, which won the American Political Science Association's 2005 Richard F. Fenno Prize for best book in legislative politics.

Nelson Kasfir is professor of Government, emeritus at Dartmouth College. His most recent work has focused on rebel governance—how guerillas choose to organize civilians politically, administratively and economically during civil war. He co-edited *Rebel Governance in Civil War* (New York forthcoming). He co-authored "The Rise and Ebb of Uganda's No-Party Parliament" in Joel D. Barkan, ed., *Legislative Power in Emerging African Democracies* (Boulder CO, 2007). He has also written on African democratization, civil society, no-party rule, and rural political economy. He edited *Civil Society and Democracy in Africa* (London, 1998) and has supplied the Uganda chapter to several editions of Freedom House's *Countries at the Crossroads* (New York, 2004, 2006, 2010, 2012).

Robert Mattes is professor of political studies and director of the Democracy in Africa Research Unit at the University of Cape Town. He is also a co-founder and senior adviser to the Afrobarometer, a regular survey of public opinion in 35 African countries. His research has focused on the development of democratic attitudes and practices in South Africa and across the continent. His published works include *Public Opinion, Democracy and Markets in Africa* (Cambridge University Press, 2004) and numerous articles in journals such as the *American Journal of Political Science*, *British Journal of Political Science*, *World Development*, and others. He holds a Ph.D. in Political Science from the University of Illinois, Urbana-Champaign (1992).

Michael L. Mezey is professor of Political Science at DePaul University in Chicago. He earned his B.A. from the College of the City of New York and his M.A. and Ph.D. at Syracuse University. He served on the faculties of the University of Virginia and the University of Hawaii before joining DePaul University's faculty in 1977 as chair of the Political Science Department. From 1993 through 2005, Dr. Mezey served as Dean of DePaul's College of Liberal Arts and Sciences. He is the author of four books: *Comparative Legislatures* (Duke University Press, 1979), *Congress, the President, and Public Policy* (Westview Press, 1989), *Representative Democracy: Legislators and their Constituents* (Rowman and Littlefield, 2008), and *Presidentialism: Power in Comparative Perspective* (Lynne Rienner, 2013).

David Ndii is a Rhodes Scholar and holds a doctorate in Economics from Oxford University. He is currently the chairman of Zimele Asset Management. He has vast experience in economic research and policy analysis having worked with numerous think tanks and governments both locally and internationally. He has previously held the position of chief economist at Equity Bank, Africa's leading micro-finance bank, served as an economic advisor to the President of Rwanda, economist with the World Bank, and taught at the University of Nairobi. Dr. Ndii also helped draft clauses on revenue allocation and finance in the new Kenyan Constitution.

Stephen Hippo Twebaze currently serves as a policy analyst with the National Resistance Movement. He is affiliated with the Centre for Basic research and a research associate for African legislatures project (ALP). Previously he worked for SUNY/CID as the Local Program coordinator for the Uganda Parliamentary Research and Internship Program (PRIP). He has also been governance advisor to the Secretary General National Resistance Movement. In addition Mr. Twebaze co-authored "The Rise and Ebb of Uganda's No-Party Parliament" with Nelson Kasfir in *Legislative Power in Emerging African Democracies.*

Lightning Source UK Ltd.
Milton Keynes UK
UKOW03n0153090517
300757UK00001B/18/P

9 780739 180686